Travel and Work with Adventure Around the World

Ralph Lloyd

Copyright © Ralph Lloyd 2014
This book is sold subject to the condition that it shall not, by way of trade or otherwise, be lent, resold, hired out, or otherwise circulated without the publisher's prior consent in any form of binding or cover other than that in which it is published and without a similar condition including this condition being imposed on the subsequent publisher.
The moral right of Ralph Lloyd has been asserted.
ISBN: 1501054333
ISBN-13: 978-1501054334

DEDICATION

My dear departed mother who told me, "Never mind what people think."

CONTENTS

CHAPTER 1	1
Making the Decision To Go	**1**
CHAPTER 2	5
How to Show Proof of Funds to Get Visas	**5**
Going for Visas	*5*
Appearance	*5*
Credit Cards and Debit Cards forget Solo Cards	*6*
Traveller's Cheques	*6*
Return Tickets	*7*
Keep Small Currency	*7*
Methods of Sending Money From the UK	*7*
Building up ID	*8*
Legally Changing Your ID	*8*
If You Are Working Illegally and You Overstay	*9*
Permanent Residence	*9*
CHAPTER 3	11
Money and Travels	**11**
CHAPTER 4	19
A Trip Marred By Immigration Problems	**19**
CHAPTER 5	24
Thailand	**24**
Kevin's Story	*25*
Thai Women	*30*
Beer Talk	*35*
Television	*35*
Crossing the Road – Almost Impossible Like England Beating Germany at	

Football	*36*
Wheelchairs	*36*
Vaccinations	*37*
Transport	*37*
Religion	*37*
Sightseeing	*38*
Face	*38*
Insurance	*39*
Hospitals	*39*
Dogs	*39*
Driving	*39*
The Deep South	*40*
Scams	*40*
One Law for the Rich, One Law for the Poor	*41*
CHAPTER 6	43
Hong Kong	**43**
Places to Stay	*44*
Working in Hong Kong	*44*
CHAPTER 7	45
Israel	**45**
CHAPTER 8	55
Greece	**55**
Working on Boats and Yachts	*57*
Bar Pimps	*57*
CHAPTER 9	58
Canada	**58**
Crime	*58*
Climate	*59*

The North: The Yukon and The North West Territories	*60*
Telemarketing	*63*
Farm Work	*63*
Health	*64*
Drinking	*65*
Getting In and Working	*66*
Being Local or a New Immigrant	*66*
Film Work	*69*
Youth Hostels and Backpackers Hostels	*69*
Applying For a Canadian Social Insurance Number	*69*
Canada Opens Door to More Skilled Workers!	*70*

CHAPTER 10 — 71

Australia — 71

Economy	*73*
Working Legally As a Holiday Traveller	*74*
Tax File Number	*75*
Working Illegally	*75*
Getting Work	*76*
Fruit Picking	*76*
Sugar Cane	*79*
Health	*80*
Working in the Cities	*81*
Telemarketing	*82*
Getting Around	*82*
Driving Around	*82*
Sport	*82*
Outback	*83*
Drinking	*83*
Working Holiday	*83*

Hitching	83
A Weird Scenario	83
Gun Fanatics	84
Recommended Reading	84
STOP THEIR DOLE	84
Harvest Calendar	85
Work and Travel – It's On!	88
Contact Numbers	89
Tax File Number Application	91

CHAPTER 11 — 98

New Zealand — 98

Modern Times: Once We Were Socialists	99
Once We Were Hunters – Today We Go Shopping	102
Getting In and Working	103
Beer	105
Getting Around	105
Skiing (June-October)	106

CHAPTER 12 — 108

United States of America — 108

Recent History	109
What Bullshit, Guns Don't Kill!	110
The Australians, Canadians and New Zealanders Are Now Making This Mistake Also	110
Black and White Movies	111
Considerations	112
Working In America – The Dream	113
Big Bucks But No Small Change (This article from 1996)	113
Money	115
Getting In	115

Arrival – Getting Past the Enemy	*115*
Entry Restrictions	*118*
States	*118*
Dope	*119*
Police State	*119*
Drink	*119*
Gambling	*120*
Drive Away Cars	*120*
Health	*120*
American Football is for Wimps!	*121*
Police	*123*
Life in Prison	*123*
Cat Killer Gets 21 Years	*124*
Statutory Rape	*124*
Flag	*124*
The State Knows Best	*125*
Modern Technology	*125*
Wildlife	*125*
Jobs	*126*
A Nice Little Earner – No Tax – No Social Security Card	*126*
Agriculture	*128*
Men Working With Women	*128*
Fishing Boats in Alaska	*129*
Natural Disasters	*129*
Religion	*130*
Catholic Church	*131*
What Did The Catholic Church Have To Hide?	*132*
Work and Visas	*132*
Summer Camps	*133*

Born in the USA	*134*
APPLICATION FOR US SOCIAL SECURITY CARD	*135*
CHAPTER 13	142
Mexico	**142**
A Few Crucial Pointers	*148*
Conclusion	*149*
Jobs	*149*
Note	*149*
CHAPTER 14	150
Women Travelling Alone	**150**
On a lighter note	*152*
CHAPTER 15	153
Don't Upset the Powers That Be	**153**
CHAPTER 16	157
Immigration and Over-Population	**157**
Population	*158*
Indian Subcontinent	*159*
Indonesia	*160*
Mass Migration: People on the Move	*160*
Vietnam's Boat People	*161*
League of Nations – Forerunner Of Today's United Nations	*162*
Sri Lanka	*163*
CV gets tourist barred from UK	*163*
A different type of farm work	*166*
Bob's Story – briefly	*176*
CHAPTER 17	181
Having Made the Decision to Work Abroad	**181**
USA and Canada, Except Quebec, Are Easier Than Europe	*181*

There Is A Third Way	*183*
Hereditary Peerage	*186*
Do It, Stop Talking, Just Go	*187*
To be British	*189*
My Hero's	*189*
BRITISH NATIONAL INSURANCE CARD	*189*
IRISH APPLICATION CARD	*190*
Undercover Cops	*194*
Story number two	*195*
The Weak Link in the EU – For South Africans	*196*
Under Twenty-six Only	*200*

A Personal Note from the Author

Dear Reader,

This book explains in detail how to work in the USA, Canada, Australia, Israel, Thailand, and New Zealand, **with or without** work permits. It is also my own story of travelling and working from Alaska to Zimbabwe with plenty of different and sometimes exotic destinations in between and generally having a fantastic time in the process!

You can work in the USA without a 'Green Card' – make big bucks then explore Mexico and even the Pyramids of Central America! Or you can work in Israel – then experience the majestic splendour of the Pyramids of Egypt! Or work in Thailand – then explore and see the exotic delights of Asia. New Zealand may be on the other side of the globe, but jobs are plentiful, the economy is booming, and they watch *EastEnders* and *Coronation Street* on TV. It is a sporting and Nature paradise – and you can make heaps of cash, and then explore the South Pacific! You can do all this and much more. I've done it myself and by reading this book you will be able to learn from my experience (and mistakes).

I've often thought that I should write a book of my adventures and reveal my know-how to others. Well here it is! I only wish a similar book had existed for me years ago as it would have saved me much time, money, and many 'hard knocks' on my travel adventures.

Ralph Lloyd

PS. There are some people who, upon reading this book, may disapprove of many of my exploits and frown upon some (or perhaps all) of my political and personal views which I have formed from my own experiences of life.

ACKNOWLEDGEMENTS

Nick Cooksey – Bahrain. Kevin Harron, Ali Dawood – Thailand. Peit Gildenheys, Jeanette Woolridge, Penney Vahn, David Spasiojevic, Marcus & Kim Breg, Debbie Paszyniski – Australia. Peter Guichard, Giles, Bob & Jane Flynn – USA. Big Belfast Bill, Les Scott, Barbara De Brussac, Jean Le Chanche – Canada. Amotz & Jasmin Tall – Israel. Jan Pattie – Sweden. Margo Houlihan – Ireland. Winnie Sommers – Belgium, Epp Hunt – Estonia, Peter Bailey – France, Charles Urban – South Africa. Kalopie Economou – Zimbabwe, Dimitri & Joe Economou – Netherlands, Viking Eric – Ecuador, Mike & Sheila Collins – Scotland UK. Andy Leadbetter, Simon Smith, Tom Shaw, Nathan Griffiths, John Webb – England, UK.

ABBREVIATIONS USED

EU: European Union
FBI: Federal Bureau of Investigation
GI: General Issue.
NRA: National Rifle Association
PLO: Palestine Liberation Organisation
PATU: Police Anti Terrorist Unit.
R&R: Rest and Recreation.
RAR: Rhodesian African Rifles
RLI: Rhodesian Light Infantry.
SAS: Special Air Service
VAT: Value Added Tax.
YHA: Youth Hostel Association.

CHAPTER 1
Making the Decision To Go

"Travel is fatal to prejudice, bigotry and narrow-mindedness – all goes to real understanding. Likewise tolerance, or broad, charitable views of men and things cannot be acquired by vegetating in our little corner of the earth all one's lifetime."

- Mark Twain

Hopefully, when you've read this book, it will help you make a decision that will definitely change your life – hopefully for the better. If you are in your late teens, early twenties, or any age bored with Britain, or wherever you live, fed up with your job, and even if you don't have a job – I will help guide you on your way to adventure and new challenges. All it requires is a firm decision and commitment to get up and go, and of course, a few pounds, dollars, euros or whatever hard currency you may possess.

A common defeatist attitude for not going is, 'I've no-one to go with,' 'I'll miss the football season,' or, 'I'll miss my buddies down at the pub or disco.' There are pubs and discos all over the world! Once you get up and go in the order of travel I've set out, you'll meet plenty of friends from all over the world who will give you addresses and leads on new pastures. I still regularly travel around the world, working and checking out old buddies and girlfriends from different continents (some between marriages – theirs, not mine). Remember, a major asset we all have in Britain and the new commonwealth is that we all speak English as a mother tongue. If you are fortunate enough to speak more languages then travelling is even easier, so brush up on other languages – it's never too late to learn. Over the years I've learnt passable Hebrew, French, Afrikaans, Shona, Venda (Zimbabwe and Northern Transvaal), also some Spanish. When I went to school, if I'd been taught languages I would have found travelling and life so much easier, instead of five years learning Algebra, (what's the point when one can just use a calculator) which I never grasped or had the faintest idea what it was about. Not much good to you when you're trying to buy a loaf of bread in North Africa whereas, if you speak French, it's literally a piece of cake. Travel breeds confidence which breeds success.

In my short lifetime, I've seen the world getting smaller, borders closing up, and immigration officials getting stricter and more sophisticated in blocking travellers and generally messing up your plans and future. I will deal with immigration officials later in this book.

When I first went to Canada in '73, the immigration asked me if I was a tourist or an immigrant, they gave you a choice, that was the beauty of having a British passport in those days. What a missed opportunity to get immigrant status in Canada! At that time, Australia, New Zealand, South Africa, Rhodesia – all had open door policies for the UK and many other nationalities. Even the USA was easy to get into. As these places are closing for permanent settlement it's still possible to travel and work and skip from continent to continent. Remember, you're not on the other side of the universe if you feel lonely in Australia – you're only a Skype phone call a way, also email keeps you in touch with loved ones or eighteen hours on an aeroplane from your family and friends. Everyone gets down from time to time, so don't cop out and go home just because you're a little homesick. It's only natural and will pass. If you do go back, you'll find that nothing has changed.

In the 60s it was possible to migrate to Australia for £10 – it took six weeks on a ship, and when you arrived you were regarded as a whining £10 Pommie. Return air fares, doing it without migrating, was £500 return. In the early 60s that was a year's wage. Today a return ticket around the world is only around £1200. Now plenty of workers around the world earn that per week, so with air travel, opportunities are opening up. Countries in Asia are now desperately seeking English teachers for their emerging economies, especially countries like China, Thailand, Japan, Indonesia, South Korea, Taiwan, Vietnam, Cambodia and Laos, India, Pakistan, Sri Lanka, Singapore, Malaysia and Brunei are all ex-British colonies, so they have little need for English teachers as English is well entrenched in their societies. Same as the Philippines, thanks to the Americans. Burma was also an ex-colony but through fifty years of hard-core nationalistic socialism under

General Ne Win and other despotic generals, English has gone into steep decline, but is now making a strong come back due to the country becoming free and opening up to travellers, tourists and business investment. Singapore, Hong Kong, Malaysia and Brunei have plenty of jobs for highly skilled workers usually company postings, but not always. It is possible to use their English language newspapers, the internet and employment agencies to get jobs. Unskilled jobs are mainly done by other Asian nationals from the not so well off nations.

In the Philippines, unlike its South American ex-Spanish colonies, English is spoken everywhere. Spanish is hardly spoken today anywhere. Such is the relentless ever-increasing demand for the English language. Spain ruled the Philippines for 300 years, left its religion (Catholicism), but not its language. The Dutch ruled in Indonesia for 300 years and left neither their language nor their religion. Whereas the old Empire and colonies have all gone, except for – The Falklands, Gibraltar, some Caribbean and a few Pacific Isles are all that remain of a once global empire.

There are now twenty-eight countries in the EU (European Union). After being in their system of paying tax and social security, in most of them we are able to claim sickness and unemployment benefits. If you are already collecting benefits you can arrange to have payments transferred to another EU country for three months whilst looking for work.

Although this book is not about sponging off welfare systems, I believe welfare is for the needy. If you've made the effort to buy this book and get up and go, you have obviously more about you than those you are about to leave behind, contented living on unemployment benefit smoking dope, gambling drinking, watching television and DVDs and blaming all their woes on the government of the day. (Alright for short periods, like a couple of weeks). I myself left home two months before my seventeenth birthday with £12 in my pocket, I was itching for excitement and adventure. I have never collected welfare or the dole – only sickness benefits. Don't get stuck in the welfare trap it's a dead end a road to nowhere.

There are definitely not the jobs there were years ago in any of the western nations. When you were unemployed in the 60s and early 70s the Labour Exchange (the forerunner of today's Job Centre) used to send you jobs through the mail. Nobody could foresee large scale unemployment as the norm. Machines, robots, and computers have taken the jobs. So many jobs have been lost forever from the factories, the mines, docks, farms, merchant navy, the fishing fleet and armed forces the list goes on and on. Now not only does one have to be able to read and write one has to be computer literate to be able to do a CV, unheard of years ago. Nobody had a CV when I was a youngster. Also, more and more women have entered the work force over the years consequently reducing the job vacancies even more. This is why you have to be more adaptable, more willing to do anything that's legal, and not be frightened to get dirty, work up a sweat, work long, unsociable hours, not complain about being exploited, and look upon hard physical labour as getting paid for a 'work-out'. Expect to get aching muscles. I've worked in 45°C in the Middle East, Africa, and Australia, and I've also worked in -40°C in the Canadian Arctic Circle. Too much heat is like too much cold, you try and get out of it. You can always move on when you've banked a few bucks. Nothing is for ever except paying taxes and being dead. This is all character building and will hold you in good stead for later in life.

If you are learning something useful stick with it a while – it can always come in handy a few years later. Say a few years down the road you buy a house, a car or a boat, or a ski chalet; if you've spent years around construction sites and can now do most jobs. You'll save yourself a fortune on renovating and repairs. Also, no tradesman builder or mechanic will be able to pull the wool over your eyes, so to speak!

So you have to be more adaptable than your parents, who could get jobs for life with big powerful unions to look after them for all their working lives. Learn as many skills as possible, and get as many tickets and licences as possible. This gives you more scope in the world job market. Talking of working in the heat, a few years ago I was repairing war damage in Kuwait after the Iraqis left in a hurry at the end of the first Gulf war. Although it wasn't a good time for me, it wasn't forever. I saw it and experienced the aftermath – the oil fires and the destruction. It wasn't that, that bothered me. There's no beer in most of the Muslim world. At least when the Iraqis had the place one could buy a drink. That doesn't seem long ago at all. I'm still the same – bit less hair maybe. Some of us remember Desert Storm. Kuwait is now free – half the male population have a sort of vote, but of course the women don't. There are jobs galore in Kuwait as no self-respecting Kuwaiti will lower himself to working menial jobs only prestigious jobs, government officials and such. They live off oil revenues from the State. Unfortunately for westerners, all the jobs are at the highly skilled end of the job market. All other jobs are done by Asians and people from the Indian subcontinent and North Africans.

CHAPTER 2

How to Show Proof of Funds to Get Visas

Going for Visas

In lots of countries immigration officials will pull you over to check you out for funds, even if it's a country with no visa entry requirements. Always remember these uniformed protectors of the state are the enemy. They can change your life. They are out to stop you. They have incredible power. They only answer to their supervisors, who are cast from the same mould. If you don't have a work visa and you are planning to work, don't carry work clothes or CVs or job offers with you – post them. They also check your address book for snippets of information. If you are on a holiday visa never ever mention work – even voluntary work mentioned will get you barred. Do not carry any *How to Work* books with you.

Appearance

It can save you heaps of hassle if you dress smart, cover up tattoos and take out earrings. Clean shaven and no pony tails are also good. Shoulder bags and wheeled suitcases are not as practical as rucksacks, but draw much less attention. Also, having loads of stamps in your passport attracts attention. I change my passport frequently. Who wants to brag about stamps in their passport anyway! Also if you wear a suit you can ask to be upgraded to business class when you check in for your flight. This I have done a number of times. You do not have a second chance to make a first impression. This quote mainly applies when you are going for job interviews, also at job interviews don't be late be early.

Credit Cards and Debit Cards forget Solo Cards

Most credit cards have a £2000 plus limit on them. A must in the USA – you cannot hire a car without one this applies to most other counties as well. Great for instant cash anywhere in the world. Watch your spending and don't lose the card. It is a good idea to keep your pin numbers separate from credit and bank cards – the best bet is to memorize them. If you're withdrawing cash with your card try to only use the withdrawal machines inside banks, as now there are very sophisticated skimming devices placed over the face of the cash machine these take your details then the fraudsters drain all your cash leaving you in a right pickle then the major hassles begin, your holiday/travelling can be but on hold or at worse ruined so be warned. Go inside a bank.

Have a mixture of cards, cash and traveller's cheques Emergency money can be transferred through **Western Union** or **Money Gram** Make photocopies of all your important documents and cards leave one copy with a friend or relative.

Traveller's Cheques

You can double the face value of your traveller's cheques by claiming to have lost them on a bus or train, etc. The first step after losing them is to go to a police station and fill out a lost property form, then inform the traveller's cheque company who are duty bound to replace them. Then you are showing at borders twice as much money. Don't lose your nerve when reporting the loss, even if you are questioned. Never try and use the original ones, as then you are in deep trouble. After the Rhodesia fiasco I carried dud traveller's cheques for years. (See chapter 4.) Same method for doing insurance scams. By doing insurance scams you are entering the criminal world, which can lead into wasting your time in jail. We are more than likely only on this earth once, so you don't really want to waste your time in jail, not to mention you end up with a criminal record which then gives you loads of hassles in the future which I've had happen to me. I'd rather pay for my haircuts and chose my own hairstyle also most countries have lousy prison food, some third world counties you only get food that is brought in by relatives or friends or in some places you have to buy the food. Although you can end up in the clink through no fault of your own, rounded up by being in the wrong place at the time, in these situations you have to have access to cash to get you out.(Third world jails are a great way to lose weight – heaps of.)

Return Tickets

Return legs of tickets are often advertised on hostel notice boards. This used to be a great way to get around, and a great way to dispose of half a ticket, but unless you are leaving from an obscure airport, in say the Congo, forget it. Due to worldwide terrorism boarding passes are checked against passports everywhere. You might be able to still get away with it on internal flights. Return tickets or onward tickets are advisable as they usually don't cost much more than single tickets.

GOOD TIP TO REMEMBER: If you are in a country and you need an extra visa extension, and they require proof of a ticket, buy the ticket just before you need to, to show to the relevant official. Then go back to the travel agent (use a big established one), hand your ticket back, and say you've changed your mind. There is usually no surcharge within twenty-four hours. I've used this method twice.

Keep Small Currency

Recently I was stuck in Manila (Philippines) airport for twelve hours. The airport restaurant and shops didn't accept credit cards, and the banks did not accept British £50 notes (too many fakes around), or Thai Baht. I only had $200 Australian traveller's cheques, and I wasn't going to cash one of these and be left with Philippine pesos, so I had to just hang out for twelve hours and use the free water fountain for the sake of not having a few lose low value hard currency notes.

Methods of Sending Money From the UK

By Nat West Bank Draft

This is a bank guaranteed cheque – costs around £20 a good method for taking large amounts of money.

Travel Insurance

A good idea is to make sure you shop around for a good deal, prices can vary a great deal also read the small print, lots of companies look for a **way out** when it comes to paying out. Remember if you're buying travel insurance from a UK based company they charge 20 per cent VAT (damn criminal) one is supposed to be responsible for one's self and you get hammered with VAT. Regular insurance is 5 per cent VAT.

Sterling Transfer

Costs about £20 – sends money direct to your overseas bank account.

Urgent Transfer

Same as above in less time – costs about a third more.

Traveller's Cheques

A safe way to take spending money – can work out expensive, but well worth the cost for the peace of mind. Don't forget to record numbers on a separate piece of paper.

Building up ID

Start off with easy to get ID such as a library card, blood donor card, store cards, electricity/gas/water/telephone bills, open water diver certificate, rent book, then driver's licence, bank book. This is how one can build up false ID if you overstay. Use a hotel to get an address, i.e. Bondi Lodge, 82 Fletcher Street, Bondi – leave the Bondi Lodge off – the mail will still arrive.

Legally Changing Your ID

If you get deported from a country for overstaying, you can change your name quite easily by deed poll – costs less than £100. Then rebuild your new ID all legally. Then you can re-enter the country that deported you. Most countries give out passports if you have one grandparent from that country. Many people from the UK have an Irish grandparent. I myself have an Irish grandmother.

Americans, Argentinians, Chileans, Canadians, New Zealanders, Australians, white South Africans, white Zimbabweans and white Kenyans nearly all have a grandparent from within the twenty-eight member EU. Having an EU member state passport gives you a lot of scope for travelling and working. Although now many countries are installing finger print and iris recognition at port of entry. So it doesn't matter what your new name is you'll come up as what was originally entered. This change has all come about because of ever increasing worldwide terrorism.

If You Are Working Illegally and You Overstay

An immigration official I know in Sydney told me that nearly all the tip-offs about Brits who overstay come from overheard pub beer talk or from jilted lovers.

If immigration comes after you it is quite often that some do-good citizen has tipped them off, so keep your mouth shut about working illegally. If they come after you they will not be spending heaps of time and effort to track you down. They will follow a few set procedures. They will check with the public utilities first – gas, water, electricity, telephone – to see if you have any of the amenities in your name with an address. Then they will check with the driving licence department to see your licence address and the address on your tax certificate, so make sure you no longer reside at the address you used to get your ID. The same with your driving licence, bank book and tax file number. They will only spend a few man hours on you, unless you've gone down the criminal pathway and then put you back into their files and move on to the next victim.

REMEMBER: you are not a criminal unless you have built up false ID and then use it fraudulently.

Permanent Residence

It is possible to obtain permanent residence by fictitiously advertising a job vacancy from a fictitious company, and you then guarantee to hire yourself, as nobody else has met the company requirements. You, of course, have a glowing CV with impeccable credentials. This method I've known a few daring enterprising travellers use in old South Africa. I've known a couple of people get their residency in Australia also, using this method. With today's laser photocopiers, all sorts of qualifications and titles can be made up to suit the appropriate situation.

In the USA I know that the Irish Mafia, the 'Westies' who control the west side of New York, do a complete ID pack in your name for $5000-$15,000, depending on how urgent the need. Going further back, all of us travellers in the then Rhodesia had the appropriate tradesmen's licences as there were no labouring, menial jobs around for whites.

There were some hilarious stories doing the rounds complete, incompetent, chancers, turning up for jobs that they had bluffed their way into. My buddy, American Pete, had at least a dozen fitter jobs before one of them lasted more than a week. When he got started he didn't even know what a hacksaw was.

CHAPTER 3
Money and Travels

The saying goes, 'money is not everything.' Wrong! The person who said that (probably a man) was more than likely a millionaire. The saying has been around for so long now that the guy is probably now a multi-billionaire.

Money doesn't buy you health, but it buys you the best doctors and after care. Ask any member of any worldwide Royal Family (trouble is, you can't get to them to ask). Money, most importantly, gives you options on where you can go what you can do. You don't have to get fat and lazy, though I might be tempted to – for a while anyway. Most of you will experience money problems. Unless you win a lottery or inherit, it will be the lack of money, not the abundance of it and with money one can live anywhere on this earth with little or no immigration hassles.

As most of you who travel are going to be young and will have a rucksack, you will quite often be asked to show sufficient funds for the length of your stay, or when you get visas at embassies and consulates. Twice over the years I have had my plans seriously affected by not having sufficient funds to show at borders. I will tell you how to get around this in the next chapter. One of these occasions changed my life drastically.

In the early 70s I was making my way to Australia, going the old hippie overland route – a well worn road, full of adventure and excitement with lots of friends made. A big regret is that I didn't have much money so I had to move faster than I wanted to do. Lots of you will experience this. It does help if you have well-off, understanding parents to help you out now and again, but don't go running to mummy and daddy every five minutes or you will lose your self-respect and your sense of achievement. However, no point in starving, begging, stealing and prostituting oneself. (Keep those needles out of your arm or these unsavoury things could happen to you). Anyway, as I was saying, I always keep getting sidetracked when telling a story.

The route started in Amsterdam. The now defunct magic bus stopped in Istanbul via Athens for the early island hoppers. Two days break in Athens – everybody saw the Acropolis and sold half a litre of blood at the local hospital which paid £7. (Two days labour to earn that in those days.) Bus stopped in Istanbul. Cheap dirty dives and heaps of bed bugs thrown in for nothing. Across Turkey by train, and as one went further East the further back in time one went. By the time we reached Erzurum, the border of the old Soviet Union (now Armenia) and Iran, it was like we'd gone back a hundred years, apart from the odd military truck. There were no roads, only mud tracks – horses transported everything. There was no electricity, just kerosene lamps and wood burning stoves. From here we crossed over to Iran. This was the Shah's Iran. His secret police had all the Mullahs behind bars back then. The first things one noticed was the prosperity of the place after Eastern Turkey, electricity, paved roads, big American cars, all paid for with the incredible oil wealth. Men and women in western clothes.

Now, after the Islamic revolution everybody's happy and contented the women are covered up and locked up in the home when they go out they have to have a male relative escort more freedom though than in Saudi Arabia. Every Friday the Mullahs at prayer time froth at the mouth and scream death to the Great Satan (America) and recruit and train and send martyrs to eradicate the Jewish Satan (Israel).

After hitch-hiking all the way through Iran, we went back to the last century again – Afghanistan. The first town inside the border was Herat, where everything was horse drawn with lanterns in front at night. In those days Afghanistan and Nepal were the Mecca for the hippie culture; blocks of hash the size of chocolate bars selling for about the same price as chocolate bars. Here, as in Nepal, hippies smoked until they ran out of money, or their lungs collapsed. What an introduction these people had to our western culture.

Next stop en-route was Kandahar, where a century before half a British army died from dysentery chasing the elusive Afghans, all part of Kipling's Great Game. As it was the beginning of summer, and no electricity, there was no fruit and veg to be had anywhere. It was a vegetarians worst nightmare. The only food available was nan bread and mutton. The sheep were slaughtered in the street as was needed. I swear, as the meat was hung up you couldn't see it for flies. Needless to say, the next day I'm rapidly wasting away with dysentery, delirious with dehydration, and slipping in and out of consciousness. The two guys I'd teamed up with got a horse-drawn cab and literally dragged a doctor out of the local hospital, who saw me and wrote out a prescription. Off they went, and somewhere got the necessary drugs to fix me up.

How many doctors made house calls in the West in those days? Even less today. I wonder if that doctor has survived through all the years of occupation and civil war. I really hope so. Four days later I'm strong enough to take a broken down bus ride to Kabul with my two buddies. All I dare eat is one boiled egg per day and black tea, as tea has boiled water. A week later I'm strong enough to climb the mountain with my two buddies, Ray and Billy, and look upon the panoramic view of Kabul.

From Kabul we entered Pakistan through the infamous Khyber Pass, and passed all the old forts which kept the Afghans and Pathans out of the British Northwest frontier, through the Swat Valley where all the gunsmiths plied their deadly trade. One could buy umbrellas that were secret guns, also pen guns – all an amazing armoury of guns. On through the cities of Pakistan, into the Indian Punjab. It was so refreshing to be able to look upon women again after the Muslim world. In the Muslim world the hospitality is in abundance, but it's all male. You seldom see or meet the women. Once inside India you embark upon the railway system, criticised as the means to exploit an Empire of days gone by. Well, all I can say is I'm sure glad we did some exploiting – I'd hate to try and get around India without it.

First stop Amritsa – the Sikh's magnificent holy temple is here. Everyone is free to visit and stay and eat at the temple. No set time, but after a couple of days the temple authorities ask you when you are planning on leaving. Two days is more than enough for a non-Sikh. Only half of the Sikhs live in the Punjab. The rest are scattered around the world – known as the Jews of India.

As I stated before, when you are short of money you have to get a move on in one direction, so most of India and Nepal was out for me due to lack of cash. Ray had left us now, and Billy and I were on the train from Amritsa. The cops come on the train and 'shake down' every westerner with a rucksack and long hair. Billy has a bag of grass that he hasn't hidden. The cops' eyes light up with glee, the sergeant says, "Okay, you guys. Come with us now to the prison and wait to see the magistrate some time in the next week, maybe. Today is now Friday. Or you can pay an admittance of guilt fine and I take the evidence." Two hundred Rupees, then about £10. A lot of money considering the ladies of the night had cost about fifty pence only the day before. Billy started to argue and get smart with them. I changed his mind.

Fresh in my mind was an experience I'd had in Morocco a few years earlier wrongfully arrested for hash in Marrakesh, I spent ten days in jail before, thankfully, the British Consulate got me out. I doubt if people are so lucky today to get looked after by their consulates. I don't recommend third world jails. You get a free head shave (all my John Lennon hair gone), it's brilliant for rapid weight loss as you have to fight the cockroaches for mouldy breadcrumbs, and it doesn't do your head any good witnessing barbaric beatings and fighting off Arab homosexuals who take a shine to European teenage blue-eyed boys.

Also, hitch-hiking around France picking grapes in between mega hangovers, the cops were always searching us for drugs, looking for a bust to make. Grape picking – in spite of automation it is still possible to pick grapes i.e. on near vertical slopes. I suggest if you want to pick grapes before setting off to read *Guide to Vineyard Employment in France* by World Publications. Also the job centres in France are called Agence National pour I'Emploi (ANPE).These days though you have to compete with Eastern Europeans.

Cops have been known to set you up and bust you in many countries – Nepal, Morocco, Goa, Thailand, Bali just to name a few also watch out for spiked drinks in bars and night clubs and boiled sweets offered by new found friends on buses. Please don't let this negativity put you off. It's all part of the course.

REMEMBER THIS WHEN YOU TRAVEL: Never carry anything illegal. Never carry conflicting IDs. Cops, when you are young, are out to get you. The more arrests they make the quicker they move up the promotion ladder. Don't have the often-said macho attitude, 'If I'm in a jail, at least I'll get fed.' Maybe in the West, but not in the Third World. Cops will harass youngsters as the youths are usually unaware of their rights so they make an easy target.

Next stop was Agra. The Taj Mahal – very impressive building apart from the graffiti, impressive garden grounds. I wasn't very impressed with the Channel Lake. I didn't expect it to be only 18" deep. After this we just had to check out the local brothels. These details will be in my X-rated travel book, along with other abundant escapades.

Next stop en-route Varanasi: The Hindu's holy city for cleansing oneself in the Ganges river, and at the end of your life to be cremated on the steps of the Ganges and your ashes thrown in the river. The Hindus believe in reincarnation so the rigid caste system keeps people in the bottom caste happy and contented called (Dalit's, the untouchables) to be excrement shovellers, born to be shit shovellers, and if you're good and subservient in your life then in the next life you will come back a caste higher and you'll be giving orders to the shit shovellers. And so you move up until you're at the top – a Brahman. They are the rulers and aristocracy.

Great fun to go and watch all the stiffs being burnt. The road leading down through the city onto the river front was crammed with deformed, pitiful beings I guess waiting their turn to be cleansed so they can come back in the next life as a healthy person. Bit of a bummer if one comes back more deformed in the next life. On my way down to the river through this ocean of deformed people, one of them managed to clasp both his arms around one of my legs, and as I'm walking he's desperately pleading with me to give him some money. I gave him some loose change, but as I'm walking I'm literally dragging him along, fastened to my leg. I guess he figured I was going to be his lifelong provider until I had to shake my leg to get him to release me.

A few other stops, then on to Calcutta a month before the rainy season. Hotter than hell, tarmac on the roads melting and squelching in front of your very eyes, people everywhere. Eight million refugees from the recent war in neighbouring Bangladesh only added to the already chaotic stampede of humanity. Going around the back streets of Calcutta at night, one felt safer than being in New York and definitely safer than Johannesburg. Such is the passive and tranquil nature of Hinduism.

Land borders to Burma (now called Myanmar) are blocked, so a short plane trip to Rangoon (now called Yangon) capital of Burma. At this time Burma had been opened up to foreign visitors for a one week stay only (this was only the second year open). Everyone brought in a carton of cigarettes and a bottle of Johnny Walker whisky, sold them on the black market, and travelled and lived there for one week living on the proceeds. An amazing country, Burma. After two days I had my first solid shit since leaving Europe. All the times that I've been and passed through the Far East, I've never been back. I think it's mainly because I'd like to spend a decent amount of time there.

The Burmese people were so friendly, and especially to the British, more so than to other foreigners. They had fond memories of British rule – definitely a lot better than the Marxist socialism they had then. Now they are embracing a free market economy like their other successful Asian neighbours. The military have now relinquished power.

It was so refreshing after India not to be hassled all the time. In India it seems everyone wants to practice their English on you, i.e., "Where are you from?" – answer England. "Where are you going?" – answer Australia. "What is your name?" – answer Ralph. "My name is Jamdin. What is your profession?" etc… on and on, "I would like to come to your country. I have many friends and relatives in Southall and Leicester. Can you give me your address in England and will you sponsor me to come to England?" Well if you have many friends and relatives in Southall and Leicester why don't you get them to sponsor you – so get lost and leave me alone.

After checking out the impressive colonial buildings I headed up north to Mandalay by another turn of the century train (eat your heart out all you train spotters in anoraks). The wooden carriages were leaking and falling to bits as we were moving. After Mandalay we went by Jeep to a mountain top hill station for the old colonials, escaping the summer heat. The houses and horse carriages were straight out of the film *Gone with the Wind* with every building falling to bits. At that altitude, European fruit, veg and dairy products were grown and made, but of course only for local consumption due to the spoilage factor of moving them with no transport or refrigeration.

Back to Rangoon and on to Thailand, short hop on a plane. As I said, the land borders were closed then. This is my first of many visits to Thailand. I will go into Thailand later in this book (under Working in Thailand).

I've teamed up with some other fellow travellers now. We stay in the cheapest dive near the down-town railway station (The Pepsi Hotel) as we are all going to go separate ways by train. That night we smoked some Thai grass that is so strong I can hardly stop myself from floating off into space. We decide to visit a brothel just up the road, a real Thai brothel leaking tin roof as it's the rainy season, a cock-fight going on downstairs, money changing hands on the outcome.

More details in my X-rated travel book. Later, back at the hotel, a few beers and another smoke. Now I'm completely gone. I've really lost the plot now.

Since leaving Istanbul where I got devoured by bed bugs, I've had about a dozen sores on my body that have not gone away. I've tried to keep them clean and treated, but with the heat and dirt, and your body always getting run down (i.e. dysentery, etc.) they are constantly weeping pus. I decided to get rid of these sores once and for all, bearing in mind that now I'm feeling no pain whatsoever from the effect of the smoke. One of my room mates has a sharp pointed pair of scissors and I start to dig at the roots of these eternal damn sores. I drift off into the deepest hallucinogenic sleep of my life.

The next day I'm in deep trouble. All my sores are glowing red with inflammation, swelling and weeping. The glands under my arms, between my groin and in my throat are also swelling rapidly. I need medical treatment, like yesterday. I went to the pharmacy – he says I'll need penicillin and anti-inflammation drugs, pain killers and a hospital – probably cost me about $1000. I've got £250. I decide to buy a pile of his pain killers, no prescription needed. I drugged myself up to the eyeballs with these pain killers, as I'm hurting real bad now.

I get the next train to Malaysia. I've put on long trousers and a long sleeved shirt, dressed the wounds, bandaged the one on the side of my head, and try and get some rest. I also realise I can't cross the border into Malaysia totally out of my head on pain killers, I'll have to let them wear off awhile so as to be alert for the customs and immigration officials that are always a pain in the neck. Just before the border the train is slowing down, so I get up to go to the toilet. Just before the toilet is a metal grill luggage cage, and just as I'm about to go past, the train jams on its brakes and I go crashing into the steel mesh. Every single sore on my body bursts open and I scream with agony. Anyone who's into pain – this was the ultimate.

After reaching Malaysia's capital, Kuala Lumpur, I depart the train and hitch-hike to the south-east coastal town of Malacca (now called Melaka), an ex-Portuguese colony. I've headed here as I know it's cheap living, huts and YHA on the beach, and a hospital that's within walking distance. I know all this as I'd been here before with my parents, who were with the British military in Singapore a few years before. I don't believe in sponging and scrounging, but sometimes you have to in order to survive. I knew Malaysia had first-class English speaking free medical facilities. Thailand didn't and still hasn't a free one, but their quality has now improved.

What a relief getting to that hospital, having my wounds frozen and swabbed out. My left forearm was as thick as my calf muscle by now. The pus that came out was hard and came out as thick as a garden worm and two foot long. I became a day patient for ten days, each morning having wounds treated and a penicillin jab every day in alternate bum cheeks, by pretty Birmingham accented nurses. Today the scars from these wounds look like entrance rounds from a .22 calibre gun. After I had recovered, I was on my way. I hitch-hiked down to Singapore and went to the Indonesian Embassy for a visa. The month before, they stopped giving out visas to foreigners with less than $350. I was now down to $200. I knew from the travel books around at the time that I could have made Portuguese Timor, which was only a $20 ferry ride from Darwin, Northern Territory, Australia, where at that time work was in plentiful abundance. Pub notice boards even had jobs chalked up on them. I guess the Indonesians had brought out these rules to stop foreigners from getting stranded in their country. It could also have been a prelude to stopping foreigners from going to Timor, as later they invaded and severed links with Darwin.

One week of going around applying for work as a roustabout with foreign based offshore oil drilling companies yielded no luck – too young and no offshore work experience. Being so desperate for employment I ended up being ripped off for half of what I had left on a so called job promise from a con-artist. Finally, I had to go cap in hand to the British Consulate to get myself repatriated – bailed out twice in four years. This had to stop! If you've read this chapter you should have learnt a few pointers:

- Don't try and cover too much ground with too little cash.

- Take out insurance.

- Desperation breeds vulnerability.

- Never carry illegal substances.

- Carry a small medical kit.

- Don't let anybody keep your passport 'for safe keeping.'

- Pick up hotel/guest-house card in case you get lost on your first foray around town.

CHAPTER 4
A Trip Marred By Immigration Problems

"Hard work never hurt anybody," said the Supervisor.

– Stuart McCauley

Towards the end of 1977 I was heading up to Zimbabwe which was then a completely different country called Rhodesia. I'd come down through Africa as far as Kenya. I would have liked to have carried on travelling overland as flying around Africa in those days (as in these days) was very expensive due to lack of free enterprise in the air industry with state monopolies being the order of the day – screw the passengers for as much money as possible and never mind about filling up the planes.

Tanzania was the next country south of Kenya, but at that moment in time the border was shut. Never mind tourists, trade and commerce – African leadership pride was at stake, so a minor disagreement between the two countries had closed the border.

To go east was the sea and to go west was Uganda, which was not such a good place to be under Idi Amin. White faces were getting robbed by police and army check points were all over the place. Black faces were ending up face down in rivers as crocodile meat. As I wanted to stay in Africa for a few years I was shortly going to need work, and not having any professional qualifications the only places for me to work were either South

Africa or Rhodesia. I flew into Johannesburg and within a few weeks I found the place to be very oppressive, being an Afrikaner apartheid police state. Little things like getting a bus for a job interview were a real headache. Six buses would go by but one couldn't get on them as they were designated for 'blacks'. You had to wait in the hot sun until a 'white' bus came along. Such petty bullshit – only a car driving Dutch Afrikaner could think that one up.

"Harsh ideology – a crazy concept, born of prejudice and fear," – General Jan Smuts.

I'd heard on the traveller's grapevine that Rhodesia was the place to be, and if you kept to the cities there were plenty of jobs to be had. The Rhodesian men were all in the army fighting for their country's very survival, so companies wanted people with no military commitments. Also, there were plenty of Rhodesian girls and women around as their men were tied up on the borders. It sounded great, so off I went. I hitch-hiked up to the border Beit Bridge. I crossed over the border and was going through immigration with a rucksack on when this immigration official's eyes lit up. He decided I was not coming into his country. He hated the British – Britain was to blame for all his country's woes. Not themselves, mind you – Britain and the British. Forget the fact that thousands of British were fighting for them in their crack units; RLI, RAR, SAS, Grey Scouts, PATU and Air Force, and maybe even a few in the Selous Scouts, not to mention all the support units. Bearing in mind that at this time Rhodesia was a 'white' country, the government was desperate for young white men to replace those that were leaving every day due to the war that was in progress. All men that were libel to do military service were doing six weeks in and six weeks out this was having a huge strain on the economy, not to mention family life.

I was coming in to settle for a while so I didn't have an onward ticket, and my funds were low. This immigration official says, "No." I expect all the women in his life probably said 'no' to him, so now he's got power in a uniform and he says, "No," to me. "You don't have enough money." After the episode in Singapore a few years earlier I made sure I'd have enough money in my bank in the UK for emergencies like this, so I showed him my bank account statement. He was still not letting me into his country – he hated Britain and the British. "I want to see cash money for a ticket from Salisbury (Harare) to London," he said. Nothing for it but to walk back to Messina on the South African side of the border and send a telegram to my bank in the UK (no faxes in those days).

Well, here I was in Messina. I was thinking I would be able to handle a couple of days, but no more, as the place was regularly recording the hottest temperatures in South Africa and hardly anybody wanted to speak English. In this place the Boer War was still going on in the minds of the locals. (This is the area where Breaker Morant and all the Aussies ran riot at the turn of the century during the Boer War of 1899-1902: Read *Scapegoats of the Empire*). Well, at least I would hear from my bank soon and be able to pick up the money from a bank in the town. Major shock and horror was in store for me when I heard from my bank. The statement read to the effect that I had had my foreign exchange allowance for the year and they could not send me any more money as they would be breaking exchange control regulations. "What the hell," I said to myself! Well, the Labour government of the day had finally taken the 'Great' out of Britain and made us a third world nation, making thousands of people criminals for having to smuggle money out in suitcases if one wanted to have more money than the official allowance which was a miserable £300 per year. So there I was, a casualty of their making, stuck in a hell hole in the Northern Transvaal. (Four years later I was managing an avocado farm in the Northern Transvaal, less than fifty miles from Messina, after my Kruger-rand gold coin smuggling exploits were over. More in my book about African Adventures). Regardless of what anybody says about Margaret Thatcher, she scrapped exchange controls which stopped people like myself getting into dire straits in strange lands.

Well, what the hell to do now? I decided I wasn't going to work in South Africa and I was going to get up to Salisbury, Rhodesia. I went back down to Johannesburg to hang out for a while until I got something sorted out. Who did I know well enough to borrow a wad of money from for a few years? At this stage of my life I had loads of good friends around the world, but most of them were in the same or similar position as myself, and getting hold of half of them would be an event in itself. I decided the pleasure of lending me a wad of money would fall on a mate of mine who was now in Edmonton, Alberta, Canada.

Les Scott was a great pal of mine. We had quite a few jaunts together, working in Copenhagen as hotel kitchen hands and checking out the friendly Danish girls. We had been construction labourers in Jersey the Channel Isles, also labouring in factories and building sites in Birmingham and had adventures in Morocco and Canada together. In Copenhagen before I got a job as a kitchen porter I was so broke I was living rough and eating out of bins. I reckon I'm immune to hepatitis. I've known countless people who have come down with various forms of this disease, but I've never suffered from this one. Les and I had both been greatly traumatized by the IRA pub bombings in 1974 as we were both regulars of those two city pubs (Tavern in the Town, and the Mulberry Bush) and we were up the city on that frightful Thursday night. Twenty-one killed and one hundred and eighty two injured many of the injuries were very serious, I've never had much time for the IRA after that. So much for hitting military targets.

I phoned him up, but alas he had no money. However, all was not lost – he would borrow money from Viking Eric the Dane, (now lives in Ecuador) another close buddy who was around in Edmonton with him. After the money arrived I hitch-hiked back up to the border. It was easy hitching in Africa in those days but don't hitch in South Africa today.

So as I go back through the immigration channels, that bastard is there again. He recognizes the fact that I now have sufficient funds and he now decides I have to deposit enough money for a plane ticket out of the country, which is only refundable when I get a residence permit or leave the country. Now I'm down to my last $20 and Christmas is in two weeks. It's very difficult to get jobs in the southern hemisphere around Christmas time due to the fact that it is also the long summer holidays.

Hitch-hiking was easy due to the fact that most traffic in rural areas went in military convoys. Salisbury was a great place with very cheap accommodation, interesting and adventure minded travellers away from the map, and diary brigade travellers. With the aid of some of the seasoned travellers around, I worked out how to get my money back.

In my haste to get to Rhodesia I hadn't checked the travel books around. If I had I would have found out that there was another route into Rhodesia at that time – a rail route through Botswana into the Western Rhodesian city of Bulawayo and according to all the travellers I spoke to they had no immigration hassles doing this route. So I borrowed money from a new found friend, American Pete, and bought a rail ticket from Salisbury to Gaborone in Botswana. Then I went along to the immigration office in Salisbury, showed them the ticket and told them that l was leaving. They gave me my money back. I then went straight away to the railway ticket office and said that I'd changed my mind and was staying – so I received a full refund. Now I had a whole wad of money for Christmas.

My further adventures in Rhodesia and Zimbabwe warrants a book in itself. Briefly, I started to follow my earlier advice about staying in the cities and by becoming a swimming pool lifeguard I got myself into too many hassles with so called available women. I then landed myself a job as a cattle ranch manager: two ranches – 36,000 and 14,000 acres, four African soldiers under my command, sixty workers and their families. All this responsibility – what a tremendous challenge. Once my boss said to me that I'd never make a Rhodesian because I worked too hard. Now I was reading Wilbur Smith novels at night and acting out the characters in the day, game hunter and all. I was able to get this job due to the cattle working experience I'd gained while working on Kibbutz's in Israel. Who said unpaid work was a waste of time? That's what I was told when I went to Israel by mates up the pub who didn't have the balls to go anywhere or do anything. I finally quit this job after myself and my buddy, American Pete who was staying with me at the time came under a mortar barrage. If it had been my land I probably would have had a different outlook.

Pete said to me under horrendous noise, "Do you realise we are only three days hitch-hiking away from the beaches of Durban?"

I later met that immigration official again in a bar in Beit Bridge. I told him what he had done to me before I kicked the hell out of him, in spite of being in front of witnesses. I got off being charged due to the fact that he went for his gun when he was gaining consciousness. Under the law there you had to hang up your weapons upon entering bars and hotels. He hadn't done so – I had. The patrons disarmed him.

Now his Rhodesia has gone forever. Taken over by Robert Mugabe's ZANU.PF party. Everything that the Rhodesians said would happen has happened. Instead of – come to Rhodesia and see the Zimbabwe ruins. It's now come to Zimbabwe and see the Rhodesia ruins. I go on the web site www.zimbabwesituation.com every day for curiosity. A very interesting YouTube video worth watching is Africa Addio made in 1966. (Farewell Africa). A bit over the top on the Cape Town segment. (Don't watch unless you have a strong stomach). If any of you are interested in Africa I recommend reading *The Shackled Continent* by Robert Guest. For Rhodesia, *Top Secret War* by Col. Reid Daley, *No Mean Soldier* by Perter McAleese.

- Check out routes.

- Have enough money.

- Work cheaply or for nothing if you are learning a valuable skill or trade.

- Read about the country and place you are going to. You can never have enough information.

- Check out whether a return ticket is needed. Some returns are not much more than singles.

- Always pay back money and favours. Never burn your bridges.

CHAPTER 5
Thailand

If you are thinking of working in the Far East then Thailand is a great place to start. Bangkok has the best variety of budget places to stay in Asia at 150 Baht – 500 Baht, dormitories (depending on the exchange rate £1 = 50-56 Baht, USD $1= 30-34 Baht, EUR 1 = 42-45 Baht, AUS $ = 28-32.

If you are not a high flyer commodity dealer, or a high ranking company employee who can get posted to the Orient, don't despair. There are plenty of job opportunities to be had for English teachers. It is still possible to place ads in the English speaking Bangkok Post or the Nation newspapers. For teaching English one to one, another good source of information for what's going on in BKK is the monthly Metro magazine. Plenty of Vietnam war films such as *The Killing Fields*, which required Caucasian GI extras, are made in Thailand plus Van Damm-type Kung Fu films. **Remember** what I wrote earlier – desperation makes you very vulnerable, so beware of handing money over to employment agencies who promise the earth but deliver nothing. Most film jobs are advertised in the paper.

Throughout the Far East over the last forty years there has been a great wave of so-called English teachers, many of whom do not have English as a first language. Due to this fact I would strongly advise one to take the RSA Cambridge Certificate TEFLA (Teaching English as a Foreign Language for Adults). This is an internationally recognised qualification. It is offered as a full-time intensive course over four weeks and as a part-time course over twelve weeks. Its main aim is to provide pre-service training in teaching English as a foreign language to adults (TEFLA). The Certificate is intended both for people without previous teaching experience who wish to enter the profession, and for those teachers who have no previous training in this particular field.

IMPORTANT: The course is very intensive and requires a total commitment. Everyone around the world today is plugging into the internet and that is in English. So is the world's aviation traffic control, also lets not forget the inroads that popular music has made over the last half a century around the world. The English language is pushing relentlessly everywhere, so by having this qualification the pressure to bullshit your way into a job will be off.

Kevin's Story

A couple of thoughts for new teachers in Thailand.

My friend Kevin, whilst teaching one of his first lessons in Thailand, was approached by a sweet young Thai girl who came to his desk and asked, "Can I have a look at your dick?" Kevin looked at her for what seemed like ages trying to think of something appropriate to say, when she reached across his desk and took hold of his dictionary. He later found out that 'dic' is the common word used by Thais when referring to a dictionary. He never got round to telling me whether he was relieved or disappointed when she made a move for his dictionary not his dick.

Another thing first time teachers in Thailand should be aware of is that most of the Thai female students, who appear interested in you, are only being friendly, and if you make advances to them you will probably scare them off and they will drop out of your class. Be patient and perhaps ask an experienced 'old Thai hand' for his opinion about what is really going on. For God's sake don't flash your dick.

You can find out about these courses by contacting your local college or library or as most people do now Google or Bing everything. If you don't fancy hanging around Britain to do this course, the same courses are available in Thailand, Australia and New Zealand. There are fifteen centres in Australia. The one in Sydney is the only one that runs every month. Although the course costs more in Australia than the UK, the cost of living in Australia is less than the UK and Sydney accommodation is cheaper and much more plentiful than, say, London. There is also better fun and lifestyle to be had in Sydney than in London. Anyone who disputes me on the quality of life comparing Sydney to London, try taking a ride on the London underground in the summer time rush hour. One is jammed in like sardines in an oven. No air-conditioning, not to mention the outrageous ticket prices.

Inquiries in Sydney to: Australian TESOL Training Centre, Australian College of English, PO Box 82, Bondi Junction, NSW, 2022. Telephone: (02) 389 0249 Fax: (02)389 6880.

There are 100 centres in the UK and overseas. For a full list contact: UCLES, 1 Hills Road, Cambridge, CB1 2EU. One of these centres has now opened in Bangkok. Of course get the latest up to date information from the internet.

When entering Thailand get a three month visa from the Thai Embassy. If you don't they will only give you one month at port of entry and for an extension you will have to go out of the country and then come back in. Thailand has land borders with Malaysia, Laos, Cambodia and Myanmar (Burma). Remember when applying for a visa you can only apply for a tourist visa as a working visa can only be obtained for you by a company. As you don't yet have a job you cannot get this. You are not supposed to work on a tourist visa, but this is not a major problem as most English teachers do not have work visas. After your three months is up everyone takes a bus or train to one of the neighbouring countries (a visa-run) and renews their visa. Now you can only do this 'round trip' three times after which a work permit is required. Your employers will sponsor you for a permit if you've made the grade.

For the latest up today information visit: www.khaosod.co.th, www.coconuts.co/Bangkok/Manila/Singapore/News.

Or my favourite site which I visit every day www.thaivisa.com/

Try and get a three months non-immigrant visa in the UK. Then you won't have to leave while applying for your work permit. This is for people with qualifications.

Thai people in general are very friendly and hospitable. There are exceptions to every rule, so don't get lulled into a friendship where drugs are concerned. The Bangkok city jail is full of westerners who thought they were onto a sure thing smuggling dope back to Europe, Australia or wherever. Many of them are now doing life sentences, hoping for a King's pardon which are issued on his birthday. Westerners have been hung in Malaysia and Singapore (barbarous nations). Thailand also has the death penalty, but is not carried out for drug offences, at least not on foreigners (Farangs) or as Thais say falang as many Asians struggle with pronouncing 'Rs.' When you're called a falang it is not derogatory, apparently it came from the Thai word for Frenchman, why Frenchman, well they were the ones who were all over SE Asia (Indo China) for 200 plus years.

Even small quantities of grass can require a massive bribe to get you off. Amphetamines that were readily available across the counter in pharmacies have now been moved up to a Class A drug, alongside heroin, so are now illegal. This was not brought about by westerners buying them, but by Thai truck drivers that were pushing their bodies to the limit and then crashing their trucks, usually killing people in the process. Also, a growing number of students were taking them so that they could stay up all night to study for exams. Talk about being desperate to pass!

Don't try and belittle the Thai people. They are a proud, strong and independent race. Respect their culture and their heritage. Their Monarchy and religion is out of bounds for negative discussion; **Lese Majeste** is a law that forbids taking about the Monarchy in a negative light, (we had these same laws in Europe 250 years ago) as a foreigner you'd get deported, maybe some jail time and maybe a fine. A Thai national can get up to fifteen years in prison and it does happen a lot, five-fifteen years. So don't go on about how rich the Royal Family is (the richest in the world) even more wealthy than the Sultan of Brunei.

Don't pat Thai people on the head – it is an insult, like patting a dog. Also, don't point with your feet – this is also an insult. When one first arrives in a strange new environment things can seem daunting, especially if at the back of your mind you know that you have to find a job, and one knows that there is no Social Security net to fall into. This fact alone can quite often be a blessing in disguise. Now you have to economize and stay off the drink and make new friends, and just generally put yourself about to get in the know for jobs.

When foreigners arrive in a new country for work they tend to head for certain locations, usually central to the main business centres of the capitals. This is definitely a great way to meet people in the same position as oneself, and so get in the know for accommodation and jobs, however, long term this is not a good idea as you will only get to know people passing through and you won't get to know the locals. London has Earl's Court and Acton, a magnet for Australians, New Zealanders and South Africans. I know Australians who have been over for years and still cling to their cans of Fosters and VB bitter – a classic case of not mixing with the locals, and a sad sight indeed. I'm far from being a flag-waving Pommie, but I've travelled all over the world and the UK is definitely the best country for its choice of beer. So get to know and mix with the people of the country – you could be missing out on all kinds of good things. Australia has Kings Cross for the foreign travellers. The first time I went to Australia I hardly went out of the place while I was in Sydney. Everybody, sometime or another, falls into a rut, which is justifiable if you're having fun. A lot of travellers now stay in Glebe and Bondi as well as Kings Cross. Well, sorry for getting off the subject of Thailand. The story of my life – I'm always getting side tracked, usually across continents on a whim. My big problem in life is that I always want to be where I'm not.

Bangkok is where the majority of jobs are for teaching English. The Khao San Road is where the budget travellers, and travellers looking for work, generally stay and hang out as there is plenty of cheap accommodation in hotels and guest houses. Another favourite area to stay used to be around the Malaysian Hotel, Soi Ngam Duphli area, off Rama IV Road. Airport shuttles run from the airport to Khao San Road, also the Airport Link runs from underneath the airport. Pick up free fold out maps and guides to getting around Bangkok at the airport.

The Malaysian Hotel has a history in itself. It was started in the 60s for R&R for GIs from Vietnam; in the 70s and 80s it was a major travellers hotel and general hangout, often frequented by Charles Sobhraj, looking for new victims to drug, rob and sometimes kill. He has had numerous books films and documentaries about him. Check him out on **Wikipedia,** what a monster. The hotel since the 90s has been a gay boy hotel and expensive for travellers. A sad memory for me – a good friend of mine, Icelandic Jan, completely out of his head, fell or was pushed out of the top floor bedroom balcony. His sister was on her way out to meet him for a holiday. We had to send her around to the Icelandic Embassy to collect his ashes. An almost identical accident (murder) happened to my buddy, Wolverhampton Graeme, six months earlier in Johannesburg, South Africa. Remember to be careful – don't get out of it, keep control and don't lose the plot.

This area had been a westerner's hang out much longer than the Ko San Road area. Everywhere in Bangkok is dirty and incredibly noisy, but all that aside, Bangkok's biggest park, Lumphini, is only a kilometre away. Also, Phat Pong Street which has some of Bangkok's infamous night life is within walking distance now looking tired and drab, in the day time it becomes a market, more action and more fun around the Sukhumvit Road area. Also, the Lumphini Boxing Stadium before it was pulled down (to be moved to a new location) used to be well worth a Friday night to see real Thai boxing. Not the tourist version – there was plenty of gambling on the outcome of the fights as the fighting was going on.

Sadly I stopped going as the Thais started their double pricing antics which sadly is spreading all over Thailand now, they have to keep gouging the tourists for as much money as possible, maybe this is down to the fact that they don't have a welfare state and the tourist is seen as being rich a walking ATM so to speak. At the boxing stadium they were charging foreigners 1200 Baht entrance fee and Thais 3-400 entrance fee. Many of the foreigners were budget travellers with limited funds where as many of the Thais turned up in 3-5 million Baht cars and trucks, (Thai poor Farang rich they say this all the time when you ask them why you're being over charged). Thais in Thailand do whatever they like, many attractions charge foreigners up to ten times more than locals, wine and cheese from Europe has 400 per cent tax duty added whereas their products are all over the EU. So much for fair trading I sometimes wish we would be more like them.

Student cards, press cards, and international driving licences can be obtained from the Ko San Road – many discounts worldwide to be had with these cards and can also be used as a 'starter' kit for building up a fake ID. Note: Always best to post dodgy ID if you're going to Sydney or wherever your next stop is. Use 'Poste Restante' Sydney. Twice over the years I have had student cards confiscated – no charges brought although fake driving licence and passport could be a prison sentence.

A lot of the westerners in Bangkok have been around for a long time. They are a good source of information, but be wary, lots of them are living off pulling scams of one sort or another, quite often on new gullible arrivals. In the early 80s I got scammed out of $100 over a sob story that I fell for. Who would expect an English ex-public school boy to be pulling cons? I didn't, so watch out!

One used to be able to buy counterfeit $100 bills for half price. They haven't been around for a long time, although I've heard they are now back and better than ever (can end up in jail though), The US Treasury Department takes a dim view of counterfeit money and so do the Thai authorities.

An old joke (now the new notes have changed)
Why are all American notes the same size and colour?
Answer: So you can rip off blind people.

As in every alcohol drinking country in the world (most Muslim countries excluded), one has to be careful. If you are going to be a typical Brit: on 'holiday', drinking huge amounts of booze, singing and shouting 'ere we go, ere we go, ere we go,' and just being a right pain, (I avoid them like the plague), and then taking the piss out of the Thais because they are polite, passive, friendly and usually smaller than Europeans, don't be surprised if you get your head bashed in. The Thais have great confidence in themselves, which probably has something to do with the fact that Thai boxing is the major sport of the country and just about everyone is good at it, just like every inner city kid from Manchester, Liverpool, London and Glasgow knows how to play a decent game of football.

Thai Women

Many liberals and feminists in the west accuse single western men of causing and creating Thai prostitution. This is simply not so, but I'm not saying we don't help to create a demand. Thai culture is very male oriented, and to have more than one wife or concubine is common practice among the more affluent in the Far East.

Business men, when entertaining for contracts, regularly take their clients to massage parlours and karaoke bars. This has been going on for centuries, long before westerners ever went out to the Far East. Siam, the ancient name for Thailand, was a favourite stopping off port for the early sailors. I definitely know why this was so.

Although Thailand is a male dominated society, women are free and not held back and restricted and forbidden by law, as in say the Islamic societies, so you will encounter females doing every kind of job, although I've yet to encounter a female taxi driver, there are some about though, many are working ten-twelve hours per day as building site labourers in the sweltering heat and humidity of South East Asia, which is a very common sight. This kind of work, as with agricultural labouring, is done by Thai and migrant workers from neighbouring countries. Eighty per cent of the Thai population are engaged in agriculture.

As in all third world and emerging countries they have televisions and DVDs in their villages, and cinemas in their nearby towns, so of course the young people see the 'good life' and excitement to be had in the cities and off they go, which we also do in the West. As there is little or no social security, many of the girls end up in the sex industry. Thus, many of them earn substantial amounts of money which enables them to send money back home to support their relatives. Of course there are horror stories about kidnapping and selling girls into sexual slavery, but this is not the norm. Thai people love and cherish their children as much or even more so than most societies around the world. Girls are not a burden to be aborted or abandoned as in, say India or China. Even in London, Harley Street medical specialists perform female circumcision on Muslim girls entering puberty.

Don't assume that all Thai girls are on the game, so to speak. It's not so. Just as not all Liverpudlians are comedians, or Mancunians support Manchester United. Assuming stereotypes can get you into trouble. When you meet a bar girl (not if, when), you will find them very willing and desirable. If you take one back to your hotel for the night, just because they are too polite to mention money, don't assume it's for free. Would you work all night for free? Of course, you meet the guys who say, 'I don't pay for sex. I've never paid for sex and never will.' Well, they are the guys who make the girls hard and callous. Sometimes these guys get beaten up and they quickly get themselves known, so when a girl talks money, it's usually because they have had one of these encounters.

Besides, apart from the one-off encounters you have throughout your life, you always pay one way or another. On a small scale getting girls drinks costs money. So does paying for taxis and taking women out for meals and the cinema although most women these days are more than happy to put their hand in their purse. How many nightclubs around the world have free entrance for women but the men have to pay? The costs usually fall upon the male. Who says you don't pay? You always pay!

Taking girls out of bars in Bangkok is usually much more expensive than say Pattaya, the beach resort south east of Bangkok (three hours bus ride). Usually you pay the bar owners – 300 baht depending on the establishment. This is added to your drinks bill when you leave. The girl gets a proportion of this amount. Then you pay anything from 1000 baht – 2000 baht depending on yourself. Double that for Bangkok. It is best to mention money before leaving the bar as this can save and avert problems later.

Remember, they also choose you when you arrive in the establishment. If you are fifty years old or older, fat and bald, an obvious sex tourist, you are more than likely going to pay more than a fresh faced twenty-five year old English speaking youth who they can have some fun with and practice their English on but not always as they know that older guys are usually less demanding and usually don't quibble about money By taking a girl from a bar and paying a bar fee, this is a kind of insurance. You know where the girl has come from.

As in all professions you get some cheats and con artists. Be careful with your money and only take with you what you will need, plus some extra of course. When I've heard of people getting ripped off, it's always girls that are untraceable. What I always do is put my wallet right in the middle of the bed between the springs and mattress when they go to the bathroom to get showered before bed. It seems obvious, but if you've checked out your room before going out you will find hiding places Also, have some 100 and 500 Baht notes so as not to pull out only 1000 Baht notes in the morning.

Of course, if you do get slack and leave your things all over the place, you will eventually pay the price, I met a woman once outside the bar system who was untraceable. When I brought her back to my hotel room I was wondering at the back of my drunken mind why she had a huge handbag with her I found out why in the morning. She had cleaned me out, a new camera, zoom lens and all. So watch out for girls with handbags anything bigger than a woman's make up bag, be suspicious. It's a right hassle cancelling and replacing credit cards and other important documents. Lots of hotels write down the girls ID numbers when they arrive back with you.

Most places have got reliable safes, so use them. Unfortunately there have been cases of people staying at small guest houses in the north of the country going off travelling and trekking, and while they have been away their credit cards have been used so take it with you when trekking. Also, whenever you use a credit card make sure it is not taken out of your sight so as to stop double run-offs. When trekking it has been known for bandits to make you sign your traveller's cheques over at gun point, although this is very rare these days it is a good idea in any country to have little padlocks on your luggage when travelling on buses and trains. It is generally accepted that you shouldn't accept drinks off locals as there have been cases of people being drugged and robbed in this manner.

Watch out for the gem stone scams, it is not possible to make money on precious stones even if they have been so called smuggled in from Burma or wherever, and they'll cut glass in front of you with them. You can only make money on stones if you have dug them out of the ground yourself. Similar scams go on all over the world I fell for it in Johannesburg in 1977. This black guy comes up to me, looking all nervous and looking over his shoulder, as if cops are about, and then he produces a fancy flip top ring holder with a diamond engagement ring and a gold wedding ring inside. So you're supposed to think, and I did, South Africa, world centre for gold and diamonds, workers all over the world pilfer off their employers, I'm onto a deal here with this ignorant black chap. He says, "Boss, boss, look at this," as he quickly shows it to you and shields it with his two hands. "Give me 100 Rand, boss. ($140 then)." Reluctantly he agrees to sell them for twenty Rand. I think I've made a killing, white man lording it over the blacks and all that. When I take my new found wealth into a back street jeweller to have the value estimated, he laughs and tells me a wholesaler down the road sells them for five Rand a set. I'm choked. I've met people who have paid 150 rand on this scam. This scam comes in similar forms all over the world.

Another scam which is practiced in Bangkok, and more so in Soho, London, it is as follows: you go into a secluded downstairs bar, usually in the daytime when no one is about, drinking patrons that is. You have a couple of drinks with a so called hostess around, and then when you go to leave you get lumbered with a massive bill. By having a couple of heavies on the door most people pay up and leave with their tail between their legs, too embarrassed to complain to the cops. In Bangkok this usually happens in upstairs Phat Pong bars which tempt customers with offers free sex shows.

This scam was tried on me in Phat Pong one hot afternoon. I had been upstairs, second floor up above the bars, to see this jeweller that I had been doing business with. When the fake, copy Rolex watches first hit the scene in London and were all the rage, I and plenty of other enterprising travellers were sending them back by post and carrying large quantities on us through customs.

Don't try this with dope as every airport in the world now has sniffer dogs running up and down the luggage conveyor belts out of view of the general public, smelling out drugs and plastic explosives. I've witnessed this first hand.

One time coming through customs I got greedy and brought fifty back with me (you see, the postal bills were adding up). I got caught and lost my watches, plus a £250 admittance of guilt fine. One of the officers said to me to write to the appropriate authorities and reapply to have the watches re-exported. I had a close friend in Bangkok, my mate Kevin, who has been in Bangkok since 1981. He started off teaching English one to one through the newspaper, and now he is head of an English college, which is not bad progress for starting out with an O'level in English. Anyway, I thought I'd send the watches to him. My reply was, "We've taken into consideration your application to re-export your forty-seven watches. We can not do this as they are counterfeit trade mark and will have to be destroyed." Well, at least those three customs officers got a perfect fake Rolex Oyster watch each. Anyway, back to the story.

When I arrived at the shop, the chap I'd been doing business with was out for a while and not due back for another hour, so I decided to have a beer and come back later. Further along the corridor was a bar entrance, not advertised at all. I figured it was probably a private club or gambling den, and rather than go down into the street, I thought, 'This place will do.' So in I went. It was quite a plush place, obviously a night time place, as I was the only person in the joint apart from two doormen who were chatting and having a smoke – both obviously ex-Thai boxers as their faces had seen better days, to put it politely. There was also one barman and one hostess. I proceeded to a corner where there was decent lighting, got the newspaper out and ordered a beer. The hostess brought the beer over, asked me if I'd buy her a drink, and could she join me. I declined both offers. I just told her I wasn't staying long as I was waiting for an appointment. No problem. She went back to the bar stool and carried on chatting to the barman.

By the time I'd finished the newspaper I'd finished my second beer. Now I asked for the bill. She brought the bill over and to my utter amazement it was 1000 Baht. Nowhere in Thailand at that time was beer over 100 Baht, bottom-end price 30 Baht – so there they are charging me 500 Baht per beer. So, obviously, I started to complain to the barman.

"What's going on," I said. "I've only had two beers. I'll give you one hundred and fifty Baht but that's it mate, no more."

Now the two door-men came over. The barman kept talking in broken English, "You pay 1000 Baht, you pay 1000 Baht for hostess."

"Bullshit – I was reading the newspaper!"

"No, you pay 1000 Baht."

Okay, then I realised this was the Soho fleecing-the-customer scam, and they were out to rob me. So I thought, discretion being the better part of valour, 'I'll pay up. I'll put it down to experience.' (1000 Baht being about £25 at that time). Of course, then I realised I had only 200 Baht in my button down top breast pocket, the rest of my money being in a money belt under my shirt. So there was no way I was getting my money belt out as I had got close on £1000 worth of Thai Baht with me. I was buying and sending a hell of a lot of watches back to the UK at that time. What to do? How to get out? Thinking quickly is not one of my major attributes in life, too much boxing I suppose. Now I had to think and act fast. The problem was, as I rapidly analysed the situation, to get out the door without getting pulverized and with my money intact. The barman didn't seem to me to be a physical problem, nor the girl, but he was calling the shots. The two doormen were the obstacle. The only option open that I could see without tackling those two guys was to take a hostage. To this day I don't know how I moved so fast. Survival instinct I suppose, the cornered rat syndrome.

In one move I turned the table over with my boot that was between me and the two guys, I grabbed the girl in a headlock, and at the same time I had picked up a glass in my right hand and I shoved it up to her face and started yelling, "I'm going out of here, or else she gets her face cut off." Well, this was obviously not what they expected. The two guys stopped in their tracks, and the girl was half screaming and crying. The barman, who I guess was responsible for everything, calmed the two guys down that had now started to come forward as I was backing onto a wall so as to keep them in front of me. To top it off the girl is now pissing herself with fear, all over me. Well, I've heard of people getting turned on by women pissing on them, but believe me it was doing nothing for me at this particular moment.

The barman's shouting above her screaming, and me yelling, "Back off or else she gets it."

He's yelling, "Okay, you go, no pay for beer." So I tell the two guys to back off to the other side of the room, and then I drag the girl to the door, push her back in, and make my quick exit. I then went and bought some Valium from the chemist to calm me down, and went and had another beer. I didn't stay long though as I was stinking of piss. (Not a recommended adventure.) I came back the following day to sort out the watches. Having 'bottle' and 'front' can pay off at times.

Overall, Thailand has less violent crime than British inner cities such as Brixton, Handsworth, Moss Side and Toxteth. Western women are very rarely pestered by Thai men – there's just too many of their own women available. I read in the Bangkok Post once of a man getting seventeen years jail for rape. When the judge was summing up the case he stated that the accused had a well paying profession and could easily go to a massage parlour or brothel that are readily available.

Beer Talk

One time I got into a little argument with a Thai guy we both had been drinking probably too much he said to me, "All Farangs are stupid (many of them are as they leave their brains behind back home)."

My reply was, "OK you tell me how many inventions have come from Thailand and what has a Thai ever invented apart from Thai boxing and Thai massage?"

Silence. End of discussion and no shouting, big sulk on his face. I nipped the potential fallout in the bud. Keep cool, keep calm the only way to be.

Television

One of the most popular soaps on TV at the present time is called *Mongkut Doc Som*. It's about a businessman with four wives all living in the same house. (What a nightmare.) Another famous businessman who was regularly in the news is Suphat Thiraparbkulowng, known as the 'Noodle meatball king'. He has eight wives and twenty-two kids. He recently bottled out of having a vasectomy.

Crossing the Road – Almost Impossible Like England Beating Germany at Football

As in all third world developing nations try not to cross the road as the automobile has the right of way. When you are on the road you are taking up their space, so you become fair game to be flattened. To me, when a person can cross a road safely, i.e. traffic stops for you at zebra crossings, then a nation has become westernised – Italy and Greece excluded – must be the Latin male temperament. To witness an Italian traffic jam is a head throbbing experience. Although the traffic is stationary everyone presses their horns as if this is going to miraculously clear their path. There is definitely a difference in temperament between Northern Europeans and Southern Mediterranean Europeans. One redeeming factor about Thai driving is that they do not press their horn – considered very rude. I will discuss Thai driving later on in this chapter.

Question: Why do Italians cross when the light's on red?
Answer: Because it's there.

Then when nations become westernised, the bicycles that had become extinct like dinosaurs, miraculously make a comeback. Needless to say, bicycles are extinct in Bangkok. The last one probably got wiped out in the late 60s. The internal combustion engine is choking Bangkok's inhabitants to death. Who says the quality of life is improving. Less than 100 years ago B/K transport was boats and rickshaws plus there was no HIV/ AIDS.

My buddy Amotz from Israel reckons a country is westernised by the state of the public toilets. He's got a good point, but Israeli drivers are close cousins to Italian drivers.

Wheelchairs

If you are unfortunate enough to have to use this mode of transport, DON' T go to Thailand. The pavements are very high to allow water run off from the monsoons and they are very narrow also most of the slabs are breaking up, and have no ramps. Also, market stalls are all over the place, and if you go on the road you will get flattened and killed. If you still want to go, I would suggest an up-market hotel at a resort where you will be catered for.

Vaccinations

No vaccinations are required, although malaria medication is advisable outside of tourist resorts. Thailand is almost free of malaria except in a few isolated rural areas. Although Dengue fever is more prevalent and can kill. There is no reciprocal health agreement with the UK.

Transport

I don't want to go into regular tour book details, but motorbike taxis are the best way to get around (except for BTS Sky train and the MRT Underground, oh boy have these forms of transport made a big difference to living in BKK) Bangkok traffic when going for job interviews, otherwise you'll be late for appointments. Lots of them provide helmets which are now required by law but not always enforced, Farangs not wearing helmets are a target to be shaken down by the cops more so than Thais. I would advise everyone to wear one even for short journeys. Don't get motorbike taxis confused with tuk-tuks which are three-wheeled motorbikes. Most taxis now have meters so you don't have to haggle over fares.

Everyone at some time or another will try out a tuk-tuk, nothing wrong with that but be prepared to be taken to jewellery shops and or tailors shops on route to your destination as the driver gets fuel vouchers from the shop owners so unless you want to go shopping best to make it clear before jumping on board.

Religion

Ninety per cent of Thailand is Buddhist. I've been all over the world and Buddhism is definitely the most tolerant of all the major religions. There's no hell and damnation bullshit heaped on you like the other religions. I'm an atheist, but when I'm on my death bed I'll get everyone in to see me – priests, preachers, holy men, rabbis, monks, ministers and mullahs – and see who's got the best deal on offer, just in case.

The high season for tourists is December – February. There is no problem with getting rooms anywhere except from December 21st – January 3rd. If you overstay your visa they charge 200 Baht per day. I've picked Thailand in the Far East as it is the cheapest destination from London. Also, you need less money here than any other 'working' countries in South East Asia. The wages are higher in Japan, Taiwan and South Korea but so is the cost of living. You would be well advised to check Thailand out before the rest of Asia and to get a feel for Asia here, so to speak. Lots of fun can be had here. I briefly mentioned the other countries in Asia in the first chapter.

Sightseeing

If you want to take a tourist sightseeing tour of Bangkok, go on a Sunday. Traffic on a Sunday is just bad, not horrendous.

Royal Thai Embassy: 29-30 Queens Gate, London, SW75JB; Telephone 0171 589 2944. Here is my idea of an ideal budget Thai hotel for under 1000 Baht. It would have to be one of the following.

- Air conditioning – the non-shaking and rattling type.

- Has to be off the main road with no traffic. It is doubtful though if one can get away from motorbikes, usually with silencers cut off, just waiting to wake you up at 5:00 a.m. after a night on the grog. Very 'cool' for Thais to rev-up motorbikes.

- Keep away from building sites as cement mixers and jack hammers first thing in the morning does nothing for hangovers.

- Dark curtains – so as to sleep in after a night of drinking.

- Reception staff – should take details of visiting female's ID cards. The same applies if you're into men/boys.

- Rooms are automatically clean, but not necessarily cockroach and bed bug free.

- Away from barking stray dogs and crowing roosters. This you don't find out about until 5:00 a.m. same as the motorbikes. Maybe they all work in unison. Catapults are a brilliant buy at fifty Baht. This is money well spent and gives great satisfaction when you pulverize a rooster's head, or turn a barking flea-ridden dog into a whimpering puppy that runs off with its tail between its legs and a bruise on its head the size of a cricket-ball!

- No Germans – so one can get near the swimming pool away from their 'reserved signs.'

Face

Asians have strong feelings of 'shame' and they are concerned with keeping 'face'. Face and shame are the two sides of an emotional coin current throughout South East Asia. Face is a person's self-esteem – if it has been shattered by careless or deliberate assault, then face is lost. Now the victim feels shame to the extent that they become sulky, uncooperative and in extreme cases even suicidal. So be careful of what you say and do to Asians.

Insurance

Well worth having: especially if one uses the motor bike taxi system.

Hospitals

There are plenty of hospitals in Bangkok. The cheapest being the government hospitals. If you are unfortunate enough to have to visit one expect to join long queues. Private hospitals are less busy, but more expensive.

Dogs

Be careful around dogs as people do get and die from rabies every year.

Driving

When driving in Bangkok watch out for motorbikes driving in between the cars, use your mirrors as you don't want to take one out, if you do hit one it will more than likely be your fault regardless of who caused the accident, as you probably don't speak Thai you'll have all kinds of hassles, the cops will come and you'll end up paying out money to the injured party. If you need an ambulance in Thailand for any reason you'll more than likely have a long wait as the Thai drivers *do not* move out of the way for emergency vehicles like in the West.

In Bangkok you do not notice how crazy the Thai drivers are as they are usually driving at a crawl. Thailand is regularly in the world's top five for deaths on the roads. Why they drive so recklessly and fatalistic is beyond me. Buying vehicles in Thailand is way, way more expensive than in the West, so using logic you would think every one would be more careful in preserving their assets and status symbol, not so. Every other week or so there is a horror story crash usually a mini-passenger van is involved. Try not to use this form of transport.

I think the reckless driving is down to corruption, it is everywhere, so people do what they want and if things don't work out, just pay some money and everything is back to normal.

The Deep South

The three southern border provinces with Malaysia have had an undeclared war going on now for over ten years with Muslim separatists who are fighting to try and join Malaysia, bombs, murder and general mayhem being the norm. Best to stay away from this area.

Scams

Thailand is a great hospitable country, with great beaches, warm clear water and cheap great food. But you can get scammed due to being too trusting and sometimes too gullible. (Can ruin your day and sometimes your trip.) Here is a list of some common scams to watch out for:

Jet-ski scam – You take out a jet ski and when you come back they point out old damage on the ski that they say you've caused, you're then surrounded by a bunch of intimidating thugs who demand heaps of money, people do get attacked and beaten up sometimes cops arrive on the scene and mediate, your relieved to see them and usually agree to pay half of the original amount, the mediators are in on the scam. Check out jet-ski scams, **Thailand, Google, YouTube.**

This can happen with motor bikes also. Do not leave your passport as a 'behind the counter guarantee', leave a passport photocopy or a driving licence then take a photocopy of your driving licence with you. You can always walk away from a driving licence 'worse case scenario' but not a passport.

Littering – This is not so much as a scam a police money making operation. I've witness this a few times on the Sukhumvit Road Bangkok, you're walking along smoking a cigarette you finish smoking and throw the butt on the ground (bearing in mind there's rubbish all over the place, especially plastic bags, Thais love plastic bags) then a cop arrives from nowhere and then escorts you to a police booth you then have to pay an on the spot fine of 2000 Baht, they have caught you as they have 'spotters' all over the place with mobile phones, also outside air con shopping centres the cigarette stub out bins have been removed, you put the butt out on the floor and guess what happens next. They seldom bother with Thais as Farangs are an easy target.

Pattaya – Police road blocks. The police will block off an intersection and pull over every Farang riding a motor bike, you will be fined 400 Baht for not having either your insurance with you or not having your passport with you or not wearing a helmet they will find something, if you refuse to pay they take the keys to your bike until you do pay. Meanwhile Thais are going on their merry way with no helmets and up to four on a bike, three to four on a bike is a very common sight in Asia.

Counterfeit goods – Are illegal in Thailand but are everywhere. A chap I know arrived in Ekkamai bus station Bangkok, he started to leave the bus station and two plain cops showed him their ID badges they demanded to see inside his luggage, inside they found counterfeit logo clothing, CDs, DVDs and Viagra all illegal but all over Thailand sold openly. He had to accompany them to the police station, they demanded 70,000 Baht on the spot fine he bargained down to 30,000 Baht.

Probably the top man in the station had sent them out to raise funds to pay for a promotion. Promotions are paid for in Thailand, maybe some on merit. Cops and immigration officials all over the world can and do search your luggage in the pretext of looking for contraband, drugs, terrorism etc.

Grand Palace closed – and temple, and other scams check out Goggle, Lonely Planet and www.tripadvisor.com. They can give better up-to-date information on these scams than I can.

One Law for the Rich, One Law for the Poor

Keep out of trouble in Thailand or if you do get into trouble make sure you have access to loads of cash, you can literally get away with murder if you are rich, god help you if you are poor.

Here are a few cases that have been in the news lately and on the internet, which the Thai authorities hate as they say it portrays Thailand in a negative light. I say tough!

Two peasants in the north of the county sentenced to thirty years jail for picking wild mushrooms in a national park, because they pleaded guilty their sentence was reduced to fifteen years.

A sixteen year old girl driving her dads car, no driving licence no insurance, kills nine people in a commuter taxi van, her wealthy mother and father 'made things right' she basally got off scot-free.

A reckless truck driver kills two Brits on push bikes, he gets the equivalent of a £20 fine (do you think money changed hands?)

So if you go to one of the islands for a full moon party, don't accept passed joints from Thais as they could quite easily be undercover cops, then when you're arrested you have to come up with heaps of dough to get off a charge.

An Australian married couple on holiday in Phuket riding their motorbike back to the hotel, pulls over onto the centre line to turn right indicating all the time, this is witnessed by onlookers and CTV cameras, is then slammed into by a drunk Thai guy in his pick-up truck. The woman on the back of the bike is killed, the guy is seriously injured and rushed to hospital. After operations and other treatment when he is ready to be released by the hospital he is arrested by the cops and charged with causing the accident, when he says I've lost my wife through no fault of my own one of the cops says to him, you can get a new wife. Anyway the chap is now in prison awaiting trial, which can take forever. The cops are demanding $30,000, 'then you can go' 'no have to go to trial'. Thank god an Aussie TV station got hold of the story, the Thai ambassador was summoned in Canberra. Thais lost face big time the chap gets to go home, I guess he'll stay clear of Thailand forever now.

Keep well away from cops, if you have to deal with them use the Tourist Police Division, phone 1155.

Thais are a law unto themselves, one sees signs like no 'Africa man' no 'Arab man' things that you could never ever get away with in the 'Civilized West' is just the norm in Thailand.

Check out www.chiangmaicitynews.com for more on these and other stories in the news.

CHAPTER 6
Hong Kong

Hong Kong is a classic story of rags to riches due to determined work ethic, unbridled capitalism, minimal government interference, low taxation and the Chinese gambling culture. There are plenty of people trodden into the dirt, but there are also plenty of people getting very rich. There are no labour and re-education camps here, as in neighbouring China. Hong Kong really took off economically after Mao Tse-Tung marched his Red Army triumphantly into Shanghai in 1948, driving the remnants of Chiang Kai Shek's army into Formosa (now renamed Taiwan) where the two China's remain at odds with each other to this day, both governments claiming to be the representatives of China. The inhabitants of Shanghai that did not want to be liberated by the Peoples Liberation Army fled to Hong Kong and Macao where they were safe. Better to be ruled by foreign devils (known as 'Gweilos') and barbarians than by communists.

In the 60s I went to school here as my dad was in the military, stationed in the New Territories. There have been tremendous changes since those days. A little over forty years ago the people were desperately poor, most of them relatively new arrivals from the mainland. Hong Kong was heaven on earth to these people after Mao's oppressive communist China. As Hong Kong is so small (about twice the size of the Isle of Wight) and in danger of being swamped with people unfortunately the British authorities had to implement very Draconian measures in curtailing the flood of humanity that was constantly descending on Hong Kong for a better life – El Dorado the Golden Mountain as far as they were concerned.

A memory that I will never forget is seeing the pitiful faces of the illegals that were sent back every day in caged trucks which passed through our village every afternoon. They were fed at the border and then handed over to the Chinese authorities, to who knows what fate awaited them – probably re-education camps to help them see the error of their ways in wanting the capitalist life. Now China is embracing the capitalist system, without democracy. They have still kept the fences up to keep their own people out of El Dorado – one country – two systems.

I have lots of fond memories from living in Hong Kong especially at such a young impressionable age. My first hitch-hiking was done here. We used to thumb lifts from the army Land Rovers – the Gurkhas always gave us lifts. I was then nine years old. Usually after school we would go through our military camp village called Sek Kong, down to the bottom end of the village and have our regular stone throwing fights with the local Chinese kids. We always had the higher ground but they used to outnumber us, so when the odds became too great we would make a strategic withdrawal back into our own camp and plot the next encounter. Better for your heart and lungs than hanging around video game arcades like today's kids. Not so healthy when you got hit on the head by a brick though.

Places to Stay

YMCA & YWCA – 41 Salisbury Road Tsinashsui, Kowloon.

Chung King Mansion – 36-44 Nathan Road, Kowloon.

Accommodation can be expensive and a hassle to get, although there are plenty of shared flats available if you're prepared to live in the New Territories or on the islands.

Working in Hong Kong

Since the hand over in 1997 the rules of working in Hong Kong have changed dramatically, when it was a colony British passport holders could get in and work with no problems. One of my big regrets was not trying to work in Hong Kong, but no one can fit everything in to one's life. If you want to find out about working in Hong Kong today. Google, how to work in Hong Kong. Heaps of paper back and Kindle books come up.

CHAPTER 7
Israel

My first trip on my own out of Europe was to Morocco in the hippie days. Israel was my second trip out of Europe. I had wanted to go to Israel ever since I was a small lad. My grandfather would tell me about biblical Israel and the part that he played in the liberation of Palestine from the Turks along with General Alenby in 1917, when they rode on horseback and camel from Egypt through the Sinai Desert up to Jerusalem – a truly twentieth century crusader.

Arriving in 1973 this was the first of many trips to Israel. Then, like now, I would strongly recommend Israel for a first time traveller going abroad to work. Whether you are a single girl travelling alone, a couple of mates, or a mixed couple, you can arrive in Israel and just about guarantee you'll find work. You can have a good time while you are there, see some incredible historical and geographical sites and meet plenty of interesting people, locals and travellers alike.

Unless you are Jewish and you are migrating there (it's not really fair that they can migrate there and nobody else can), or you are doing your Jewish bit and going to serve in the army or some other cultural experience, like planting trees, wailing at the Holy Wall, etc., or learning Hebrew, most working travellers are heading for a Kibbutz, a Moshav or an Ulban Kibbutz (which is where you learn Hebrew and work), an archaeological dig or tourist work around the resorts – but by far the vast majority are heading for a Kibbutz. Once on a Kibbutz, life as you know it will change tremendously. From now on you will be safe and secure and have an uncomplicated way of life. You will never ever experience hunger; you can have holes in your pockets as you never have to carry money; you will always have a roof over your head and a bed that is dry, warm and clean. Also, you will never be lonely or stuck for someone to talk to. Also, on most of the Kibbutz's you can drink for free.

Unfortunately, plenty of British people have found out about this lifestyle, and rather than, say being unemployed in dark, damp, miserable UK (they are better off in Israel working on a Kibbutz which is nice and secure with sunshine most of the year around. Don't mistake a Kibbutz for an 18-30 Club Med holiday camp. Because you don't have to fend for yourself it has attracted plenty of rowdy 'Brits on holiday' type – ere we go, ere we go, ere we go – drink heaps, stomp about in the disco singing *Belsons a Gas* (Sex Pistols), punch ups, puking up, then going back to the rooms terrorising the out-of-favour volunteers, smashing up the living quarters, and then not turning up for work cause 'I got a sore head.' This has caused many Brits to be thrown off Kibbutz's – both males and females. It is no good then saying to the Israeli volunteer leader, 'Ah! But we won the war, mate, and if it wasn't for us in 1940 sticking up to the Krauts and not surrendering like the frogy bastards and all the rest of Europe, you guys wouldn't have a nation, or a race.'

In spite of us winning the war, about half of the Kibbutz's refuse to take Brits on any more. Yet in the early 70s the Brits were some of the best workers, being as in those days your average twenty-year-old Brit had been in the work force back home for five years already with little or no unemployment. Nobody had an excuse for not working, whereas lots of your Americans and Canadians had only just left college and had only done summer holiday type work, so were 'still green' to coin a phrase.

Snow storms in the Sinai Desert killed Israeli soldiers in the winter of '73-'74, and snow in the winter of '92-'93 blanketed the Middle East from Damascus, Syria, to Alexandria, Egypt, Amman, Jordan, to Jerusalem. I remember working long hours in the rain and snow, and this was the norm for me as I'd already spent years of my life on building sites in similar conditions, but with the threat of getting the sack if you stopped working. Many of the Israeli's asked me to work with them in preference to some of the other nationals. So when you get on a Kibbutz, think about trying to reverse the trend so that other UK travellers don't have to suffer through no fault of their own.

Unless you work outside of the Kibbutzim and Moshavim, you will be known as and referred to as a volunteer, even though on a Moshav you are a paid worker on a collective farm, as opposed to a socialist commune worker.

It was in 1968 after the six day war of 1967 when the first non-Jewish volunteers were recruited to come to Israel to experience the unique socialist way of life. It used to be said that the only true form of communism was the Kibbutz way of life, and one was free to leave, unlike living under the old communist regimes of Eastern Europe. Also, the fruit was probably rotting on the trees due to the fact that every time Israel has a war everyone is involved. Women are called up to do military service the same as men, although in today's army women are used more and more as a support role, making cups of coffee for the officers. Although, to be fair, plenty of crucial work is carried out by women in all the armed services.

So, in the early days for volunteers, the Kibbutz's were booming. Agricultural machinery was not as developed as it is today, so the volunteers were welcomed with open arms and were urgently needed. As my buddy, Amotz, on Kibbutz Dorot told me recently when I was staying as a guest, "I was very excited when the first volunteers arrived. It gave us a completely new perspective of the outside world to talk to these new people. As we were teenagers it was very exciting to be able to mix with people from all over the world and learn about their countries." Today the enthusiasm for new volunteers has waned as many thousands have now passed through each Kibbutz, but don't let this deter you, as members are very friendly and if you are a good worker you will get noticed and known.

There was a fear amongst the Kibbutz leaders that a lot of their young people would leave after mixing with the volunteers, and to a certain degree this has happened. When a youth has finished their military service – three years for men, two years for women – a lot of them do go off travelling themselves to check out the world. Israeli's are big travellers considering the size of their country's population. I've meet plenty of them all over the world.

Amotz, whom I mentioned earlier, I met in Africa. (We had cattle in common.) He left his Kibbutz for fifteen years and then came back with a beautiful wife named Yasmin. They are now bringing their four children up as Kibbutz kids, and there is probably no better place in the world to bring up a child. Many of the founding socialist ideas have now been dropped, changed to suit the modern age, but the basic structure the Kibbutz is still the same.

As many of the young people have left for good plenty of volunteers have stayed and married into the Kibbutz. You will find every Kibbutz has these ex-volunteers that are now Hebrew speaking members. All Kibbutz's originally started out solely based on agriculture. The first one started in

1909. Today many of them have small packing and assembly plants and small factories. This has come about partly by their own success as they are so productive in say milk yields, that they now having to have a yoghurt factory or cheese factory, and the same with fruit and vegetables.

I would suggest that if you arrive in the winter then try to get on a Kibbutz in the south of the country in the Negev region, and if you arrive in the summer then try for the north of the country or by the coast as Israel has extremes of weather temperature. In the summer months you will have to compete with European university students for available places so you might have to hang around for a while to get placed unless you go through an agency which charges money and makes the arrangements for you before you leave home.

Many travellers are now heading to Greece, Turkey, and Cyprus after a Kibbutz stint. If you do this you will need to leave Israel by about the end of May or June to get in the summer season around the resorts. Ferries leave from Haifa to Greece and Cyprus It is not worth trying to pick fruit in Greece any more as there are now hundreds of thousands of Albanians doing this type of work. Remember: Greece is in the EU so you can go there first with your UK unemployment transferred for three months.

When working on a Kibbutz you will have to be prepared to start early, and be prepared to do menial jobs at first, such as working in the kitchen, the dining room or the laundry. After a stint of doing one or more of these jobs you can request what type of work you want to do. Usually the longer you are prepared to stay the better the job you will get. As some jobs require training, they don't want to waste the training on someone who is only staying for a month.

There are about 270 Kibbutz's and the volunteer intake is usually between ten-forty per Kibbutz, depending on the size and the time of year. I recommend a smaller Kibbutz as you will get to know more people and you will feel less insignificant than on one of the massive Kibbutz's that are mainly based in the north of the country.

Every three months the Kibbutz's organise camping and sightseeing trips around the country for the volunteers. These are great fun. Depending on where you are and what time of year, you might all be checked into YHA's which are all over Israel or you might all be camping. There is great fun to be had by all.

YHAs and other hostels are around Ben Yehuda Street and Dizengoff Street in Tel Aviv. When arriving do not plan to arrive on a Friday as on Friday afternoon and Saturday all public transport is closed down.

When recognised as an independent state by the League of Nations in 1948, Israel was to be a Jewish State, meaning that any Jewish person anywhere in the world has the right to immigrate to Israel. I always found this somewhat unfair to all of those Palestinians who were stateless due to numerous Arab-Israeli wars. Also, the Palestinians were born there and their ancestors were born there, whereas the vast majority of Jews had left thousands of years ago. So, say if a Jewish person is from London, they have the right of abode in twenty-eight EU countries, all the remaining British colonies and the State of Israel. I think that gives one a good scope of options. Now due to the Palestinian Intifada which started in 1987, plus PLO and Hamas terrorism over thirty years, a Palestinian State is being formed in the previously occupied West Bank and Gaza strip.

So the people who say violence achieves nothing have been proved wrong once again. Just as the Jewish State was created out of violence, so is the new Palestine State being created out of violence. Yasser Arafat, once a wanted hated terrorist had become a peacemaker and leader of his people, just as in the 70s Menachem Begin, a leader of the terrorist Irgun and Stem gang of the 40s also became a leader and peacemaker. Hence the saying 'Today's terrorist, tomorrow's leader.'

Both of these men were responsible for indulging in an orgy of murder, bombings, shootings and kidnappings. Menachem Begin was condemned by the Israeli provisional government under its first leader, David Ben Gurion, for terrorist acts against the British and for the killing of innocent Arab and British civilians. Today Jewish terrorists have streets named after them in Jerusalem. I wonder how long it will be before streets are named after the Hamas suicide bombers in the West Bank!

Many people within Israel are adamantly opposed to handing back the West Bank as they claim it is part of biblical Israel. This is why their great warrior peacemaker leader Yitzak Rabin was sadly killed, for his devotion to peace. In the middle of this 'peace' Hamas has declared war and pushed the Israelis into declaring all out war. A Palestinian Marxist remarks, 'That's what Begin declared on Arafat in 1982. That's what Rabin declared on the Hizbollah in '93. They both failed. And now Peres will fail.' – The Independent: 7-3-96.

When land is won in battle, in order to keep it the new occupiers have to either drive all the inhabitants out, kill all the inhabitants, or totally over populate the inhabitants – called ethnic cleansing. The Serbs and Croats were expert at this and so are the Chinese with their occupation of a once sovereign Tibet. Israel did ethnic cleansing in the war of '48 but was not prepared to do this in later wars, so now they have to hand the land back. Let's hope the Israeli settlers that did migrate to Judea and Samaria can live in peace under a new government, as the million or so Arabs that live in Israel do.

Israel today: From 1948-2014, a little over sixty-five years, Israel has transgressed from oppressed to oppressors. (The new old South Africa.)

Due to the break-up of the Soviet Union, Israel has had to absorb about a million or so Soviet Union Jews. This has had a great impact on the country. Many of the new immigrants were absorbed through the Kibbutz system. Also, unemployment is quite high now due to so many people coming in such a short time. This has had a knock-on effect for the prospective volunteer. In the old days before the break up of the Soviet Union, you could come and stay as long as you liked on a Kibbutz. Sadly this is no longer so. Now you have to get a volunteer visa, called a B4 visa, which is $40 and valid for three months. To renew for another three months is $40. This visa also enables you to work on an archaeological dig or a Moshav.

Working on a Moshav: is definitely not as cosy and as fun loving as a Kibbutz. You will have very little social life, you will have to work long hours, and you will have to buy and make your own food, but you do get paid up upwards of £350 per month. This is not a great deal, but on a Kibbutz you will be earning £50-£60 per month. If you learn to operate and repair agricultural machinery, this can come in handy for working elsewhere around the world. I have worked on farms in Africa, Canada, Denmark and Wales.

Israeli's are accused of being arrogant. I put this down to their achievements in science, medicine, agriculture, hi-tech industry and the military, and the fact that they have been fighting wars for over sixty-five years and winning most of them.

Hitch-hiking: I have recently heard negative reports, but Israel was probably one of the best countries in the world for thumbing lifts – still be careful if you are a woman. Public transport is cheap and plentiful. On Friday afternoons and all day Saturday public transport does not run. This has been brought about by the religious Jews pressurizing the government, putting religion before commerce.

Women Travellers: If you have been to the Southern Mediterranean countries and experienced hassles, pestering, aggravation and groping of the Mediterranean male cliché, it gets worse with the Muslim males. Turks pester you more than Greeks, Arabs more than Turks, and Israeli's can also be ungentlemanly. If you've been living free and easy on a Kibbutz, wearing skimpy T-shirts, braless with your tits popping out, and tight short shorts, to an Arab man this is an open invitation. They have all heard about the lack of morals amongst western women and seen pornography, etc. So when you leave the Kibbutz 'cover up.' I don't mean just when popping down to the beach – I mean when going to the cities and towns.

Always remember this: With Arabs their girls are unavailable until marriage. They are covered up and shut up behind closed doors. All over the Middle East, if a Muslim girl gets pregnant before marriage this brings terrible shame and disgrace to the family, so male members of the family quite often kill their own, i.e. daughter or sister (so called honour killing). This is expected and happens frequently. Also, under Islamic law if a woman gets raped she has to have three male witnesses, just to make sure she is not fabricating the whole story. This is not the case in Israel though.

If you've got blonde hair and blue eyes, this excites them even more. So cover up – and you can even wear a wedding ring and carry pictures of your husband and children. Male children have more social status than females, and never make eye contact with Arab men – look away.

Health: Some of the best medical facilities in the world are in Israel. Let's hope you don't need them. On the Kibbutz you will be covered by insurance, although on the Moshav you will have to have your own. Casualty departments of hospitals around the world are usually free, or a minimal payment.

Student Cards and YHA Cards: There are lots of discounts to be had all over Israel on buses, trains, hostels, historical sights, etc.

Security: When going to or leaving Israel allow two-three hours for check in as security is very tight. Don't smuggle anything. Even harmless things like vibrators can be very embarrassing when discovered in your case, and it will be checked out.

A few years ago an Irish girl who was pregnant by her Palestinian boyfriend checked onto a flight to Israel. Her boyfriend had something come up and so was going to get the next flight over and meet her there, where they were to get married. Needless to say she was devastated when she found out the Walkman cassette player her boyfriend had given her for the journey turned out to be a bomb. This was picked up by Israeli security. Imagine what thoughts are going to go through her head for the rest of her life. I bet any money she becomes an alcoholic, if not already.

When I left my last Kibbutz as a volunteer I was on way down to Africa. A week before I left Kibbutz Lahav my best buddy at the time, Canadian Dan, and I were grooming and feeding the horses. When I went to get feed grain out of one of the plastic dustbins, the lid had been left off I guess to be filled at a later date as there was only about an inch or two of grain in the bottom, and also about twenty or so rats had got inside, probably dropping themselves off bales of straw into the bin. Quickly I slammed the lid back onto the bin, and then we proceeded to put a hose pipe in and drowned the rats.

At times one can get bored on the Kibbutz for things do, especially if the weather is not so good, so the volunteers were always on the lookout for new pranks to play each other. Also, our afternoon football games had dried up due to the heat and the demoralised members' team that us volunteers kept on beating.

We dug a hole, chucked most of the rats inside, and buried them. The remainder we took back to the living quarters and proceeded to go inside all the girls' rooms and deposit a rat inside each soap box, and we made up a hangman's noose from piece string and hung a rat from the ceiling lampshade. When the girls finished work they all went to one room for coffee and a smoke, and of course Dan and myself were giggling like schoolboys in the room next door waiting to see what would be the outcome of our escapade.

After about ten minutes nothing had happened. We sat back disappointed, thinking the girls had seen the hanging rat and decided to call our bluff by not reacting. But just then it happened – six girls screeching and screaming and yelling and generally going nuts. They had finally looked up and spotted the rat dangling from a hangman's noose. We had to cut down the rat and the remaining hanging rats just to calm them down and make the peace.

Two hours later the six girls from the three rooms that they shared headed off to the showers before the evening meal. Of course Dan and I were following closely behind. A few minutes later the same screeching and screaming erupted again, but this time they were really mad. We had to disappear for a day or so to let things calm down and get back to normal.

One week later I was checking out through Israeli security at the airport. At least sixty-seventy per cent of security personnel that do the questioning and checking the luggage are young women of the armed forces. A girl of about twenty years of age was giving me the usual run down of questions as she searched my bag very military like and professional, which they are. She came across a packet of Drum hand-rolling tobacco. I'm thinking, oh, my Dutch girlfriend who I'd just left behind has slipped a packet of hand-rolling tobacco into my bag for me to smoke down in Kenya where I was headed. This was after I'd been asked if I had packed my bags myself, to which I replied 'Yes.' As she opened the tobacco packet I said nothing. She let out an almighty scream as she dropped the packet onto the desk and a dead rat fell out. She had dropped her veil of professionalism. Within seconds I was surrounded by security personnel pointing machine guns at me and then they whisked me away for interrogation. No charges were brought, and when things calmed down they saw the funny side. Israelis do have a sense of humour. I was on my way, but the girls had the last laugh.

(I found out later that they'd kept the rat fresh by freezing it.)

Make sure you do pack your own bags and put locks on the pockets. Even with tight security around, Israeli people do get slack. Kibbutz Dorot had ten horses stolen one night out of the middle of the Kibbutz, and they weren't stolen by Sioux Indians either. The front road entrance has a night guard, but the back entrance leading out to the fields had been left open. This was in '94. Probably outside contractors had spotted the break in security. The horses were probably ridden to Gaza which was less than fifteen miles away, never to be seen again.

Archaeological Digs: You don't get paid to work on them, in fact you usually have to pay for your own keep.

Au Pairing is in demand. Average pay is $500-$1000 per month live in – usually a one year contract.

Au Pair International: 2 Desler Street, Bnei Brak, Tel Aviv 51507; Phone/Fax – 03 619 0423

Star Au Pairs: 16 Michal Street, POB 26571, Tel Aviv 6326; Phone – O3 201 195 Fax – 291 748

Shlomi Meiri: 24 Tabenkin Street, Tel Aviv 69353.

These three agencies charge a registration fee of $150 plus.

Tourist work is available in the resorts, but competition is stiff.

Israeli Embassy: 2 Palace Green, London W84Q8, Phone – 0170 957 9500 Fax – 0171 957 9555

To join a U.K. group costs a fee.

UK Kibbutz representatives: 1A Accommodation Road, NW118ED; Phone – 0171 458 9235

Jewish Agency: 13 Leonardo De Vinci Street, Tel Aviv. Phone – 03 258 473 or go direct to Kibbutz Movement, 124 Ha Yarkon Street, Tel Aviv. Phone – O3 651 710.

Moshav: 78 Ben Yehuda Street, Tel Aviv.; Phone – 03523 0140

You should be between 18-32 for a Kibbutz and 18-35 for Moshav placement.

Visa Stamp: If you intend to visit other countries in the Middle East it is best to get your visa stamps on a separate piece of paper that will be stapled inside your passport. Most of the Arab world still does not recognise the State of Israel, so you will be refused entry with Israeli stamps.

Kibbutz Volunteer by Victoria Pylus. Before departing for Israel, I recommend reading this in-depth book about all working aspects of Israel.

For the latest up to date information go to www.ivolunteer.org.il or www.kibbutzvolunteer.com also www.kibbutzprogrmcenter.org

CHAPTER 8
Greece

"Nobody on their death bed says, I wish I'd spent more time in the office!"
– R Lloyd

If one is contemplating working in Greece, Cyprus, Turkey or any of the islands in the Aegean Sea, it is best not to arrive before the middle of April at the earliest. There is plenty of tourist work to be had around the resorts, although there are more vacancies for women than men in catering and bar work, etc. Forget about the old travellers jobs such as working on farms picking fruit and labouring on construction sites. These jobs are now predominantly done by Albanians who have flooded into Greece since the communist collapse of Albania, however, you can still get lucky if you hit a region where all the Albanian immigrant labour has just been deported for working illegally.

A great asset to have anywhere in the Aegean Sea is an Ocean Masters Yachting Certificate. This is recognised worldwide and enables you to skipper a yacht any place on earth. An offshore day skippers ticket will also get you a job. Any other experience around boats or yachts is very useful for scoring a job, and proven cooks are in demand on yachts. Once again women are more in demand than men as most crews and skippers are male oriented.

I'd rather have a horse under me than a boat as I'm prone to sea sickness.

If you decide to go to Greece before Israel it is up to you, but remember the seasons determine whether you will find work or not; not so much in Greece, but in Israel expect the summer students on Kibbutz's. Most ferry rides between Haifa, Israel, to the islands are roughly around $120. Southern Cyprus is in the EU. There are regular jobs to be had on the Greek mainland. My good friend Dimitri from Zimbabwe met his wife working at a major hospital in Athens. They have now moved to Josephine's country, the Netherlands, to live and raise their family, but who wants to work in a hot polluted city when you can have sun, sand, sex, no surf but plenty of booze working on the islands. Dimitri had learned his profession as a male nurse in the Rhodesian army. He recently said to me, "It sure is a lot easier picking up my wife to cart her off to the bedroom than it is picking up wounded soldiers in the middle of a fire fight."

English Teachers for Greece: ETFG, 160 Little-Hampton Road, Worthing, West Sussex, BN13lQT. Phone 01903 218638 /766029. Or best to check out web sites.

To claim UK unemployment in Greece for three months maximum you have to have been claiming in the UK for one month prior to leaving. Check out leaflet NI11 from your benefits office and get the transfer sorted out before you leave. Make sure you read leaflet copy UBL22 – Unemployment benefit for people going abroad or coming from abroad, and get an application form for transferring benefit. Or you can contact: The Overseas Directorate, RMAOSl3, Newcastle upon Tyne, NE98LYX, Phone 0191 225 5251 /225 5298.

Remember to take out a free European Health Insurance Card, it is not the same as insurance but entitles you to medical treatment in a European country for the same cost as paid by local citizens. This card is good for all EU countries.

My only experience of working in Greece was crewing on a yacht based in Corfu – great lifestyle, especially around the marinas at night. My problem is I'm a lousy sailor, constantly leaning over the stern puking up. Good job the Captain, Tony the Villain, was my mate from Birmingham, or else I guess I would have been fired. Even working the oil rigs of the North Sea I used to get sea sick. A company medic on one rig I was on said I was the only case of sea sickness he'd seen in three years on that particular rig, Sedco 135F. When I broke both of my legs on that rig the company medic cut away my overalls and leggings, took one look at the condition I was in and fainted on top of me. He was on the next chopper after me. He was fired. Since that dreadful day in 1976, I've suffered pain daily in my right leg, but what the hell, one has to carry on, what's done is done, can't turn back the clock.

PR work is available in the tourist resorts i.e. giving out fliers and vouchers for restaurants and night clubs this work is also available in all Mediterranean resorts as well as the Spanish Canary Isles.

Working on Boats and Yachts

A great lifestyle to be had, once you become a competent sailor. Once you get an ocean master's certificate, you're in great demand worldwide, either to be a skipper or to deliver yachts. Plenty of females hanging around the marinas.

Bar Pimps

The first time I was in Athens I had sold blood at the local blood bank. As I proceeded to stroll along in a leisurely fashion this Greek chap befriends me, and after conversing for a while he suggests we go and have a beer. This sounded all right to me, especially as he made out he was buying. Off we set down and around a few back streets till we entered this bar. Upon entering he sees one of his buddies and so went over to check him out, while he says could I get the beers, which I did. I brought the beers over, he and his buddy took a sip each and then left, leaving me to sit back and finish the three beers that I really did not want at 10:00 a.m. So as I had paid for the beers, I sat back and read the paper I was carrying. Over a period of an hour both of these guys continued to bring in punters for the bar. These days they have gotten more sophisticated and women arrive to keep you company, and then they pull the 'Soho fleece the customer' scam. These scams are only performed in the daytime when the bars are quiet, so watch out if you are on your own.

CHAPTER 9
Canada

"My experience of working and travelling allowed me the opportunity to grow so much as an individual. Day after day there were challenges to be met, and day after day I grew – both through successes and failures."

– Kevin Anderle

If you are planning on going to North America and you are under twenty-one years of age, I would recommend Canada to the USA. Under twenty-one years of age in the USA you have a lot of restrictions placed upon you which you don't have in Canada. The major down side in Canada is that it has half the jobs that the US has, and nearly double the unemployment rate.

Crime

Crime in Canada is way less than its neighbour south of the border and maybe one of the contributing factors is the lack of guns. In Canada you can only own hunting guns – not hand guns or machine guns. Canadians do not have the God given right to go out and commit a massacre like the Americans have written into their Constitution.

Climate

Don't arrive in the winter unless you are planning on working the ski resorts. Most of the skiing, and the best skiing, is in British Columbia and the south-western corner of Alberta. Although nearly everything else is more expensive in Canada than in the US, skiing is cheaper and less restrictive about going off-piste than in the US. Vancouver has jobs in the winter as it doesn't freeze over like the rest of Canada. The Pacific Ocean keeps the place very mild, similar to the south coast of the UK, but with nearly twice as much rain. If you can't handle rain don't go to Vancouver in the winter. It can also rain all summer, hence the vegetation is a temperate rain forest.

A huge mistake I made in Vancouver one winter was to quit an indoor job to take a roofing job that paid more per hour, but some weeks we were only working one day per week. All the other guys could go and claim welfare for getting laid off, whereas I couldn't, being illegal. I got fired after a few months for mentioning to the other guys that if we were a union company we would get rained off money. Somebody crept off to the boss and I was out, as we were a non-union company. Luckily all my buddies from Edmonton had recently moved to Vancouver and I was able to get an inside job, ceramic tile fixing with my buddy Les Scott.

What did help me out a lot was my boxing experience. I'd always joined boxing gyms wherever I could, and I was getting paid to spar in the down town Hastings Street gym to an up and coming contender, Big Belfast Bill. This would be the fittest time of my life. Pro-boxing is no sport and it's a hard way to earn a few bucks. It doesn't do much for your looks either.

Vancouver seems to go from one boom to another boom and at the present time is enjoying a boom compared to the rest of Canada. This is partly due to the massive influx of Hong Kong, Chinese and main land Chinese who are worried about losing their fortunes, some of whom have acquired their wealth fraudulently.

Also plenty of Taiwanese have come to Vancouver. They are also hedging their bets against China taking over their country. Vancouver has always had a very large Chinese community, similar to San Francisco, dating back to the 1860s.

Even though Vancouver is experiencing a construction boom there is still plenty of unemployment as people from the depressed areas of Canada have always come out west to look for jobs. Don't be surprised to hear an accent that is totally not North American. The Scottish-Irish accent of

Newfoundland and Nova Scotia (New Scotland) are all over Vancouver and British Columbia. Newfoundland stayed British until 1947 when it joined Canada. They made tremendous sacrifices for the Empire in the Boer War, World War 1 and World War II, as did the rest of Canada with the exception of Quebec, although more Quebecois did join up in World War II than in World War I.

Today, due to the over fishing of the Grand Banks off Labrador, the Maritime provinces, Newfoundland, Nova Scotia and New Brunswick, are having a bad recession as their economies are very dependent on fishing, fish processing, canning and packing, etc., but over the last few years things have picked up and in some places are booming due to the new found oil, gas, fracking and mining that is going on all over Canada.

The Canadian Navy threatened to sink Spanish trawlers in the summer of '94 for over-fishing in their waters. The Spanish could not understand why we did not support them as they are our EU partners. How many Spaniards died for us in two world wars, I ask? You could probably count them on one hand. What a surprise British sympathy was with the Canadians.

The Maritimes is not really the place to look for work. Although there is fruit picking in the summertime, if you want to work it has to be either Ontario, British Columbia, or Alberta. In Quebec you have to be able to speak French. Saskatchewan and Manitoba have only farming jobs in the summer. Ontario, mainly around Toronto, has regular jobs, as plenty of Canadian companies have moved from French speaking Quebec. Canada in general has bent over backwards to accommodate French Quebec by making French compulsory and the country bilingual, whereas in Quebec they have banned English and made it French only, and they keep trying to separate from Canada. Hence most of the multinational companies that deal with the US have moved to Ontario where the minimum wage is lower, productivity is higher and trading is in English.

The North: The Yukon and The North West Territories

There is very little work to be had as the oil, gas and mineral booms of the 70s are long gone, and there is also a massive slump in fur trapping due to the unpopularity of wearing fur these days. I can't shed a tear for the thousands of fur trappers who have lost their livelihood. I have seen the suffering the animals go through from the use of traps, as when I was ranching in Africa I killed plenty of predators using traps and poisoned bait, not to mention the non-predator animals that happened to get caught up by mistake. Bloody hell – if I keep on lecturing like this I'll end up becoming a vegetarian, God forbid!

If you want to go up north, pick the Yukon where there is more happening in the tourist trade than the North West Territories. I worked a summer in Whitehorse as I was able to get regular casual work out of the Government Employment Centre – CEC – Canada Employment Centre. I had tremendous fun in Whitehorse. I drove my pick-up truck from Edmonton. First I got myself the biggest dog out of the Edmonton dog pound, a cross between a St. Bernard and a German Shepherd. They used to keep the dogs three weeks before they sent them to doggy heaven. This dog had three days left before I bailed him out for $30. No self-respecting guy can drive a pick-up truck up north without a dog in the back – part of the Canadian backwoods image, along with the chequered shirt. I left him at my girlfriend's house for two days before my departure for the Yukon. She freaked out with this monster dog bounding all over the place and was glad when he went. I was told not to bring him back when I returned. I picked up a couple of hitch-hikers on the way, Mac and Steve. We camped out every night and Rex, the dog, was let loose to chase away bears and wolves. He did a good job because we never got pestered by any. When I used to go hiking he was great because he used to carry a dog backpack for me – his St Bernard breeding I guess.

Bears: If you go hiking in the woods in the springtime you should make a noise, i.e. wear bells, to warn bears with youngsters that you are approaching. Every year people get killed and mauled by bears – mainly grizzlies, but black bears can also kill and have killed. They don't stop to eat sugar puffs if you are in their way.

How do you know a black bear from a grizzly bear? It's not a joke. The black bear will climb the tree after you – the grizzly bear will push the tree over to get to you. And if a polar bear is after you, there will be no trees to climb. People who have survived bear attacks have 'played dead'. This is no doubt easier said then done, especially if the bear starts to eat you. In the far north Polar Bears will also try to eat you.

If your unfortunately marooned on an ice flow and you come across a dead polar bear, don't be tempted to eat the bears liver as all flesh eating animals have very toxic livers, sharks liver is also very toxic. Also many game animals have toxic livers, as I have found out the hard way.

A tremendous time was had in Whitehorse that summer where we camped permanently at the YHA for $1 per night. We used to go drinking at night at the 'Copper Kettle' bar which was a couple of kilometres out of town. They played great live country folk, rock music, and bands every night. The Royal Canadian Mounted Police (RCMP – Mounties, don't mess with these guys though as their history is they are a para military police force, they tamed the West not the army.) never bothered anybody about drinking and driving, and everybody leaving the place was half intoxicated, with the last frontier mentality. It was very strange leaving in the early hours of the morning the sky would still be light as we were so far north. On many occasions I saw the spectacular Northern Lights bouncing up and down off the polar cap.

Further north in Dawson City there are summer tourist jobs as they re-enact the gold rush days of the 1890s, and gambling is legal so it is a very mini Northern Vegas. As much as I liked it up north it is a very limited work season of three months, and it is a long way to go looking for a limited amount of work. Also everything is expensive, except camping out that is.

Some years before, in the summer of '76, I got three jobs in a morning in Medicine Hat, Alberta – real jobs – not catering and fruit picking type work. One had a choice of jobs then. These days if you are going to go out west looking for work, you should pick the Banff, Lake Louise area and stick to tourist type work. There are summer and winter resorts with plenty of casual dishwasher, waitress, and chambermaid type of work available. The huge Banff Springs Hotel employs over 700 people, and big hotels have a big turnover of labour. Canadian students go back to University at the start of September. They are then out of the casual job market.

If you want to check out proper jobs then the nearest big city is Calgary, but be warned, for all western cities and towns in North America (outside the tourist resorts), a set of wheels is a must. You will find life very hard without your own transport. Maybe you can team up with a partner and share a set of wheels between you. Good motors are cheap. Vancouver and Toronto are OK for public transport. A UK licence is OK for three months, but if you don't have a licence then Canadian and American driving tests are quite easy to pass. Also, I always build up local ID I got off loads of motoring offences once in the UK by having an Alberta licence and making out I was a Canadian, originally from the UK. Don't try this if the car is registered in your name though, only if someone else registers the car.

There is lots of casual work in Calgary for the annual stampede (rodeo) which attracts up to a million visitors. This is usually held in the first two weeks of July.

Whistler Mountain, ninety miles north of Vancouver, is also a year-round resort but accommodation is not as easy as Banff. Plus, if you are camping, this area gets the same rain as Vancouver (rain at the bottom of the Mountain, snow at the top), whereas Banff hardly gets any rain.

There are plenty of times when I have gone skiing in these resort towns and to get a place to stay I have slept on the landings of the fire escapes. They are all within the main buildings of the hotel so they are always heated and carpeted, and the older hotels have bathrooms and showers not attached to the rooms, so these are easily accessible. Of course, you have to have a sleeping bag.

For women a great way to get into Canada is to be a nanny/au pair or care worker. It is worth getting UK qualifications as this is a more prestigious job than in Europe. This is a way into Canada without all the bullshit immigration crap points system one has to go through to immigrate. After two years you can apply for residence status, such is the shortage of qualified workers. Then if you ever go working in the US and you get caught, you can just move back up to Canada instead of back to the UK. There is an agency in the UK, Childcare in Canada, 40 Kingsley Court, Welwyn Garden City, Herts. AL74 IIZ Phone 0170739001. Canada House or agencies in this field will provide you with up to date details also check out the book; *How to become an Au Pair*, from the how to series. Also heaps of stuff on the internet.

Telemarketing

Very popular with working travellers, same demand as Australia, New Zealand, and USA. Jobs in newspapers and employment agencies.

Farm Work

Southern Ontario grows just about everything from strawberries to tobacco. There are twenty-four seasonal agricultural offices in Ontario which issue up to date crop picking leaflets. The Prairie Provinces grow endless amounts of wheat. I drove a wheat truck in Bow Island, near Medicine Hat, Alberta one summer for the harvest which starts in August and goes through to mid-September. What the job entailed was to drive your truck alongside the combine while it empties its load of wheat, then you drive off and deposit the wheat in a storage bin or to the rail head. You'll see massive grain silos all over the Prairie Provinces. Don't do what I did. I hadn't been driving long in Canada so I was still getting used to the right side of the road. There is no problem to orient oneself when other vehicles are about. At 10 p.m. I pulled onto the main road from a field and started heading for town to drop off my last load. I'd been working since 6 a.m. After a few miles this stupid car driver is coming straight at me on my side of the road. 'What an idiot,' I thought, 'he's going to kill us all.' Before I could swerve he swerved and he ended up in the ditch. Needless to say it was me that was on the wrong side of the road. He wasn't a very happy man.

Okanagan Valley in British Columbia grows everything except tobacco, and also has packing and bottling plants. It does attract a lot of immigration raids though because of the high number of illegals that are around working.

To find out about work ask the main seasonal workers who are French Quebec hippies. Still in a 1969 time warp, they do this work year after year. A lot of animosity is caused with the locals who look down on these characters. These French Canadians also know where all the tree planting is going on. As more trees these days are being planted than cut down, most of the planting is north of Vancouver around Prince George and Vancouver Island. Tree planting companies recruit in March, start in April and finish in August. There is also tree planting in Alberta and Ontario.

The Okanagan Valley stretches down into Washington State but the fruit picking south of the border is done mainly by Mexicans. When I've worked with illegals, if you are camping and sharing rooms with them, rent a post office box number to put your documents in so that if the immigration raids the work place or living place you can run like hell into the woods. They won't hang around for long, and they can't take your passport if it is in a post office box.

Health

There is no reciprocal health agreement with the UK and unlike Australia and New Zealand medical costs are expensive. All Canadians have health coverage so you can use a Canadians health card, but make sure you remember the name and date of birth on the card. I almost came unstuck in Edmonton Hospital. I had checked into hospital with a bad case of malaria which I suspect I had caught in Malawi or Kenya three months earlier. On my second or third day in a three-man ward. This doctor comes into the ward and is calling, "Mr Les Smith please."

I just lay there thinking, 'That's funny, why is he calling my buddies name out?' I finally twigged – Ah! Ha, that's supposed to be me. So I says, "Over here doctor. Sorry for not answering, I'm still delirious and drugged up and a bit out of it."

He says, "Not to worry, I wonder if I could ask you a favour?"

I think, 'Hello, they're onto me, hell what am I going to do now! How do I do a runner in the state I'm in.'

But he says, "We have a lot of student doctors in this hospital and obviously they have never seen an advanced stage of malaria, or any stage of malaria come to that, so could I sent them in to see you one at a time and you answer their questions and let them do an examination of you, but don't tell them what you've got."

Phew! – a flood of relief comes over me. So l think, 'Why not? It's the least I can do.' The drugs were stopping the chronic fever, murderous headaches and sweats and shivers I'd been suffering with up until I got into this place. So over a couple of hours half a dozen or so young doctors proceeded to examine me and ask me all sorts of questions. This would have been all right except each one of them felt my swollen spleen which probably would have burst if I hadn't come to hospital. Feeling your swollen spleen from pressing down on one's stomach is one thing, but shoving their fingers inside a rubber glove and then inserting them up one's rectum is not my idea of fun. Maybe OK if you're a homosexual, but I'm not. The pain was excruciating but apparently they had to do this to feel the spleen from the inside. It was the size of a cricket ball on the outside. After half a dozen trainees had done this I just had to call a stop to it. I think getting found out would have been better than this. Anyway after four days in hospital I'm released with half a dozen different drugs to take at various intervals and every three weeks I had to come in as a day patient to have my blood checked so as to determine what new drug quotas to take. So my buddy Les has malaria on his medical history now. One of these days I'll get insurance.

Drinking

Canada has the same puritanical hang-ups as the USA about drinking in public. If you try having a beer on a park bench, in a park, on the street or on the beach you will get the drink poured away and be arrested if you give any lip to the RCMP you'll get heavily fined. Some of the worst hangovers I've had in my life have been from Canadian beer, murderous headaches brewed too fast with too many chemicals. Why people buy this grog in the UK when we have so many beers to choose from is beyond me.

Quebec: Has more tolerant laws about drinking. It's also the only province that allows drink to be bought outside of state controlled liquor stores. This is the closest you'll get to European civilisation when it comes to drinking.

Saskatchewan province: When you are in a bar you must sit at a table and you cannot have more than two drinks in front of you at any one time. If you want to change tables you have to get the waiter/waitress to move your drink for you. Similar laws exist in all the bible bashing Prairie Provinces.

In the cities where they have pubs where you can stand, they have fire regulations that stipulate how many people can be in the place at any one time, so a place that we would call empty, they consider it full. This creates huge queues outside waiting to get in – one out, one in, and so on. For places like the Rose and Crown pub in Edmonton you have to be in the place by 6:45 p.m. or you have to wait in a line-up for an hour or so. This is a real turn off on a Friday night when you want to go out on the town. When you hear Canadians being described as real boring conservatives, you now know why this is so. These stupid rules and regulations probably drove me out of Canada. You need to be eighteen years old to drink, unlike the USA where it is twenty-one years.

Getting In and Working

There is no visa required for a British passport. On arrival a three month stamp is issued, or six months can be obtained at port of entry by showing funds and a return ticket. It is easier to come in on three months, then when you are in apply for another three months at an immigration office that all the cities have. Do not mention you are coming in to work, just a travelling tourist.

Have any trade papers or job offers posted to you, Poste Restante, such and such a town, if you don't have an address.

Students can apply for work permits from the Canadian High Commission in London, Immigration Section, MacDonald House, 38 Grosvenor Street, WIX OAA. Phone 0171 629 9492. You must be eighteen to thirty years and have proof that you will be returning to your course studies on returning to the UK.

If you are not a student you will have to make up a social security number when going for a job. They are nine digit numbers, foreign workers start with a '9'. You might be asked to show proof of status if you use this. Locals numbers begin with '72l'. You probably won't be asked to show your card – you just have to know your number. Or you can get away with working by claiming your number is in the post. You can usually get away with this for six-eight weeks at a job and then make up a number beginning with '72l'.

Being Local or a New Immigrant

Always go on about how great the country is and don't be negative about the country. The same applies for the United States, Australia and

New Zealand. Don't go on about how great the UK is, we all know it's crap. This can avoid you being turned in if someone knows you're illegal.

A buddy of mine, Andy, who is now an American citizen, for years had a Union Jack flag above his bed. He is now totally embarrassed about the whole affair, and we still wind him up about it. He is now as American as apple-pie.

You can have a story about why you speak with an accent. My buddy, Big Belfast Bill, came over in the 70s as he was getting too mixed up with the Protestant paramilitary in Ulster. Now when someone asks my pal Bill where he's originally from as he still has a bit of an Ulster man's accent, he doesn't say Ulster or Northern Ireland or Britain – he says Ireland. So my theory is, if all the kids in Northern Ireland had to leave when they were sixteen for ten years and go around the world, when and if they came back there would be no more 'troubles'. God forbid, I remember when my granddad put me on his knee when I was six years old and told me the Catholics were the Devils own creation. At six years of age I didn't know what a Catholic was, probably thought they were creatures with horns. He had been a black and tan in the British army in the 20s doing his duty for King and Empire.

Bill's dad had served in Europe with the Canadian armed forces and the Canadians are still there now. His dad met Bill's mother who was from Ulster, and so settled in Ulster, hence he had the right of abode in Canada. So try and pick up accents. Nobody knows where I'm from with my mongrel English accent that over the years people have mistaken for South African, New Zealand, Canadian, American, English and even Irish. I guess on that one I mixed with the Novies too long (Newfoundlanders) or from when I worked around England with Irish Navvy gangs as a teenager.

Hitching with a Union Jack flag is OK, that way people know you are from overseas. Canada in general is a great place to hitch, more so out west than in the east. Over the years I have done a tremendous amount of hitch-hiking around the world. It can be a brilliant way to meet people and get the 'feel' of the place, soak up the atmosphere of the country so to speak, and get shown out of the way sights that you wouldn't see from public transport. Plus you can get to find out about local work prospects and sometimes get a running commentary on the local history and sometimes even get put up for the night. It's much more exciting than catching a bus. Sadly today hitching is dropping in popularity.

Whenever I am driving and I pass hitchers, if I can't pick them up for one reason or another I have terrible pangs of guilt and I remember the times that I have waited for lifts. I know plenty of people, great people, who would never dream of picking up a hitch-hiker, such is the controversial subject of hitch-hiking. 'They are riff-raff – you don't know anything about them – they'll rob you, rape you, murder you – they are freeloaders, druggies, alcoholics, people on the run, nasty people,' etc. These are some of the reasons you hear for not picking up people, but by far the greatest danger of getting robbed, raped, murdered or stranded is for the hitcher, not the driver.

I've had some very hairy moments, from drunk drivers who can hardly keep awake, to drunk drivers showing off and trying to scare you. A drunk French farmer fell asleep at the wheel as we were going around a bend in the Pyrenees Mountains, and if I hadn't grabbed the wheel I would have been dead at the age of twenty and so would he.

In Africa I have been scared out of my wits by a drunken African soldier driving at 160 Ks in the rain, in a Datsun with bald tyres and worn out shock absorbers, in the middle of nowhere where wild animals cross the road constantly writing off cars and with no hospital for 200 miles.

Hitch-hiking in Canada, halfway between Calgary and Edmonton, I'd been travelling with this chap from Vernon, British Columbia – a brilliant ride. We were in his new pick-up truck pulling a horse box with two horses, when a car with a drunken pair of kids hit the horse box by overtaking us on the hard shoulder. This was one of the worst car crashes I'd ever been in. My driver lost control, we turned over and over and ended up in the ditch with the seventeen stone driver on top of me. I could hardly move for a week after from aches and pains, stiffness and bruising. The truck and horse box were written off and one of the horses was killed. The other one ran off up the highway with the guy's dog running after it. The two kids were in the opposite ditch with their car written off. The passenger had a broken leg the driver was OK, until I head butted him and broke his nose, whereupon the other drivers around who had witnessed the whole affair, calmed me down and said not to give him any excuses for getting off. I did this because he started to down play the whole affair. When the RCMPs came he blurted out that I'd assaulted him.

The Mountie said, "Did anyone witness this assault?" Nobody said anything. The Mounties arrested them and said, "you must have broken your nose on the steering wheel buddy."

Always talk and be good company to your host. They are picking you up for company and sometimes to share the driving. I, and plenty of people I know, if we are driving long distances, are constantly looking to see what towns are coming up and if I pick up a hitcher or hitchers, I tell them I'm going to the town fifty miles up the road, so if the company is really boring and a down and out wino who stinks, I can easily drop them off with no hassle as I have made out I've reached my destination and they are fifty miles up from where they were. If they are good company I keep them with me. So you have to be interesting company. If you are a woman it is best to hitch with someone. If you are a couple of guys it is best to split up and meet later down the road. Try not to carry massive packs. You will lose prospective rides if your pack is too big. Usually you can manage with half of what you're carrying.

Film Work

Vancouver and British Columbia is now a major centre for making films as Hollywood is now all unionised for extras. Lots of big budget films are made in Canada now, i.e., *First Blood* (Sylvester Stallone), *The Unforgiven* (Clint Eastwood). Also many TV films and serials are made here i.e. *Northern Exposure*. Watch out for agencies that guarantee you work after you have paid a registration fee, check to see if any films are being made first. The Canadian Tourist Board can give you this information – they are in every city.

My buddy Viking Eric is now picking up movie stars from the airport by limousine and dropping them off at locations or hotels and gets huge wads of money for doing this. You won't get one of these jobs without being in the 'know'.

Youth Hostels and Backpackers Hostels

YHA's of course are a good source of information on jobs to be had. It is not a good idea to stay at them once you are working. When giving out your address to employers, try not to be staying at the address just in case the immigration raids the place.

Applying For a Canadian Social Insurance Number

Go into any Canada Employment Centre, they are all over and ask for an application form, it's two pages, it's bilingual (French, English), don't be nervous going into one of these centres, you're not doing anything wrong only asking for an application form, similar set up to the UK job centres similar offices in USA, Australia and New Zealand. Filling them out can be a bit tricky though grab a couple of copies or use a light pencil, until you're happy with the end result. Best of luck I myself never had a legit Canadian card I always used a number that belonged to a buddy of mine, my name to employers, his number never any problems. I have legit one for Australia,

New Zealand my American one got confiscated off me on my last trip to the US, more of that story under USA.

Canada Opens Door to More Skilled Workers!

As of now summer 2014 Canada has opened up for skilled and semi-skilled workers there are now eighty-nine trades urgently needed to be filled, under the Federal Skilled Visa programme, so if you're under forty this is a great opportunity to get into the real land of the free and the brave.

Go to www.ixpvisas.com don't waste any more time stop talking and get moving.

This site is great it tells you everything you need to know.

CHAPTER 10
Australia

"Work consists of what a body is obliged to do. Play consists of whatever a body is not obliged to do."

- Mark Twain

From 1787-1868 it was incredibly easy to get into Australia – all you had do was to steal a loaf of bread in the UK, then you could get a free sailing trip out here. Now in Australia it is vogue to have a great-great-grandparent that was a convict. In fact only between 150,000 and 170,000 were transported here only about 25,000 were women, which had a long lasting influence on the male dominated society of Australia for many years afterwards. Australia could have quite easily become Dutch, Portuguese or French. The Dutch and Portuguese reckoned it would be more trouble than it was worth to colonise the place, and the French were, planning on colonising the place but we beat them to it, thank heavens.

On arrival you were guaranteed work, the only snag was you didn't get paid. If you were a masochist it was great because you got yourself flogged regularly as well. In those days Australia was described as the social sewer of Britain. If one could get sent out here today for stealing, the shops in the UK would be stripped bare, such is the attraction today of Australia. After World War II up until 1972 one could still get out here for £10, hence the

£10 Pommie. Sadly, today it is difficult to migrate to Australia unless you have close relatives or you marry an Australian, or you can come out sponsored by a company which means you have to be well qualified. Australia, being a very desirable place to live, can pick the cream of the immigrant crop which it admits from around the world.

A lot of third world migrants are here due to their large extended families. Sixty per cent of non-English speaking immigrants end up being long term unemployed, so don't take Australian unemployment figures too literally (8 per cent and falling), plus Australia has more people out of work intentionally than just about anywhere else in the world, due to the generous welfare system. That's not to say there is not genuine unemployment around in certain areas. Now new immigrants have to wait two years to collect welfare – the Liberal government is in action, New Zealanders exempt.

Australia must rank second place after Israel as the best place to find work, but whereas most work in Israel is unpaid work on Kibbutz's, the work in Australia is well paid and on a world standard it is probably one of the highest paid countries for unskilled and casual work, i.e. plenty of people work for $8 hour in the USA. Nobody works for that in Australia. Very few people work for less than AUS $ 12.0 per hour and plenty of jobs pay AUS $ I5-AUS $ 20 per hour. AUS $ 1 = 90¢ US. The Aussie dollar is just about on par with the Canadian dollar and the Swiss Franc.

I put this high wage factor down to the fact that no third world country has a land border with Australia, so the place is not flooded with large scale illegal immigrants who don't speak English and who are prepared to work for anything so as to have a piece of the 'good life', like Mexicans in the USA. Australia also had a 'white Australia' policy up until the mid 1970s. Also, Australia had kept a Labour government for many years with strong union support, who have kept wages and awards high for the workers. Australia has one of the highest union memberships per head of working population of all the western nations. By resisting Thatcherism (cut everything and privatise everything – make the rich richer and the poor poorer), Australia has paid a price for a country with just about every natural resource on earth – vast mineral deposits, mountains of iron ore, tons of gold, huge fields of diamonds, oil, gas, silver, nickel, lead, uranium, zinc, coal, timber; every kind of food is grown, heaps of fish, cattle and sheep – everything except polar icecaps, plus a massive tourist and film industry.

Economy

Australia has a small population of 25 odd million plus with plenty of land, and the national debt is $260 billion dollars. How can this be! Whereas a country like the Netherlands, same population which would fit into one of the outback cattle stations, with half of their country under sea level, no natural resources except some oil, gas and tulips, and they have minimal national debt. The unemployment figures are about the same, and wages are about the same. In productivity Australia ranks low down among the western industrial nations, but who wants to work your balls off in the middle of summer I ask, when you can go and have a beer instead.

This makes the Netherlands credit worthiness strong, whereas the Australian international credit worthiness was not so good, until the mineral boom buying from China which caused their dollar to gain strength, and getting stronger since the height of early 2008-9 world downturn. In this present economy, Australia is still donating overseas aid, called Aus Aid to countries like Thailand, whose own economies have been booming until recently. Of course, the Asians will take what you give them. Twenty-five per cent of the world's billionaires are now Asians – maybe they should be tapped for contributions to the poor instead of the Aussie tax payer.

But I know where I would rather live given a choice. 'The land down under' is for me. Who wants wooden clogs and tulips anyway? And heaps of Dutch fell in with the Germans during the last war whereas Aussies fought and died for the UK in great numbers in the Boer War, World War 1 and World War II – Australians of British and Protestant background who were the most vocal in their support for what was sometimes called the 'motherland'. The then Labour Prime Minister, Andrew Fisher, gave the lead in 1914 when he declared that Australia would support Britain to 'the last man and the last shilling'. Such was their devotion to the British Empire. Australia then with a population of 4 million had more casualties than the USA who had stood by and watched until 1917.

Canada with a population then of 8 million also sacrificed more men than its southern neighbour, such was their devotion to duty also. I read recently that Australia had the highest standard of living at the turn of the century '1900' and are now ranked in the top five. I've also read that Argentina had the highest standard of living at the turn of that century '1900'. How on earth these statistics are come by I don't know.

As of 2 March 1996 the Labour government under the leadership of Paul Keating had lost power to the Liberal coalition party under the leadership of John Howard. In the previous election, held every three years, the Liberals lost it as they were going to bring in a GST same as VAT, a terrible tax for small business as I have experienced in the UK. The election before they lost out as the Labour government dropped 10 per cent off beer tax one week before the election – only in Australia! This time Keating couldn't pull it off. So as the Sun newspaper put it, 'The Lizard of Oz that Was'. Apart from being of Irish decent, I thought the guy was all right. Anybody who stands up to the monarchy is all right in my book, and he even put his arm around Queen Liz.

John Howard had promised to reform the present labour laws. At that time it was almost impossible to be fired from a permanent job. Even if you burn your bosses factory down the Industrial Relations Commission would state, that your state of mind was brought about by the 'stress of the job', so your job will be kept open for you. These labour laws have been detrimental to the growth of small business throughout Australia but because of these laws Australia has a booming casual labour pool system where agencies recruit for companies on a temporary basis, which is great for the travelling worker.

One of the first targets for the then new government was be the closed shop unionism, at that present time – dock wharfies were then earning $75.000 per year with one of the lowest productivity rates in the world. I doubt if a working traveller will ever be able to get one of these jobs, but this kind of closed shop practice will probably come to an end in the not so distant future, like New Zealand and the UK. Australia ranks second to the USA in its over legislative restrictive bureaucracy. It is the only country I know where it is law to wear a crash helmet when cycling. Australia also has more politicians per head of population than any other western democracy with stifling bureaucratic interference from public servants, blood sucking on free enterprise, with their snouts in the trough just like in the EU.

Working Legally As a Holiday Traveller

12 Month Visa

Working visas can be applied between the ages of eighteen to twenty-six. Some are given out to people with special skills up until the age of thirty. The latter group are usually checked out for sufficient funds etc. and, 'Why have you waited until you were over twenty-six to apply?' (I went to university, or I looked after my sick granny). Application forms are £78 non-refundable. Australians can work in the UK for two years on a working visa. They can apply for this until the age of twenty-seven (not fair).

On the working visa you can only work for three months with any one employer, then you are supposed to change jobs, 42,000 of these visas are given out to Brits. The Irish have also got on the bandwagon, but they get their own. They are not included in the 42,000. How do they get in on everything, and they are not or never have been part of the Commonwealth? The visa starts running out one month after it has been processed, so don't hang around the UK sorting this and sorting that. Be ready to go.

Australian High Commission, Australia House, Strand, London. VC2B4LA. Phone 0171 379 4334.

You can also apply in Bangkok if you want to do Asia first.

Tax File Number

Just about every job requires you to have a tax file number. It's a nine digit number. The forms are no longer available from the post office since '92. You don't need a working visa to get one. Tax is stopped at 29 per cent. Without one you will be stopped at 49 per cent. You will also need to open a bank account as lots of employers require you to have both of these, so make this a priority after your first couple of days in the country. With a working visa you can claim a tax rebate back when you leave. Read the tax file application.

Check for the latest up to date information off the internet on all my facts and figures as some are now out of date.

"Work – the curse of the leisure class." - R Lloyd

Working Illegally

Enter on a six month holiday visa – this can also be extended for an extra three months at $100. You can still apply for a tax file number and bank account. Maximum stay legally is one visit of six months, plus two and three month extensions at AUS $100 each. Countless Brits have got in this way and overstayed, ended up getting married or in de facto relationships (a promise of getting married), and have eventually got themselves legal.

I myself overstayed a year in the mid 80s when I left through Darwin immigration. I was taken into a room and interrogated. They wanted to know where, when and who I had worked for, and they threatened to jail me if I did not divulge all. I kept my mouth shut. I figured they were bluffing as the plane was on the tarmac and I had a ticket. If they had detained me the tax payer would have had to foot the bill (not that they would have been worried about that). I just kept denying I'd worked at all. I'd sent out my bank book – very incriminating evidence to be carrying. Finally they let me get on the plane, with a 'code' stamped in my passport. I found out later that it was a five year ban. Next time I came to Australia it was over five years plus I'd changed my passport again. Don't hang on to passports if they are full of stamps – this causes immigration to check you out more thoroughly. In those days I still possessed the 'edge' – not like in the USA in '94 when I'd lost it by being a settled taxpaying conformist business man in London.

If you are working illegally don't tell anybody. Make out you are a resident and have relatives living here, pick up the accent, and don't go on about crappy old UK. Always go on about how great Australia is, which is not at all hard to do.

Getting Work

What the government is trying to do with the three month clause in your work visa of three months per job, they are funnelling you into the enormous agricultural economy, fruit picking, packing and canning. Everything is grown in Australia. The CES (Commonwealth Employment Service) has a special harvest section in designated offices. In the cities, as well as providing a regular notice board, they have a casual labour section where you turn up at 6 a.m., but it is best to be in the queue at 5:30 a.m. As casual day jobs come in they are distributed out. If you have your own transport you get the out of suburb jobs. Some of these jobs can lead to semi-permanent jobs. Most of all be reliable and hard working, and you can be asked for by name the next time the job comes up.

I used the Brisbane one for three months in '85. One job lasted one month, plenty of others lasted three or four days. Lots of the guys you are competing against are down and outs and drunks who have run out of beer money before their next welfare cheque, and they don't have transport either. Not so long ago you could easily work your way around Australia using the casual labour out of the CES offices. One can still work one's way around Australia by fruit picking.

Fruit Picking

All the backpacker and YHA hostels in Australia have information about fruit picking – where the crops are and pick up points. As Australia is so huge there are crops to be picked all the year round, from the temperate climate of Tasmania to the tropical north of Queensland. A camaraderie develops amongst fellow fruit pickers as hardly anybody is a life long professional picker like the French Quebecois of Canada or Mexicans in the USA, so most pickers are on holiday and know they won't be doing this job forever. There are lots of drinking sprees to be had, and it is not unheard of for the odd joint or two to be passed around.

Still, watch out for coordinated immigration raids. Try and keep away from Swedes as there are thousands of them in Australia doing picking as it is the vogue place to come for young Swedes, and none of them have work visas. That will teach them to be a neutral country, and be hand in glove with the Germans as they were in the last war.

The farmers get pissed off with immigration when the fruit gets left on the trees or bushes to rot. They are doing these raids to build up their quotas of deportees so then they can point out to the government how efficient they are at their job and so get more funding off the state and look at how many jobs we have saved for Australians to do. So if you do a runner in the fields, have your passport in a post office deposit box, as I stated in working in Canada and the USA. Most locals are not interested in picking as the welfare state is so generous.

A friend of mine, Mick from the UK who lives in Freemantle, Western Australia, has been in Australia since '87 and has not done one day's work here since he arrived. He married an Australian woman to get in, they have one child, and receives heaps of $ per fortnight on the welfare. Plus if you are unemployed you receive massive public transport discounts, supposedly to enable you to look for a job, and you also get other benefits and discounts. Mind you Mick does have a bad back, but this has not stopped him totally renovating his beach house which is 300 yards away from the beach. The house is fully paid off, so is his boat and car. At least you won't have to compete for a job against him and his wife. As I said earlier, don't take unemployment figures too literally. Living on the dole makes people not only negative and depressing, it makes them tight. Mick charged me $5 to drop me off at the airport. I've dropped plenty of people off at airports during my life and I've never charged anyone anything. God forbid if I ever start to charge people! So with this amount of money do you think he's going to pick fruit for a living, with his bad back! The guy can hardly do his shoe laces up as he's so fat. When he went over to the UK recently for a three month summer holiday to show off the baby, he and his wife signed on the UK welfare system. No wonder single men get pissed off, as we pay the lion's share of society's taxes and take the least out of the system, plus we're expected to fight the wars when needed. Not to mention that men in most countries have to work longer then women before they can retire.

If I was in his position with a regular fixed income I'd be off gold prospecting every day, as plenty of people earn $10-$30,000 per year prospecting with metal detectors in WA (Western Australia). In '92 a 22 kilo nugget was found near Kalgoorlie with a metal detector. It was found one metre down and one metre across from an old gold mining shaft that had been combed countless times with detectors. With prospecting it is good to have a regular income such as a pension or welfare cheque to cover day to day expenses such as eating, until you find the big one, which are around dry river beds after a flash flood.

Right, where was I? Back to picking. As a teenager I and countless other teenagers used to head over to Jersey, the Channel Isles, in April to pick and pack potatoes and tomatoes all summer. Packing is much better than picking, as your back stays upright. Remember we've spent hundreds of thousands of years getting our body to stand up right, so when one spends all day bent over picking it obviously murders one's back.

After I left Brisbane, Queensland, I headed up to Bowen to pack fruit as I hate picking. Bowen is 600 km south of Cairns, which is a party town where everyone goes to take diving courses which are probably the best value in the world, plus you learn on the spectacular Great Barrier Reef. One tip before signing up for diving (before I get back to Bowen) – if you are an asthmatic don't pay to go and have a medical which everyone is required to do before starting the course. All asthmatics fail a medical, so why pay a doctor $100 for him or her to tell you you've failed. The same applies for perforated ear drums. This is a con that the diving centres are working with the doctors. This con needs to be eradicated.

I only packed tomatoes in Bowen for a couple of weeks as I was basically just cruising up the coast with my best Aussie buddy Marcus, checking out the members of the opposite sex on the tropical coastal island resorts. On the way down from Bowen to Brisbane we had a panel van full of travellers. Of course a Queensland cop pulls me over to check us out. One of my passengers is a Kiwi and they find dope in his bag. This is reason enough to take us in for questioning and searches. I'm cursing luck because I know that in one of my bags I've got a shoe box with all my relevant papers in it – my passport which is already six months over my allocated visa, plus I'm in the process of building up a new ID and they are all stacked together. When we reach the police station everyone's gear is searched, six of us in total. My gear is last, and they haven't found anything else on anybody except the Kiwi guy. When the cop comes to my shoe box I'm trying to distract him so he doesn't check out the passport and other IDs. He's thumbing through every item quite methodically. The passport and other assorted pieces of ID are at the end of the box and he's getting closer to them. I've almost resigned my fate to getting arrested when just before the incriminating evidence there is a pile of twenty or so photos which he pulls out for a look. Thank God they were of Thai girlfriends in various semi-pornographic poses. His eyes are popping out of his head now.

Phew, a breathing space for me. I say to him, "All right aren't they mate?"

He says, "You bet. Fair dinkum mate, where do you get these?"

I tell him, "In Thailand mate, the best place on earth for a bachelor."

He says, "Yeah, really, go on mate."

I say, "You bet. Are you a single bloke?"

He says, "Yeah."

I say, "Where do you have your holidays mate?"

He says, as he's still gaping at the photos, "I go fishing mate."

I says, "Well, why not go up to Thailand? There's heaps of fishing up there plus heaps of beautiful women, as you can see."

We carry on a mates conversation like this for about five minutes and he gives me my photos back. He's lost interest in the rest of my shoe box. I owe a lot to those girlfriends. No doubt he's found out the joys of the East. I still had the 'edge'.

The moral of this story is never carry conflicting IDs in the same location. Don't carry dope. The Kiwi guy got busted. If my van had been a boat, speaking hypothetically, I would have had it impounded. So don't carry dope on yachts either, for the owner's sake.

Sugar Cane

Opened up Northern Queensland, lost half of the tropical Daintree Forest in the process. Must have seemed like a good idea at the time. Today I'd rather have the forest and buy the sugar from Brazil or wherever.

There are no jobs to be had in the sugar industry as this industry is in decline and the seasonal jobs go to locals. Gone are the days of chopping it down with a machete, it is fully automated today with harvesters, etc. In the days of old the Queensland sugar industry had a labour dispute. Some headstrong union labour set fire to the cane fields just before harvesting time. After the fires had run their course it was discovered that the cane was still standing and intact. What had happened was that only the outer brush had been bunt off and the cane was easier to get at for harvesting. This method of harvesting was then copied throughout the sugar cane world.

Countless lives were thus saved due to the fact that the poisonous snakes that inhabit the cane were roasted.

Health

Australia has a reciprocal health agreement with the UK. To go and see a doctor will cost money for an appointment, but clinics and casualty departments are free. If you are going to spend a long time in the outback exploring, you might want to consider insurance in case you need to be air lifted out in an emergency. Burke and Wills, an Irishman and an Englishman, never had insurance and they died. (Two intrepid explorers of the nineteenth century who walked from Melbourne to the Gulf of Carpentaria and back looking for the inland sea.)

There is no danger from wild carnivorous animals (although if you are a woman you might think that some of the outback men are wild carnivorous animals) – only reptiles, insects and fish. Some of the most venomous snakes in the world are found here, also poisonous spiders. One variety, the red-back spider, is only found in Sydney. Why couldn't they go and live in Canberra where all the politicians live. The other poisonous spider, the funnel web, is found all over.

Crocodiles inhabit the tropical regions so stay out of the rivers. Crocodile hunting was banned in the early 70s. Then they were not a problem. Today they have Jurassic Park varieties with huge appetites, so look out for 'No Swimming' signs that show either a shark, crocodile or jelly fish stingers. You don't want to be a statistic – remember, Crocodile Dundee was fighting rubber crocs. One of my heroes is Vic Haslop, the world famous man-eating shark hunter. Hated and despised by the 'greenies', he regularly gets called out all over the world to sort out 'man-eaters'. Sharks also munch on people all over Australia from time to time, even 30 km from the sea, in the city rivers. The box jelly fish (stingers) are also found in the tropical north from October – April, can and do kill people, but at least they don't eat you. Vinegar is the antidote to their stings.

Alligators in the Southern States of the USA are culled and hunted with licences creating an industry which employs many thousands of people. Why can't Australia do the same with crocodiles, so as to limit the spread of these Jurassic type monsters, which are feeding not just on fish but livestock and isolated Aboriginals out hunting and fishing. I'm sure that the tourist industry would benefit as well.

A great many Australians have died from melanoma skin cancer which is far more dangerous than all the above – so respect the sun! Wear hats and sunscreen block. The Victorians covered up and milky white complexions were all the rage!

While I was working in Brisbane on a self-employed basis I gashed my arm on a piece of sharp steel. I quickly wrapped my arm in a towel and drove to the casualty department of the city hospital, where they fixed me up and told me to come back in two weeks to have the stitches removed. No problem using the hospital. I wish I'd been working for a company then as I could have had paid leave. Two weeks later I was up further north on one of the islands with my buddy Marcus, fraternising with members of the opposite sex. He took the stitches out for me with a Swiss army knife. In those days Marcus had the looks and physique of a Baywatch movie star. Today he is living off welfare in Adelaide and eating himself to a heart attack with the waist line of Paverotti. Life is good in the land down under. To be poor in the UK is the pits – in Australia it is OK. Disposable income is much higher down under.

Working in the Cities

If you speak Japanese and or Chinese you will get a job right away in the tourist industry. A few years ago the powers that be wanted to drop visas for Japanese as they desire to visit and spend heaps of money in Australia. The veterans from World War II, led by the RSL (Returning Serviceman's League) were up in arms and the government had to back down.

The tourist board want all holiday visas scrapped. The government makes heaps of dough out of visas, but they lose out on a lot more tourists that would come here if there was no visa bullshit. It is estimated that more than $1 billion annually is lost to the tourist industry. But bureaucracy is bureaucracy and by scrapping visas some civil servants wouldn't lose their jobs, but would have to be shuffled around to another government department, which would make waves.

As I stated in the beginning of this chapter, it is almost impossible to be fired from a permanent job in Australia, so now companies are using temporary and casual labour to get around this problem. It is more expensive for them in the short term, but not in the long term. This state of affairs is beneficial to the working traveller. The Sydney Yellow Pages phone book has fifteen pages of employment agencies who specialise in every form of employment (Perth has fourteen, Melbourne – fifteen, Brisbane – ten). Some of the employment agencies are international, others are home grown. Here are just a few: Drake Industrial, Able Industrial, Kirby Contract Labour, Manpower, plus heaps of agencies who specialise in office, computing and secretarial staff. There are also many vacancies for nurses, au pairs and nannies. There are labour pools in the cities for office furniture removals and exhibition hire work. I did thirty shifts for ASM Exhibition Hire. In '96 at $12 per hour, no tax. With ASM you need a bank account number, tax file number and $30 worth of tools – they tell you what tools to get.

Telemarketing

Very popular with working travellers – huge demand average pay AUS $18 per hour. Newspapers and agencies are always advertising for newcomers.

Getting Around

If you work out your route before leaving the UK you can get great discounts on internal flight and bus passes. Check with travel agencies who specialise on Australia, plenty are advertised in the Exchange and Mart, Time Out, TNT magazine and the Sunday news papers plus the internet.

Driving Around

There is a car market for travellers in Kings Cross, Sydney. Lots of the vehicles are kitted out for camping and touring – also many trips are advertised on hostel notice boards. For a very in depth book about Australia I recommend *The Lonely Planet* and *The Rough Guide*.

Joke: Bruce and Sheila walking over Sydney Bridge.

Sheila: Bruce, I'm pregnant, and if you don't marry me I'm going to jump off this bridge.

Bruce: Well Sheila, not only are you a good lay, you're a damn good sport, an' all.

Sport

An outdoor sporting paradise. Australians definitely don't like losing, especially at cricket or any other sport and especially not to the Poms. Not unknown to revert to underarm bowling to win. Win at all cost. No medals for losing.

Outback

The terrain reminds me so often of Africa, alas with few animals and heaps more flies, but the bird life is spectacular. A good money making scam was smuggling parrots eggs out of the country for huge profits. These days one can expect to receive a prison sentence equivalent to smuggling heroin, so don't be tempted. Just look at the birds and try not to see $ signs.

More of a 'buzz' in the African bush. Australia has less animals but more flies than Africa.

Australian High Commission: Australia House, Strand, London, WCZB4LA. Phone 0171 379 4334.

Drinking

Pubs, bars and hotels – similar set up to UK. Nothing like North America. No under 18s. Tips not required as in North America.

Working Holiday

Information sheet from: Australian Outlook, 3 Buckhurst Road, Beschill-on-Sea, East Sussex, TN40 1QF. Phone 01424 223111. Enclose an A4 stamped, self-addressed envelope.

Hitching

The backpacker murderer who terrorized NSW hitch-hikers for years has now been captured. For more about hitching read under Canada.

A Weird Scenario

Fireworks and crossbows are illegal, and have been for years because they are too dangerous. As everyone knows, if someone throws a banger behind you, you are in great danger of having a heart attack when it goes 'bang'. However M16 Armalite automatic assault rifles were perfectly legal up until May '96. They have only been made illegal since a local Rambo went 'ape shit' and shot thirty-five people dead. I have seen first hand what military assault rifles do to people. The general public does not need to own these weapons – they are over the top for shooting rabbits.

Australia now has a successful buy back scheme – let's hope the USA will follow their lead somehow I doubt it will happen.

Gun Fanatics

My experience with gun freaks, whether they be in Australia or the USA is that generally they tend to be males with large bellies, and little dicks. Bow and arrow hunting is the only way to go, from horseback, a true warrior's sport.

Recommended Reading

Live work and Play in Australia by Sharyn McCullum, *Workabout Australia* by Barry Brebner and *How to Live and Work in Australia* from the How to series. The best free budget travellers guide to Australia and New Zealand is TNT's *Travel Planner*. Gives up to-date information on visas and finding work – has six up-dates per year and can be obtained at travel agents and branches of Waterstones bookshops or ordered by phone on 0171 37333377.

An article taken from the Sydney Morning Herald 1996

STOP THEIR DOLE

The Kids Who Refused Jobs in Paradise

Shane and Bindy Paxton yesterday turned down food, accommodation, and AUS $ 245 clear a week.

Community Outrage

The three unemployed youths who shocked Australia by refusing jobs at a tropical island resort should have their dole payments cancelled immediately, the business community demanded yesterday.

"It would send a message for people out there to get off their bums," Small Business Association of Australia spokesman John Fowler said.

"There are lots of jobs out there, but some people are just lazy bastards."

His reaction was typical of most people who watched on national TV as Mark, Shane and Bindy Paxton turned down jobs at South Molle Island, in the Whitsundays, because the boys would need to have hair cuts and their sister didn't like the colour of the uniforms.

The job offers were made when the resort manager Kevin Collins took pity on them after they were featured on Channel Nine's A Current Affair in a report into long term unemployment. The TV show flew them up to Queensland for interviews. The three were offered food, accommodation, board and $245 clear a week for work as a kitchen hand, gardener and waitress.

But Mark, sixteen, and Shane, eighteen, both sporting pony tails reaching to their backsides, astounded Mr Collins by refusing his offer when he insisted they would have to have the regulation haircut. Bindy, twenty took her job and was sent to be fitted for a uniform. But she quit less than an hour later when she discovered the uniforms were green, insisting she would not wear any colours but purple or black.

So the Paxtons returned to their western Melbourne homes and the dole queue!

Harvest Calendar

New South Wales

BARHAM - Summer - Oranges, Tomatoes - (050)32-4571 - 4hrs west of Albury.

BATHURST - Jan – Feb - Peaches, Nectarines - (063)31-1588 - 3hr train ride from Sydney.

BATLOW - Dec – May - Apples, Stone fruit - (069)47-2077 - 5 hr train ride from Sydney.

BILPID - Nov – May - Apples, Stone fruit - (045)77-1100 - 1 hr bus ride from Richmond.

BOURKE - Nov – Jan - Cotton - (068)72-2511 - Train Syd-Dubbo, then bus. May - Grapes, Citrus.

COFFS HARBOUR. All year - Bananas - (066)52-1433 - On Pacific H'way & train line. Sept – Nov. Berries.

COWKA - Sept – Oct - Asparagus - (063)42-1088 - Train Syd-Bathhurst. Then bus.

FORBES - Jan – April - Apples, Grapes - (068)62-2055 - On Melb.-Bris bus route. Stone fruit, Vegetables

GRIFFITH VILLAGE - Dec – Mar - Grapes, Citrus - (069) 69-1100. Train Syd-Orange, then bus.

MOREE - Nov – Jul - Cotton - (O67) 52 -3100 - On Melb-Bris bus route, Train Syd-Moree.

ORANGE - Dec – Apr - Apples, Pears - (063) 61-4144 - 5 hr train ride from Sydney. Stone fruit

YOUNG - Nov – Dec - Cherries - (063) 82-3366 - Train Syd-Cootamundra, then bus.

Queensland

AYR - July – Oct - Tomatoes - (O77) 83- 0666 - On Bruce Hwy. & main train, Capsicums line.

BOWEN - Jun – Dec - Tomatoes, Beans -(077) 86-2161 - On Bruce Hwy & main train Corn, Capsicums line. Zucchinis, Mangoe, Rockmelons

BRISBANE AREA - July – Sept - Strawberries, Onions - (07) 250 -3111 - See Brisbane Section. Potatoes

BUNDABERG & CHILDERS Apr – Jan - Tomatoes, Citrus, Peas - (071) 53 -7555. On Bruce Hwy & main train. Capsicum, Beans, line. Melons, Zucchins, Squash, Pumpkins, Avocados.

CARDWELL - All year - Bananas, Sugar cane - (077) 76-4111 - On Bruce Hwy & -INNISFAIL – (070) 61-5555 and main train, INGHAM line.

GAYNDAH - May – Sept - Citrus - (071) 61 1677 - $44 bus ride from Brisbane.

GYMPIE - May – Nov - Beans, Squash, Cucumbers. - (074) 82- 0699 - On Bruce Hwy & main train line.

MAREEBA - Sept – Dec -Tobacco, Mangoes - (070) 92- 8111 - Bus from Cairns to Mareeba, DIMBULAH - then car.

Harvest Calendar

NAMBOUR - July – Oct - Strawberries - (074) 41 31 77 - 2 hr. bus ride from Brisbane.

SUNSHINE COAST Feb – Mar Ginger.

STANTHORPE Dec – Apr - Apples, Grapes - (O76) 61 6555 - 3-4 hr bus ride from Brisbane - Pears, Tomatoes, Lettuce

TULLY - All year - Banana, Sugar Cane - (070) 68 2820 - On Bruce Hwy & main train line. Melons (esp. winter)

Victoria

ARDMONA - Jan – Apr - Pears, Apples - (058) 29 0002 - Train Melb-Shepparton. Stonefruit

COBRAM - Jan – Mar - Pears, Peaches - (058) 72 2360 - Train Melb – Shepparton, Apricots then bus.

ECHUCA - Feb – Apr - Tomatoes - (054) 82 0400 - Bus from Melb.

AREA - Oct – Dec - Berries

MILDURA - Feb – Mar - Grapes, Citrus fruit - (050) 219 5000 - 8 hr bus ride from Melb.

NYAH - Jan – Mar - Grapes - (O50) 32 0400 - 6 hr bus ride from Melb.

ROBINVALE - Feb – Mar - Grapes - (O50) 22 1797, 7 hr bus ride from Melb.

SHEPPARTON - Jan – Apr - Pears, Stonefruit - (058) 230 300. Apples

Tasmania

HUON VALLEY - Jan – Apr - Apples, Cherries - (O02) 64 1744. 30 min. bus from Hobart.

SCOTTSDALE - Mar - Hops - (O03) 37 1833. - 30 min. bus from Launceston.

MERSEY VALLEY - Feb – May - Apples - (O04) 27 I103 - Close to Devonport.

South Australia

ADELAIDE HILLS - Mar – Apr - Apples, Pears - (O8) 366 0400 - Close to Adelaide.

BAROSSA VALLEY - Mar – Apr - Grapes - (O85) 22 0400 - Bus from Adelaide.

CLARE VALLEY - Mar – Apr - Grapes - (O85) 22 O400 - Bus from Adelaide.

COONAWARRA - Mar – Apr - Grapes - (085)162 3337 - Bus from Adelaide.

THE RIVERLAND - Jan – Apr - Grapes - (085) 8O 1111 - 3 hr bus ride from Adelaide. Oranges, Stonefruit,

Northern Australia

KATHERINE - Oct – Nov - Mangos - (089) 741 655 3 hr. bus ride from Darwin.

Western Australia

CARNARVON - Mar – Apr - Bananas (099) 141 1107 - Perth-Darwin bus route.

DONNYB ROOK - Jan – Apr - Apples - (O97)11088. Bus from Perth. Small Crops

KUNUNURRA - Jul –Nov - Melons, Bananas, (091) 68 1211 - Perth-Darwin bus route. Vegs

SWAN VALLEY - Feb – May - Grapes, Apples - (O9)2741344 - Suburban bus/train in Perth.

Work and Travel – It's On!

It's ON! Finally the 'bloody' draught has broken!

Work! Yes good old fashioned Australian labour! Get yea backpack, water bottle, billy, sleeping bag, tent, dust down that forgotten slouch hat, polish up those tattered GP boots and get your backside to the country! It's Pumping!

Apples, asparagus, bananas, blue berries, cherries, cotton, grapes, onions, prunes, tomatoes, pears, avocados, mangoes, melons, pineapples, peaches, apricots, strawberries, tobacco, sugar, fish, hops, lobsters, crop seeding and mining. It's all there for the picking! Instead of shying at home during the semester break, bored and penniless, travel this fantastic country of ours and fill your pockets full of money. Tone those muscles and tan those boas, feel good and explore. If you want a peace of the action, like lots of money, travel, the opposite sex or hell even the same sex (well, it is the twenty-first century). Put your finger on the dialler and phone one of the following numbers!

Try John from Why Walk Tours first, he runs specialist trips to work areas; Tel: (O2) 548 28 84. Book your transport through the Bus Booking

Centre, they give between 10% – 50% off for TAFE Association and ISIC card holders; Tel: 368 0299.

Contact Numbers

New South Wales
Why Walk Tours Tel: 548 Z884
Ballina Job Centre Tel: 066 866 833
Macadamia Plantation Tel: 066 895 269
Batemans Bay Job Centre Tel: 044 751 900
Bourke Job Centre Tel: 068 722 511
Cooma Job Centre Tel: 064 521 788
Griffith Job Centre Tel: 069 691 100
Leeton Job Centre Tel: 069 532 899
Broken Hill Job Centre Tel: 080 877 155
Cuffs Harbour Job Centre Tel: 066 521 433
Mudgee Job Centre Tel: 063 721 266
Orange Job Centre Tel: 063 912 700

Northern Territory
Alice Springs Job Centre Tel: 089 S97 122
Darwin Job Centre Tel: 089 464 877
Katherine Job Centre Tel: 089 721 655

Queensland
Atherton Job Centre Tel: 070910666
Mareebs Job CentreTel: 070 928 111
Ayr Job Centre Tel: 077 830 666
Bundaberg Job Centre Tel: 071 537 555
Cairns Job Centre Tel: 070 422 222
Emerald Job Centre Tel: 079 824 622
Bundell Job Centre Tel: 075 703 922

Gympie Job Centre Tel: 074 820 699

Narnbour Job Centre Tel: 074 413177

South Australia

Mt. Barker Job Centre Tel: 08 391 2644

Berri Job Centre Tel: 085 801 111

Gawler Job CentreTel: 085 226 814

Angas Park Farm Tel: 018 839137

Angas Park Fruit Co. Tel: 085 642 O52

Tasmania

Devonport Job Centre Tel: 004 246 244

Huon Job Centre Tel: 002 641 744

Hobart Job Centre Tel: 002204 068

Launceston Job Centre Tel: 033 371833

Victoria

Ararat Job Centre Tel: 053 522 595

Bendigo Job Centre Tel: 054 342 730

Shepparton Job Centre Tel: 058 320 300

Colac Job Centre Tel: 052 314 277

Echuca Job Centre Tel: 054 820 400

Mildura Job Centre Tel: 050 221 797

Western Australia

Albany Job Centre Tel: 098 424 800

Carnarvon Job Centre Tel: 099 418384

Bunbury Job Centre Tel: 097 255 455

Esperence Job Centre Tel: 090 714 467

Geraldton Job Centre Tel: 099 641 420

Kalgoorlie Job Centre Tel: 090 211 011

Kununurra Job Centre Tel: 091 681 211

Manjimup Job Centre Tel: 097 711 088

Tobacco Park Work Shop Tel: 097 721 228

Instructions for Getting a Job

1. Pick up the phone and dial one of the numbers above find desired position and accommodation.

2. Book your transport through the Bus Booking Centre Tel. 368-0299. It is advisable to buy a return ticket.

3. Contact Work-A-Bout Australia for your seasonal work 'bible' Tel. 068-84-7777 or Fax.068-82-9023.

Tax File Number Application

Tax File Number application or enquiry for an individual.

PLEASE READ THIS PAGE AND THE BACK PAGE CAREFULLY BEFORE COMPLETING THIS FORM.

THIS WILL ENSURE THAT UNNECESSARY PROCESSING DELAYS ARE AVOIDED.

Who should use this form?

Use this form if:

- you have never had a Tax File Number or

- you are not sure if you have a Tax File Number or

- you know you have a Tax File Number but cannot find it on any tax papers you have.

PROOF OF IDENTITY MUST BE PROVIDED

When you lodge your form you must provide appropriate **original documents** which prove your identity. If appropriate proof of identity is not provided with the form a Tax File Number cannot be released to you.

Appropriate Proof of Identity documents are listed on the back page.

When completing this form please print clearly in ink using **BLOCK LETTERS**.

Do not use correction fluid or covering stickers.

Tick the appropriate boxes.

Make sure you answer all the questions otherwise we may have to contact you for the missing information.

This may delay getting your Tax File Number.

Having difficulties?

If you need help to fill in your form or you have difficulty providing enough proof of identity. Please contact the Tax Office for assistance.

Privacy of Information

The information requested is required by the Income Tax Assessment Act. Some of the information may be given to other government agencies that are authorised to receive it. These include the Departments of Social Security, Veterans Affairs and Employment, Education and Training.

Where do you lodge your completed form?

You can take your form and proof of identity documents to:

Any Tax Office.

If you cannot take them personally, you should mail your form and proof of identity documents to the Tax Office Branch nearest to your postal address for service of notices. Your documents will be returned to you by certified mail. See mailing addresses on this page.

Your Veterans Affairs office, if you need to give them your Tax File Number.

Your Social Security office, if you need to give them your Tax File Number for a benefit other than Family Payment.

Your Student Assistance Centre or most CES offices, if you need to give Employment, Education and Training (DEET) your Tax File Number.

If you lodge your completed form at Social Security, Veterans Affairs or DEET you only need to provide the relevant department with the proof of identity documents required for your income support payment.

The mailing addresses are:

AUSTRALIAN TAXATION OFFICE

NSW.
PO Box 9942 Albury 2640, Bankstown 1688
Chatswood 2057, Hurstville 1493
Newcastle 2300, Parramatta 2123
Penrith 2740, Wollongong 2500
GPO Box 9942, Sydney 2001

VIC.
GPO Box 9942 Casselden Place 3001
PO BOX 9642 BOX Hill 3128
PO Box 9990 Geelong 3220
PO Box 9942 Cheltenham 3192. Dandenong 3175 Moonee Ponds 3039

QLD.
GPO Box 9942 Brisbane 4001
P0 Box 9942 Chermside 4032, Townsville 4810
Upper Mt Gravatt 4122

TAS.
GPO Box 9990 Hobart 7001

SA.
GPO Box Pulteney 5001
GPO BOX 1198 Waymouth 5001

WA.
GPO Box 9942 Perth 6848
PO Box 9942 Cannington 6107

NT.

GPO Box 1198 Waymouth 5001

ACT.

GPO Box 9942 Canberra 2601

How will you receive your Tax File Number?

We will mail your Tax File Number to the postal address you show on this form within 28 days of receipt in the Tax Office.

It would help us if you don't enquire within this period regarding the progress of your application.

A Tax File Number will not be issued at the Enquiry Counter or over the phone.

TAX FILE NUMBER APPLICATION

Proof of Identity Documents

When you lodge your form at a Tax Office you must show documents from the Category A and Category B lists which prove your identity.

You must show original **documents, not photocopies.**

If you mail your form and proof of identity documents, your documents will be returned by certified mail.

If an original proof of identity document is in a language other than English, a written translation should be provided, certified as a true and correct copy, by an authorised translation service e.g. Department of Immigration and Ethnic Affairs, an appropriate embassy or professional service.

From the lists of Category A and Category B documents on this page, you must provide:

2 different category A documents: A A

OR

1 category A document plus: A B

1 category B document

OR

3 different category B documents: BBB

If any of the documents are in a previous name, you must provide an additional document which shows how your name was changed (e.g. a marriage certificate).

If you are under 16, you need only provide one document (category A or B)

If a parent (or guardian) signs this form on behalf of a child under 16 years of age, full proof of identity must be provided for **both** the parent and child.

The parent (or guardian) must also establish their relationship with the child and provide a link document.

Please note: it is not mandatory for a parent to sign on behalf of a child under 16 years of age.

Category A documents

A01 Current Australian Passport

A02 Current overseas passport with evidence of immigration status

A03 Certificate of Australian Citizenship

A04 Australian Armed Services discharge documents

A05 Document of appointment as a Justice of the Peace

Only one of these four that is less than 1 year old and issued from an **Australian university, college or school.**

A06 a degree

A07 a school examination certificate

A08 a school examination report

A09 a student ID card with photo

Please note: A06-8 not acceptable if B16-18 supplied

A10 Certificate of identity issued by the Department of Foreign Affairs and Trade

Category B Documents

B01 Full birth certificate **(an extract is not acceptable)**

B03 Notice or advice of pension (where name and address match those on this form)

B04 Current Australian driver's licence with (where name and address match those on this form)

B05 Divorce papers (decree nisi or decree absolute)

B06 Current Commonwealth or State public service ID card with photo and signature

B07 Marriage certificate

B08 Adoption papers

B09 Maintenance agreement registered with the family or Magistrates Court

B10 Declaratory Certificate of Australian Citizenship

B11 Tradesman's Right certificate

B12 Rates notice (where name and address match those on this form)

B13 Nurses Registration Board documents

B14 Current medical contribution book provided membership is more than 12 months old (where name and address match this form)

B15 Title or deed to real estate, or registered mortgage papers on a home or on a property

Only one of these three that is **more** than 1 year old and **issued from an Australian university, collage or school**

B16 a degree

B17 a school examination certificate

B18 a school examination report. **Please note**; not acceptable if A06-8 supplied

Only one of these three where name and address match those on this form

B19 a current home contents policy

B20 a current life insurance policy

B21 a current car insurance policy

B22 A current International Drivers Permit with photo

Only one of these four that is **less** than 1 year old and name and address match those on this form.

B23 a bank account statement

B24 a building society account statement

B25 a credit union account statement

B26 a finance company account statement

One or two different types of legal documents that are **less** than 1 year old, from this list

B27 summons

B28 bail paper

B29 restraining order

B30 police order

B31 discharge certificate (from prison)

B32 parole order

CHAPTER 11
New Zealand

Captain Cook took possession for the British Crown in 1770. The French had hoisted a flag there the year before in 1769, but fortunately they did not stay. If they had it would probably still be a colony like Tahiti or New Caledonia and they would probably be detonating atomic bombs underneath the volcanic mountains to see what would happen. Then Britain would not have had all those loyal patriotic New Zealand soldiers who volunteered for us in countless wars to die for the 'Motherland' – a tremendous sacrifice was made.

The first white tribe on the scene were the Dutch; the incredible explorer Able Tasman named the place New Zealand in 1642. The Dutch never stayed as they were too preoccupied with the 'Spice Islands', the Dutch East Indies, now Indonesia. I don't think the seafaring Portuguese made it here, although someone will probably correct me on this. The Vikings definitely didn't their claim to America is more than enough for the Danes, Swedes and Norwegians.

As everyone knows, the place was not unoccupied. The Maoris, a Polynesian race, were here first. They arrived probably from the Hawaiian Islands round about 1350. Their folklore states that seven waves of migrants came in their long canoes, probably over a period of a couple of hundred years. Anthropologists claim that other Polynesians were here before them around about 950 AD.

Being as there were heathen ferocious warriors and practising cannibals who had not discovered the Christian virtues of civilisation and hard honest fulfilling work, to save their souls they had to be brought around to seeing the errors of their primitive ways. Europeans had stopped the good sport of 'witch' burning by now, so were well and truly enlightened in Christian enlightenment. I don't know why the Maoris didn't want to change their ways, I mean, who wants to be a hunter, warrior, fisherman anyway when you can go and work down a coal mine.

Two wars and numerous skirmishes later, over a period of more than ten years, they finally saw the errors of their ways and agreed to share their land, which then could be cleared and cultivated for the settlers arriving from Britain, and quite a few from the overspill of the New South Wales colony.

The British had learnt from their experience in the Americas about letting in non-British stock – a costly war of independence in 1776. So strictly controlled British immigration was to be the order of the day, and no convicts, although a few resourceful escapees, had made it from Australia.

The first settlers escaping British poverty and exploitation brought with them revolutionary social concepts – one was free education for all, natives included – a huge social leap for the times, also the vote for women in 1898 making New Zealand the first country to do so.

Modern Times: Once We Were Socialists

This was the beginning of New Zealand's love affair with social welfare, that in later years (the 1930s and 40s) the whole western world was to copy and use as a role model in setting up their own welfare states. New Zealand had become a laboratory for the world. Sadly, today the welfare state is being broken up. The economic realities of being a progressive competitive trading nation requires this action to save itself from apathy and decay. For too many years New Zealand had stagnated, the population was acutely decreasing, mainly the productive youth were leaving, mainly to Australia. The incentives to strive and get ahead were gone because of high taxation – the country was in decline. The same story worldwide – 'Why should I carry the burden of taxes on my shoulders,' while other scroungers and parasites live off the welfare state from cradle to grave and expect it to be their God given right, getting locked into welfare dependency.

A basic human characteristic is that if one can get something for nothing, one will, regardless of the final outcome. Also when something is free it loses its value.

Since the late 1980s New Zealand has undergone the most radical economic transformation of any western industrialised country, with extensive privatisation, the dismantling of many welfare systems, abolition of subsidies and tariff barriers and a plethora of corporate regulations and union power. The results have been a while in coming, but New Zealand now boasts one of the lowest inflation rates in the main twenty-four industrialised nations, and the lowest budget deficit for a decade.

What European countries would give to have a growth rate and unemployment rate of NZ.

But what government in Europe would dare to follow New Zealand's lead and do extreme measures like cutting the dole money by 30 per cent. Hence many of New Zealand's dole bludgers have moved over to Australia where they have right of abode.

New Zealand led the world in socialism and will probably start to lead in capitalism in the not so distant future. You know a country has become capitalist when you see a mobile dog washing business advertised and operating successfully.

Australia, as of June '96, three months into a new government, is looking at the New Zealand example, whose international credit worthiness is much stronger than Australia's now. Already Australia's Prime Minister, John Howard, has started to cut government jobs and has brought in a new law forbidding new immigrants from collecting dole payments for two years after arrival. I think this is mainly aimed at third world migrants that come into Australia on the family reunion scheme and are unskilled, uneducated, speak no English and have no chance of getting a job, so now the family have to support them instead of the taxpayer. Every new immigrant falls under this category, except New Zealanders.

God knows what my buddy Mick, who lives in Perth, would have done if he had to wait two years for dole money when he arrived. Probably lived off his savings I guess – he breaks out in a sweat just talking about work. (See under Australia for more on Mick).

This beautiful majestic friendly country is roughly the same size as the UK or Japan, but with only 3.5 million people in it and no snakes. This country is like a world in miniature, where most of the wonders of nature can be found, a number of which are very unique. In the North Island, sub-tropical rain forests, in the South Island, temperate rain forests. There are live volcanic mountains with hot spring geysers erupting, and the country has an abundance of lakes, rivers, forests and mountains with skiing. New Zealand has an equable climate, with winters similar to that of Southern Europe (North Island), but with summers more like Southern England or Northern France.

Talking about France, the French have not been very popular over recent years with the Kiwis, going back to 1986 when French secret service agents, with about as much cunning and flair as Inspector Clouseau, sank the Rainbow Warrior, the flagship for Greenpeace that was moored in Auckland harbour at the time, in between monitoring French nuclear testing in the Pacific. The Rainbow Warrior was out of action, one mechanic was killed and the two secret service agents were quickly arrested, tried and convicted.

This was state sponsored terrorism, putting France on par with countries like the old Iraq, Iran Syria, Libya and the present day North Korea. The two agents, to be fair, were only carrying out orders, but nevertheless received life sentences for murder. Within eighteen months the New Zealand government released them into French custody to serve out the rest of their sentences in France – which meant freedom. Why did the New Zealand government let them go? Because France threatened to block all New Zealand exports into the EU.

How many Kiwi soldiers paid the ultimate sacrifice on French soil in two world wars? This is the kind of repayment you can expect to receive off the French for bailing them out. Ten years later the French were still letting off atomic bombs on Mururoa atolls in French Tahiti. We all know that they work – so why keep testing them? You may wonder why does France need nuclear bombs – who is going to invade France? Surely they are not still terrified of the Germans? Germany has no nuclear bombs, so next time around the French can bomb the Germans.

I suppose France does need to protect itself because when they get invaded half the population surrenders, puts their hands up and collaborates with the enemy, and then waits for Britain and America to come and rescue them. When they do fight they use the Foreign Legion to fight for them.

In 1940 when their country was overrun, most of their Mediterranean fleet was stationed in Oran Algeria, then a French colony. We begged and pleaded with them to come out and join us, to fight the Germans to help them get their country back for them. But being indecisive and reluctant to fight they refused, so we had to sink the fleet to stop the Germans taking possession. Thousands of brave young French sailors died on that day. Britain desperately needed ships; we had to go begging to the Americans for fifty old World War 1 destroyers. To cap it off most of the remainder of the fleet was in Toulon mainland France. One year later the same situation as in Oran they would not come out and join us to fight, but this time they scuttled the ships rather than get blown to bits by the Royal Navy. A few of their ships were in British ports in early 1940, just as well we grabbed them before they could set sail. The French sometimes don't do themselves any favours what so ever!

Kiwis themselves are adventurous travellers, many of them staying away for many years doing 'the big overseas trip', usually the first stop being Australia so as to increase their funds by working there. For the size of their population, a large percentage do 'the big overseas trip', so in spite of the country's isolation, the population are very knowledgeable about the rest the world, although a hell of a lot of them like the rest of the world refer to the UK as England and the English instead of Britain and the British, which I found very surprising for a nation that is mainly made up of British stock.

Without a doubt, the English more so than the Welsh, Scottish and Irish, are the world's best migrants, becoming the 'mainstream' of the population in all the European Protestant English speaking countries of the world, assimilating more rapidly than any other nationality.

Once We Were Hunters – Today We Go Shopping

12.9 per cent of New Zealand people are of Maori stock, although anthropologists claim there are no full-bloods left. Over recent years Maori autonomy, self-determination and nationalism have been spreading. This is partly due to the treaty of Waitangi signed in 1840 at the end of the Maori wars, which gave them certain rights and privileges in exchange for land. Today Maoris are a 'special interest group' being able to claim certain perks and privileges of the state. This in turn causes a 'them and us' mentality amongst other New Zealanders, especially as many Maoris are less than an eighth blood line.

Similar deals I have seen all over the world with indigenous peoples. Well intentioned ideals to safeguard people from poverty and exploitation usually do the reverse and keep people indebted to the state, instead of becoming 'one' nation, 'one' people.

Since the UK joined the EU in the early 70s and then started to sever agricultural trading links with New Zealand and Australia, both countries have looked to Asia for trade and commerce, and being politically correct have allowed large scale Asian migration – so one is constantly reading in the daily papers about being 'alienated', 'swamped' and 'overwhelmed' in my own country.

There is a certain criteria for certain races. If you let in large scale Italian migration you will get great stone mansions and great pasta restaurants, but you will also get the Mafia as part of the Italian package. If you let in Chinese and Vietnamese you get cheap fried rice and noodles, but in the same package you get Triads and heroin, although the vast majority will be hard working and enterprising. The illicit drug trade is the second largest global industry, beaten only by the arms trade. What a world we live in!

Getting In and Working

Don't smuggle fruit – very heavy fines. They are protecting their fruit industry from foreign plagues and pests. If they still had hanging one would probably get hung for this offence.

No visa for the UK is required if coming in as a tourist. Remember, don't mention work to the immigration official, only holiday six months' stay is automatically given, other nationals only three months. You might be asked to show an onward ticket, plus NZ $ 1200 per month for your stay. Unless you are looking really down and out there should be no problem getting in.

One year working holiday visas are given out to UK citizens on the eighteen to thirty working holiday scheme. The forms (A. 1000) have to be in by March and the working visa starts in May. You can also apply for a working visa when you are there, at one of the seven immigration offices throughout the country.

To use the government employment services and the employment agencies they will require to see your work visa and your IRD number which is your tax number (Inland Revenue Department). Getting a job yourself, i.e. through the newspapers, knocking on doors, and the yellow pages, all you need is your IRD number which is very straightforward to get. All you do as soon as you are in the country is to take your passport to the Inland Revenue office, fill out the tax form, hand it over with your passport and wait ten minutes for processing. You are then issued with a tax card which is required from you by all employers.

It doesn't matter if you only have a holiday visa in your passport. In the unlikely event you are asked why you require a tax card, you can state that it is to open a bank account, which is always a good stand-by answer.

You may be on the other side of the globe but many things are British here. They drive on the left, they watch Coronation Street, EastEnders, Heartbeat, and many more British TV programmes. Even the phone boxes are British Telecom models, plus British weekly newspapers are available everywhere.

New Zealand is a sporting paradise, with trout fishing and rugby, the best in the world. The South Africans think that they are the best but they're not. There is plenty of rivalry with Australia. New Zealanders always remind you that they came to New Zealand, whereas the Aussies were sent.

If you are a Welshman you will feel at home here as sheep are everywhere, and Wellington boots are sold everywhere. Great times can be had and still can be had for those of you who get up and go. At the time I went lots of my friends were unemployed in the UK and were doing absolutely nothing with their lives.

Many New Zealanders trace their ancestry back to Scotland, there is heaps of Scottish culture here, but unlike Nova Scotia in Canada, the Scottish descendants down here have learnt to speak English, leaving their unintelligible drunken Glaswegian dribble behind, i.e. 'Ya ken wat I meen Jimmy' – 'Ak, eye.' – Scottish 'You know what I mean James' – 'Yes, I do.' – English. When I worked doing exhibition hire display I was in a Scottish work gang, I ended up being the interpreter as none of the supervisors could understand a word that these guys spoke.

I have also witnessed Glaswegians getting so frustrated in Thailand with the Thais as they just cannot be understood, I recommend any Glaswegian to go and live in Edinburgh for a year or two to learn the Queens English before setting off on your travels.

Kiwis themselves do hype on about the foreign ownership of their country. The Japanese, Chinese, Taiwanese and Koreans are buying up golf courses and condominiums. So what? They can't take them out, and they do create heaps of jobs. Tourism is now New Zealand's biggest industry, with the above four nationalities spending the most money. The Japanese can't believe how cheap food is down here. In Japan one has to be a millionaire to eat steak due to the Japanese government's agricultural protectionism. The Japanese, Taiwanese and Koreans idea of a global economy is to put up protectionist trade walls around their own country and then flood the world with their own goods, like Europe is doing with its EU agricultural policy and systematic structural barriers.

Agriculture and forestry are second and third in importance. There are heaps of casual temporary jobs in all three industries. 30,000 fruit and vegetable related jobs are available on an annual basis. There are more jobs and higher salaries in the North Island with one third of the population living in and around Auckland. There are 800,000 people in the South Island – the remainder are in the North Island outside Auckland.

Overall, wages are lower than Australia and most things are more expensive then Australia, but there are more jobs here, less unemployment, a bright future.

Beer

A really good selection here, second only to the UK for choice. There are plenty of ales, bitters and stouts, not just lager, lager and lager as in Australia, Europe, Canada and Africa. Water is also safe to drink. If you fall off a bar stool and bash your head, there is a reciprocal health agreement with the UK. Official age for drinking is twenty. Patrons seldom asked to show ID, unlike the USA.

Getting Around

Good roads and public transport. Hitching is a common mode of travelling. Most travelling workers who come here to work do a tour of the country. Some before they start work, to have a look and to see where the jobs are. Others do the trip after they have finished work, before they move on.

A great way to do this trip is with one of the unorthodox bus companies that take you to all the out of the way places to see and do heaps of adventure type activities, then stopping at late afternoon where there will be loads of hostels around. If you like the area you are in and want to carry on with your activity, like trout fishing or whatever, you can stay and then get on one of the company's other buses coming through later on in the week, usually every day. This way you will also get to know more people. This way of travelling is ideal for the single girl/woman. There are plenty of people to meet, lots of information collected, as in hostels all over the world.

Tip: When I'm moving daily, I wash one article of clothing every time I have a shower. This stops build up of unwashed clothes, which annoys other people. The hostels are good quality, with plenty of reductions around New Zealand with a backpacker/YHA/student card, fifty per cent off internal flights. YHA's tend to be the most expensive and where the Japanese and Korean travellers go, being as most of them are strictly tourists, not working, so not much work information is gained from them.

The two main bus companies mentioned, Kiwi Experience and Magic Bus, operate all over New Zealand. The West Coast Explorer is a South Island bus only. Kiwi Experience is more of a party type bus. The Magic Bus has better buses with more room. Both are good value for money. Both buses have heaps of rowdy Brits, fortunately the thug type haven't made it here yet, only the good natured type. On the Kiwi bus I travelled on, the self-appointed entertainment officer was Tony Hull and his assistant, Drew Bradshaw which resulted in a fun time with a holiday type atmosphere for all. Three well known white lies in N.Z.

(1). My dad played for the All Blacks. (2). My grandmother was a Maori princess. (3). I was only helping the sheep over the fence, officer.

Everybody travelling in New Zealand is carrying a Lonely Planet book – great for flora, fauna, places to stay and places to see. But not much good for work opportunities – you're better off with *Seasonal Work in NZ* by Andrews Publishing.

If you are into slaughtering wildlife, most animals can be slaughtered at will as they have all been introduced, now making themselves so called pests, so deer, pigs, cats, foxes, rabbits, weasels, stouts, ferrets and possums and many more feral creatures can all be blown away once you acquire a firearms licence.

Skiing (June-October)

The best skiing is on the South Island. As there is no ski in-ski out type accommodation in the snow fields one has to commute to the ski fields by shuttle bus. Lifts are operated efficiently, like in North America, unlike at some of French resorts. Also, one can afford to eat on the mountain, unlike in many of the European resorts. 1,500 plus casual jobs are available at the twelve commercial ski fields. It is best to send in application forms before the end of April. Application forms are available from the government employment service offices, or on site.

My first day skiing in the southern hemisphere, Coronet Peak, staying and partying in the resort of Queenstown, a great resort town with loads of happy hour bars, not like expensive Europe. Watch out for Japanese kamikaze snow-boarders that have taken up seasonal residence. I got 'taken out' by one flying off a precipice, hurtling towards me, I couldn't hardly see him as he was in an all white ski suit, one of my major bugs in life is skiers that wear white ski suites, they are so dangerous to themselves and to other skiers, as they can not be seen against the white of the mountain especially in a 'white out', also if the snow patrol have to go looking for them they are camouflaged so putting the rescuers lives in danger also. I remember seeing Prince Charles skiing in Switzerland in an all-white ski suite (enough said) the word plonker comes to mind. I was out of my skis and concussed – the first and only time I've been carried off a mountain by the ski patrol. How embarrassing!

If I make loads of dough from this book I will take up heli-skiing to get away from the commercial runs, and no more digging holes and pushing wheelbarrows for a living.

Departure tax: NZ $25 when leaving.

New Zealand Tourism Board and High Commission:
80 Haymarket Street, SW1 1/4 TQ Phone: 0171 930 8422
Fax: 0171 839 4580.

Ralph's good beer guide for countries in this book, quality and variety:
1) UK
2) New Zealand
3) Mexico
4) Australia
5) Canada
6) USA
7) Hong Kong
8) South Africa
9) Israel
10) Thailand
11) Zimbabwe

Kiwi fruit picking starts in Tauranga from 10 April. Phone Danny or Jo for more information on (07) 578 5064.
Yes, we are close to the city.
Yes, we do have tent sites.
Yes, we can pick you up from the bus, train, or plane.
Yes, we have games to play.
Yes, Tauranga is the place to be.
This work is 'Piece-Work' with the average pay of $12 - $18 per hour.
These types of posters are everywhere in New Zealand.

CHAPTER 12
United States of America

"Liberty has never come from government; Liberty has always come from the subjects of it. The history of liberty is a history of existence. The history of liberty is a history of limitations of governmental power, not the increase of it."

– Woodrow Wilson

The USA has always been a great attraction for people wanting to work, travel and settle. The USA has tremendous diversification. Within one country one can find just about every climatic condition on earth, from desert to Pacific island beaches (Hawaii), and every condition in between i.e., pine rain forests, hardwood woodlands, prairie deserts, mountains, Everglades and frozen tundra (Alaska).

This has to be my favourite country for variations of climate and landscape, plus the majority of the people are very helpful and friendly.

But if you're: under twenty-one years of age, I do not recommend the USA. There are far too many hassles placed upon you by the overbearing legislative, bureaucratic bible bashing, conservative authorities who have passed a multitude of restrictive, authoritarian laws to stop you just having a good time. Also many counties have night-time curfews imposed upon teenagers by the authorities, the powers that be, curtailing basic human rights – the freedom of movement.

For a nation that is forever going on about freedom and democracy, I find it quite ironic that there is probably less freedom and more oppressive laws than just about any other western nation, except maybe Japan, Singapore and Switzerland.

You have freedom of information, (more so than in the UK) you have freedom of speech (although you could get yourself sued), but you don't have freedom of action. Saying that, one is free to arm oneself with just about any conceivable portable weapon on this earth to protect your constitutional God given rights because it says so in the constitution. But when the constitution was passed, if I'm not mistaken, America had no standing army, and there were wild bears and wolves in your back yard. Meanwhile, marauding wild Indians were trying to keep the land or were trying to get back what they had already lost. In addition outlaws; and desperadoes were trying to rob you of your possessions and rape your women folk, so in those days I would definitely have armed myself to the teeth, just as I did in Rhodesia when wild animals and wild people were all over the place.

With all the guns all over the place it's not surprising that America averages between 35,000 to 40,000 gunshot deaths per year, roughly half of which are accidents and suicides. They are brainwashed on guns. How often do you see a cinema or television film without guns? Usually the weaker the plot, the more we see a proliferation of guns. With these gunshot fatalities 35-40,000 per year, year on year, do the maths on that over a twenty year period it's frightening. Whereas the UK averages less than 100 a year and in Japan they have less than 50 per year.

Recent History

When one considers that 58,000 Americans, mostly kids, lost their lives in Vietnam in eight years, you don't have to be an Albert Einstein to realise that America is at constant war with itself, because of the availability of guns. The NRA gun lobby always quotes that 'people kill – guns don't.'

Ultraconservatives, like Charlton Heston, are always going on prime-time TV adverts supporting this reasoning. The best book I've read about the aftermath of the Vietnam War is; *Kiss the Boys Goodbye* by Monika Jensen-Stevenson, well worth a read.

What Bullshit, Guns Don't Kill!

A great many of those 58,000 war fatalities were conscripted in the first place and were considered old enough to die for their country, but were not allowed to vote or have a drink because they were under twenty-one years of age. What an unbelievable con. Many Americans are really quite naive and have very little world knowledge as they seem to only concern themselves with what is happening in their own state.

They all refer to the UK as 'England', even Presidents such as Ronald Reagan, who congratulated the English army on retaking the Falkland Isles, "A heroic victory for the English army," he said. Bit of an insult to the Welsh Guards families, whose boys died in the sinking of the Sir Galahad, and the Scots Guards families whose sons died at the battle of Mt. Tumbledown, George Bush senior also thanked 'our' gallant ally 'England' for our contributions to the Gulf War effort. No wonder Scottish and Welsh nationalism is on the increase as they get referred to as English all the time especially by the Americans, (more so than anybody else). They will never it seems in a thousand years learn the difference between the UK, GB, and England.

President Obama knows the difference though (I personally think he's the best president since Kennedy) not just for knowing these differences.

The Australians, Canadians and New Zealanders Are Now Making This Mistake Also

With all the laws, regulations and restrictions placed upon one, people are prone to rebel and crack up, 'go off the rails', to coin a phrase, and quite often they happen to pick up a gun, and go 'ape shit' and commit a massacre. One can get off murder charges if one is rich and famous, i.e., O J Simpson, otherwise the justice system is renowned for its cruel and medieval prosecutions. That does not say much for justice in a so-called civilised country. If found guilty of murder, the state will exact its revenge by usually keeping the guilty person locked up in a cage on Death Row for ten or more years and then it will either gas, poison, hang, shoot or fry the victim. They have yet to start boiling the victims or carrying out public beheadings like in the barbaric medieval state of Saudi Arabia. We might yet get to see public executions on Sky TV in the not so distant future.

To exact revenge, the state will do its utmost to get it, even if the prisoner requires, before execution, a heart triple bypass operation to keep him or her alive. I mean come on, surely he or she is going to end up in hell anyway. Does it really matter? This has happened. As anyone who believes in the Lord Almighty will doubtless tell you, he's destined for hell, regardless. So why give the victim a triple bypass operation costing the tax payer countless thousands of dollars, when out on the streets 40 million people were terrified of getting sick until Obama care finally came along as they now have insurance cover, whereas before, there was none. So how on earth can you have and promote preventative medicine when people couldn't afford a basic check up. No doctor wants to earn a normal salary.

So when a humanitarian president comes along and says, 'Let's get rid of guns, let's have a western world type health care i.e., like our northern neighbours Canada.' The powers that be, the special interest groups, bury the guy and nearly bankrupt him in the process. Bill Clinton failed with his second turn in office to make America a 'gentler place', whereas George Bush senior failed.

I'll never forget George Bush senior on the White House lawn with the Emir of Kuwait. The President was 'chomping at the bit', dying to say the magic words 'Freedom and Democracy', but of course he couldn't. Kuwait had never had freedom and democracy and still doesn't and probably never will in my lifetime.

The Emir got his country back, and today thousands of American ex-soldiers are dying slowly in excruciating pain due to chemical poisoning and Saddam Hussain still had his country until George Bush junior came along.

Black and White Movies

What a sight to see old films of elephants being electrocuted so they would know how to fry a human being, and this is in the country of 'human and animal rights', but not so long ago it wanted to bomb a nation back to the 'stone age'(North Vietnam).

They were so paranoid of these communist nations they termed the scare 'reds under the bed'. Under Senator McCarthy, along with his two loathsome lieutenants, Cohn and Schine, they routed out and destroyed countless lives. In Hollywood they had misguided informers such as the then actor Ronald Reagan to help them in their quest to purify America of this evil red scourge. Commies there, commies everywhere. The only good commie is a dead commie.

Considerations

Some times in life you have to make a decision on where to go next. That is, if you're not in the travelling mode, you can always stay put in one place where you were born, on the dole, vegetating.

When making a move, you can just get up and go, but by doing that it is usually better to have quite a few bucks in your pocket, unless the cops or immigration are after you, then you have to move sharpish.

Otherwise it is best take a few options into consideration before moving on to your next adventure.

1. Things like have I got anyone to travel with. It makes living a lot cheaper if one has a travelling partner or partners, plus you can bounce ideas off each other.

2. Buying and renting cars is a big consideration to look at when going to the USA or Canada.

3. Access to a telephone when looking for work, not such a problem today as every one has a mobile phone.

4. Have I got any good buddies/girlfriends where I'm going? Can they put me up and for how long?

5. What's the employment situation like where I'm going? Are they in a recession and hard times, or are they experiencing a boom?

6. Can I get a legitimate work visa, i.e., why go the US if you're twenty-five years old, when you can get a work permit for Australia up until the age of twenty-six? Why let this opportunity pass you by? Take it and go the US when you're twenty-six or older.

Also very important is the time of year you want to go. It's no good arriving in a Rocky Mountain resort in April and expecting to find a job. What you'll find is that the ski resorts are closing down for the season and are laying people off left right and centre, and it's too early for the summer season to take on the out of work casuals.

When I went to Aspen Colorado. I'd missed the snow. Had to make do with going roller skating. Make sure you time your seasons when travelling.

Also remember that the Southern Hemisphere has its seasons opposite to the Northern Hemisphere.

Working In America – The Dream

The great American dream is to get rich, have a great lifestyle, kick back and kick ass. Great for a few. Most people who get rich have to work in a very competitive environment. Although it is a low taxation, thriving, entrepreneurial culture, people work long and hard with the least amount of holidays of any western nation, except Japan. The rewards are there, the US probably has more self made dollar millionaires per head of population than any other nation. This is due to the work ethic. It used to be quoted as the 'Anglo-Protestant work ethic'. Today this is not so much in evidence, as now America is changing its racial and religious balance of population.

Unless you are highly skilled in a trade or profession, you will probably be travelling around working for a minimum wage of between $7.50- $10.00 per hour depending on what state you go to. It's really tough to live on these wages, so try and get a job with some sort of perks if you're on the minimum wage, i.e., tips and or food and board.

Big Bucks But No Small Change (This article from 1996)

Washington, Friday: Members of the United States Congress have voted themselves three wage increases in five years and now pay themselves $133,600 (AUS $ 172,000), or about $64 an hour.

But recently the Republican-led Congress refused yet again to allow a vote on raising the minimum wage by 90¢ to $5.15 an hour.

President Bill Clinton and his Democratic allies in Congress have tried repeatedly over the past two years to raise the minimum wage, but each time Republicans have fought it off, arguing it would cause a reduction in jobs for the lowest paid.

Mr Clinton said after yesterday's vote in Congress, "It was time for Republicans to give 10 million Americans an immediate pay increase.

"With every day that the Republican leadership continues to stall, the value of the minimum wage continues to fall closer and closer to a forty year low," he said. **Sydney Herald Correspondent – Pilita Clark May '96.**

Also Congress has very generous allowances and perks.

Another reason to consider Australia is that the minimum wage in Aussie is nearly double the American one.

In the US there are steep fines for employers who hire illegal, undocumented workers. This is probably what keeps the wages so low as there are literally millions and millions of non-English speaking migrants. I have read recently that it is estimated that one in seventy-six people are illegal immigrants. Somehow they get by, and heaps of these people don't even speak English. So don't worry too much about being undocumented. That is not to say the Immigration Department won't throw you out as they have to throw out Europeans to stop the civil rights people accusing them of harassing just Chinese and Hispanics.

Now I get back to what I've said before – forget about speaking like an English person ("Oh, but your accent is so neat") – forget it. It's OK for chatting up members of the opposite sex, or same sex if you're that way inclined. To blend in use words and phrases like; alright you guys, what's happening, cool it, take it easy man, have a nice day, awesome day man, truck, gas, etc, etc.

If people asked me where I was from, I would tell them I was a Canadian of British origin. Most Americans (except those living on the border with Canada), think that Canadians can live in America. To people who queried me even more, I would tell them about my ex-wife who was from New Jersey. Actually we just cohabited for a summer in Denver. At the end she went back East and I went West, an amicable arrangement. So obviously if I was married to an American, and I was from Canada, I was almost 'apple pie!' You can always claim an American dad or mum if anyone asks, was American servicemen and women have been stationed in Europe for over seventy years now – about time they went home, in that time, heaps of people in Europe have been born to American servicemen and women, in and out of wedlock.

Once you are sounding like a native, you can use lots of the facilities. I used to use the American equivalent of the British Labour Exchange, now the UK Job Centre. I've used these centres in Australia and Canada as well.

In the phone book these departments come under State Government Departments, Job Service Centres, Employment Development Departments or Employment Security Departments. In America they come down heavily on people out of work. We've all heard about 'work fare'. I bet quite a few people in the UK and Australia are sweating already, dreading the thought of having to work for their unemployment benefit.

A lot of uneducated people with large families get trapped on welfare, as they get free health care cover. Once they get back into the workforce, unless they are able to score a 'decent' job, they have to then sort out their own health insurance and it's not cheap either (thank god for Obama care). Before they always had to pay the first thousand or two dollars of any bill they received.

America has little compassion for the unemployed who they consider parasites, scroungers and spongers, so be prepared to work hard. Working construction sites in Colorado and Nevada, I've had rapid promotion by showing them I could do the job and was willing and able. 'Only in America man,' as they say.

Money

In the US there are no class barriers, only money barriers. Financial apartheid is in operation. In the summer, the national unemployment rate is usually 5.5% to 7.5% in the winter months it rises a few percentage points more. No other western nation except Japan, has this few people out of work, New Zealand is not far behind.

What would any European nation give to have these unemployment figures? This is in spite of the millions of illegal immigrants. Maybe it's got something to do with the low taxes and the American mentality of, 'if you want it, go out and get it', and 'anything is possible,' 'just do it,' 'can do,' an attitude only in America people thinking positively.

Getting In

To live permanently in the US, you have to have a green card. It's easy to get if you're wealthy, marry an American citizen or have close relatives to sponsor you. If you don't, it's not so easy as American immigration officials are notoriously suspicious of all visitors entering the US.

For a country that has one of the toughest entry restrictions in the world, I find it amazing that they have a worldwide 'Green Card' lottery every year, at £20 per ticket. Usually about 50,000 green cards are given away. Britain gets no quota. Ireland usually gets about half of the allocation. So much for the British 'special relationship'. It's more like 'bail out the Irish.'

The 'special relationship' is dead, gone and buried, in World War II when the, Americans practically bankrupted the British Government, bailing us out in order to carry on fighting – so they then could spread their rising tide of global 'American monoculture' worldwide.

Arrival – Getting Past the Enemy

If you have a full British passport, there is no need to apply for a visa from the US Embassy any more. On arrival in the US, you apply for a visa-waiver, which is valid for ninety days. This can be renewed once inside the country.

Another option is to apply for a six-month visa on arrival, but then you could get 'grilled' heavily. This grilling is extremely uncomfortable, totalitarian to the uninitiated. Make sure you have sufficient funds as they will count your money. You need about a $1000 per month. Any addresses and phone numbers of relatives or friends are handy as they quite often 'phone these numbers'. Don't give a 'phone number' of a friends friend, as the person could say he's never heard of you.

Bear in mind that since 9/11 (I really wish the Americans would not write the date backwards it's the 11th of the 9th) they have increased their powers with the Home Land Security Act. Under this act you have no rights whatsoever, they can do what ever they want, and they do. Don't be a smart ass and don't make any jokes. Don't mention any work whatsoever, paid or unpaid, unless you have a full working visa. If you don't have a Q1 or H1B visa don't even joke about work. Don't let the bastards trap you into saying, "I might do a little work for board and keep."

Get current and up-to-date information from the internet.

Don't carry addresses of employers, CVs, working clothes like overalls and steel toe-capped boots or trade certificates. Post them beforehand to a poste restante or a friend.

A girl I once knew, had her letters read out in front of her on arrival. In her letter her Aunt had congratulated her on her new job opening in New York. Needless to say, she was on the next plane back home.

Don't carry this book, or any other working guides such as **Work Your Way Around the World** by **Susan Griffiths**. By the way, her book is a very in-depth book about working from country to country. Well recommended for travelling and working around the world. As it is now in its thirteenth edition, some of her facts are sometimes out of date and so are some of mine.

Keep stressing that you're a travelling tourist. Whatever period you stay, three months, six months, or nine months which is the maximum, you must then leave for the same period before you can re-enter again. But if you stay nine years without leaving, and you've supported yourself, this is a way to qualify for a green card. I know plenty of Brits in California who've gotten green cards using this method, when it was seven years.

It is estimated that there are over 200,000 Brits living in California alone. They have their own pubs, newspapers and football teams. I've gotten casual work out of these pubs. I spent a couple of years slipping in and out of the US and Canada. When my time was up in one place, I'd checkout through a border crossing to keep my visa legal. I did this on both borders. Then my friends would come and pick me up the next day – a car full of Canadians or Americans apparently just crossing over to fill up with gas, or going skiing, or returning from skiing with skis on the roof. Remember that Americans and Canadians cross each other's borders without needing passports.

Since 11 September 2001 attacks, immigration and Homeland Security have been beefed up considerably now quite often checking passports and other ID. If you're originally from South Asia i.e. India, Pakistan, or somewhere else in that region and you've got a beard you'll be pulled no doubt about it, they say they don't do racial profiling but they do. Make sure you have local ID. Remember the enemy immigration people are trained to pick up foreign accents, so if you do this method, don't talk.

It helps to 'lose' your passport now and again also, or put it in the washing machine, so as to get a replacement passport free of border stamps. I've also hiked around border crossings. It is best to do this at night, so make sure you have a compass and a map. I've done this in places ranging from Montana to Waterton National Park in Alberta. There are no lions around like the bush in Africa – just a few bears (there was a saying in Africa, when you need a gun, you really need a gun).

When I was working and travelling, I was always ready for the immigration. Remember, they are the enemy, they outnumber you and they have everything on their side, they are **untouchable** – the same as our Royal Family.

When I was refused entry into the USA in January 1994, I had been a respectable businessman. I'd settled down in London for five years and had been paying my taxes and taken out a mortgage. Basically, what I'm saying is that I'd become 'Mr Respectable'. If I'd only kept my mouth shut nothing would have happened to me as they had nothing on me. I just thought that they had heaps on me. They had nothing. They only pulled me because I'd just come back from one skiing holiday and was only back in London for four days before turning around and going back out for another holiday. In retrospect, they must have figured that I'd come back to take up a job offer.

I now take my skiing holidays elsewhere, best to go to France, it's cheaper and far more scope, the three valleys area covers three times more area than all the skiing in the US and this is only a quarter of the ski area of France. I then folded my business, rented out my house and started working and travelling again, so as to regain the edge that I'd lost by being a conformist.

The immigration official said to me, "Don't take it personal."

I did, I was out of pocket big time and I missed the best powder snow that Steamboat Springs, Colorado had, had for years, they don't care about you spending money and helping the economy – hence this book. Hopefully I can help other people get past the enemy.

At the same time that I was sent back, a young girl on my plane was also sent back. She had told them she was going to work as an au-pair. Needless to say she had no work visa.

Entry Restrictions

The following will be refused entry to the USA unless a 'waiver of ineligibility' has first been obtained. If you fall into this category you have to go for an interview with an immigration official at the US Embassy in London, for him/her to grant you a 'waiver'.

A. Anyone afflicted with a communicable disease.

B. Anyone with a criminal record. (In the US a criminal record stays with you forever. In the UK a criminal record is wiped clean after ten years. I'd forgot this when I was pulled over). So forget about anything that is older than ten years.

C. Narcotics addicts or abusers and drug traffickers.

D. Anyone who has been deported from, or denied admission to the USA within the previous five years.

A waiver of ineligibility, is a real hassle to get, but can be obtained without an immigration lawyer who will charge you a fortune.

Can be a good idea to enter from Canada, if you feel insecure about getting in from the UK.

It doesn't help if you are dirty, scruffy and generally looking down and out. Remember. immigration officials are notoriously tough and unpleasant. Many of the immigration officials would not be out of place doing ethnic cleansing with the Serbs or Croats in the former Yugoslavia.

States

Every State has a Governor and a Legislative Assembly. They make their own laws and these can vary considerably from state to state. Some states execute for murder, in numerous fashions as described earlier, others don't. More and more states are starting to abolish it (good job to). California had a brief respite from executions in the sixties (a time for hope and a time of change), hence Charles Manson never got gassed. America is starting to reverse the trend of drifting back to the European Middle Ages.

Dope

Some states are very liberal Colorado, Washington others are totalitarian, i.e., you can live in California and grow grass for your own consumption, but if you happen to work in the neighbouring state of Nevada, you won't be allowed to smoke it as it's illegal.

Police State

One Christmas and New Year, I was skiing in the Lake Tahoe region. The town of Lake Tahoe is a gambling town inside Nevada, although most of the residential part of town is in California. That New Year's Eve, thousands of people were celebrating in the streets on the Nevada side. Exactly on the state line, California had put up a wall of armed police officers to stop people crossing over. They were fully decked out in riot gear. They had shields, helmets, clubs, CS gas, dogs, guns – the works. They were like the police forces in the old communist block countries; such as the East Germans, who used to patrol the Berlin Wall, and this is the Land of the Free which gave the world a movie star President who put the Soviets on 'red alert' in 1983 with his speech about the evil empire. 'Only in America man.'

I must take my hat off to Ronald though as he did bankrupt the USSR into democracy, he did spend the US into incredible debt, and interceded in the savings and loan scandal that almost bankrupted America. In between, he performed his legendary TV cartoon watching.

Drink

America is amazingly backward and hung up compared with the laid-back European attitudes towards alcohol. You have to be twenty-one years of age to drink in all States. In some they have an 11 p.m. curfew on under twenty-one year olds. You will be asked to show ID everywhere! Drinking on the beach or in a public park can get you arrested and your drink poured away, same as in Canada (eighteen to drink in Canada). If you're a woman and you go topless on the beach, you'll also get arrested. Unlike Australia where topless bathing is the norm.

Some of the states are completely 'dry'. Other states may be 'wet', but counties within these states may be dry. When they had prohibition that lasted fourteen years, it was a complete failure, established the Mafia who then moved into other lucrative illegal enterprises as they had developed a huge infrastructure from their enormous profits.

According to numerous books that are out now and documentary TV programmes, it's now common knowledge that the legendary crime fighter, Edgar Hoover. Who was the head of the FBI for fifty years was on the Mafia payroll along with his assistant guy lover (what a joke).

Gambling

No such thing as going into a bookies shop and placing a bet as it is highly illegal. If you want to place a bet, you have to go to the race track meet, or visit gambling towns like Reno, Las Vegas, Atlantic City or an Indian reservation that has gambling. Otherwise you have to use the Mafia who run the numbers system. The Mafia gets stronger and richer and the government loses out on taxes from gambling. It makes no sense to me at all.

Drive Away Cars

Great way to see the country, good idea to share expenses. If you're on your own, team up with someone from a hostel. Join the Youth Hostel Association before leaving the UK and get the *North American Handbook*, or get *Jim's Backpacker's Bible* by Jim de Cardova. This book is excellent I used it all the time when travelling around the US.

Basically, you're delivering cars for people or companies. I've had great trips doing this. I once took a Buick from Seattle, Washington State, to San Francisco, California. I took a slow drive down Highway 101, the coastal route. The drive away companies give you a full tank of gas to start you on your way, the rest you put in yourself. These companies are advertised in the 'yellow pages', under Drive-away Service Company or Auto-mobile Transporters. You can stop where you want to en route, so camping is a good way to go. You do have time limits on your delivery trip though. Arriving ahead of schedule can sometimes get you a bonus from the owner.

Health

Best medical treatment in the world, if you can afford it, or if you have the right insurance cover and it doesn't run out halfway through the treatment. Plenty of people are frightened to change jobs and start up in business on their own as they will be without cover for themselves and their family until they take out their own cover. If you're a construction contractor, with a family, medical cover is steep, plus you always pay an excess, which is the first few thousand dollars, of any bill. Hence, forty million Americans have no cover and are terrified of getting ill. You constantly read about people getting shunted around hospitals. These people are victims who require long term treatment; such as burn victims who do not have adequate medical cover. It's not unknown for them to die while being shunted from hospital to hospital.

Most major cities have a down-town charity hospital where the queues are horrendous and the treatment is basically Third World standard. I waited all day in one once and every time a slab victim, gunshot victim or auto crash victim came in, they jumped the queue. So it took me forever to get to see an overworked doctor.

Also, lots of down-town suburbs have medical students who run donation clinics. They are limited in what they can do for you. Their treatment is usually confined to giving bandages, stitches and ointments, pills and advice. Getting to see a doctor or going to a hospital costs money. Remember this and get dental work done before leaving your own country.

Every medical practitioner is insured up to the hilt to cover their ass in case of malpractice lawsuits. Some surgeons are paying in excess of $100,000 per year liability insurance cover. These costs of course are passed on to the general public. Your bill is also pushed up, as doctors cover their asses by referring you to someone else higher up. They often refer patients to a specialist for a second opinion, just to make sure they don't leave themselves open for malpractice suites. This they have to do as half of the world's practising lawyers are in America, prowling around like sharks looking for victims of malpractice to represent. Everybody in America is terrified of getting sued.

I wonder how many Americans, over the years, have come over to Europe and been treated for free in our hospitals – it makes one wonder. Hopefully now **Obama care** will end all of this nonsense.

American Football is for Wimps!

One Sunday afternoon I was playing American football with some buddies of mine. We were in San Rafael which is a great, laid back place just north of San Francisco. It was one of those lazy, fun afternoons. We had a barbecue, joints and hidden beer. A great time. The game started, and as girlfriends were playing as well, there was no rough stuff. Suddenly I was tackled by three players at once, down I went and snap, my femur bone broke. There was big panic for a while, but someone got it together to call an ambulance (no mobile phones in those days). Off I went to the hospital and had an operation. As my leg was in traction, there was no chance of doing a runner.

'What in damnation am I going to do now,' I thought. I was lucky to get into the hospital in the first place without an insurance card, I remember when they wheeled me in and a couple of my buddies told the receptionist that my wallet with my documents was back in my bag and it was still on the pitch with the others.

On my third day in bed, the Ward Matron came to my bed with a clipboard and heaps of papers. 'Oh, oh, I'm in big trouble now,' I thought. I was telling myself, 'what the hell, my leg is not fixed yet, they can't throw me out, they'll just have to bill me.' Of course this happens to thousands of people, they get billed and have to sell their house, car and whatever they can and take out loans, just to pay off their hospital bills. It happens every day. 'No problem, I'll just sign for my thousands of dollars of treatment, and when I get out I'll shoot off back to Africa, via Asia. I was planning on going anyway in six months time, I'll just have to go sooner rather than later.'

Three years earlier I'd broken both my lower legs while working in the North Sea. I was helicoptered off and then spent months in Aberdeen Hospital having four operations and skin grafts. It took me two years to get over that. All these years later, I'm still in daily pain with my right lower leg.

Anyway, the matron said to me, "Mr Lloyd, we haven't had your insurance details yet for our records." I was drugged up, trying to come up with a feasible answer, none of which made any sense to her. She then said to me, "Mr Lloyd, you don't have any insurance cover, do you?"

To this question I replied, "No, I don't, you'll just have to bill me and I'll pay off my bill in instalments."

Thereupon she said, "Just sign here, please." I asked her what for and she told me that a few years ago one of their long-term elderly women resident patients had died and she had left her considerable fortune to the hospital. The money was to be used for charity purposes, people who could not pay their bill. (Glad she never left it to a cats' home.)

Holy smoke! This was like winning the lottery, four weeks in hospital in traction and then let out with a full leg cast and no bill to pay, except the ambulance bill for $120. What unbelievable luck! Of course the hospital does not advertise the fact that this wealth was left to the unfortunates who can't pay their bills or else the place would be inundated with charity cases.

Going to America – getting insurance is a pretty good idea. Someday I'll get some. When getting a job, see if any medical coverage is included in the job package.

(Daniel Boon never had insurance when he trekked through the Appalachian Mountains.)

Police

Helpful to tourists. Remember to carry your driving licence with you at all time when driving or you'll get charged. No ifs or buts.

Don't give them any lip as we all know what happened to Rodney King, and he were proved innocent of any wrongdoing, just doing their job. Obviously Rodney King threw himself onto the police batons. It's all on video if you want to see him do it.

A few years ago, a British tourist in Florida was walking home to his motel one night after a few drinks, singing his favourite football song as Brits on holiday do, not doing anyone any harm. Unfortunately for him a woman copper took it upon herself to tell him to shut up, whereby he told her, in good old British tradition, to 'go and get stuffed.' She pulled out her gun and shot him dead. Being a woman, she said that she felt her life was in jeopardy. Well I believe in female equality, but don't start the 'woman under threat' crap when it suits you.

Cops all too frequently reach for their guns and shoot people dead – you can see examples of this on YouTube. One I remember seeing recently was a cop in Seattle, Washington. He told a Native American who was walking by whittling a piece of wood to put the knife (a little pen knife). According to relatives of the poor chap he was partially deaf. The cop said after he shot him four times that he thought his life was in danger. To me, many cops want the power to be a 'big shot' – 'Look how tough and important I am but have no balls to go and join the army, where the enemy fights back.'

So watch out for cops; they can be extremely hazardous to one's health.

Life in Prison

Many states today are bringing back the 'three strikes and you're out'. This is an attempt to reduce the ever-increasing crime rate. What it means is that on your third serious criminal conviction, you automatically receive a life sentence. Never mind about the hardship this causes other family members.

Now the USA has four times as many people in prison as the UK per head of population. The UK has the highest amount of prisoners in the EU per head of population.

A well-meaning law to help the overworked police, but the temptation to upgrade a charge or 'frame' someone so as to get them locked away for good is just too great.. This law will not solve any long-term problems, it will only cause more problems and make petty criminals hard-core cons. It's cruel and medieval prosecution

Cat Killer Gets 21 Years

Louis Weala from Milwaukee was sentenced to twenty-one years in prison for shooting his pet cat. This sentence is an example of what you can receive if you fall afoul of the law. I myself love animals but this sentence does seem a bit over-the-top. Prisons are nice places so make sure you **keep out**.

Statutory Rape

Meaning that even if your partner is willing to indulge in a sex act with you, if she/he is underage, you are in deep trouble – usually it's a prison sentence, not a slap on the wrist like in the UK and the rest of Europe. The legal age in some states is eighteen, others sixteen.

Flag

Americans being extremely patriotic proves my point that you don't need a Royal Family to be proud of one's country. Israelis and the French are also very patriotic and they have no royal families. Also, the Germans are very patriotic, though we have to watch them as they tend to get too carried away at times.

Anyway, don't mock or burn a US flag, it could really get you shot.

My king, Harold, died with an arrow in his eye in 1066, a true warrior. All the others since then have all been pretenders. William the Conqueror, a foreigner, made himself King. Later, when the Plantagenet lineage ran out, we brought in another foreigner, William of Orange from Holland. Since then we've had loads of foreigners from Germany, Greece, and from other European states. Richard the Lionheart, although a Norman not a Saxon King, is still one of my heroes. He died from a crossbow bolt in the neck at a time when leaders led from the front, not from behind a desk.

Oliver Cromwell, another one of my heroes, got rid of them once. It's a pity Tony Benn wasn't listened to a bit more – he'd get rid of them too.

The State Knows Best

The adoption of statutes providing forcible sterilization of the feeble minded, is supposed to show that the state knows best. This was an enforced sterilization programme where countless thousands of people lost their basic human rights. The sterilizations were carried out over a thirty year period. Sounds like Nazi Germany to me, but this was happening in the USA up until the 50s. Many permissive, unmarried mothers, had forcible sterilization. Sweden had forceful sterilization up until the 1970s. While I'm on the subject of Sweden. A strange lot indeed, must be the long dark winters they have to endure, with too much or not enough alcohol but back in the 1960s, Australia's first global superstar was 'Skippy' the bush kangaroo, a worldwide sensation, back then only ninety countries in the world had TV. Skippy was shown all over the world and was loved by everyone. Sweden the only country in the world refused to have the show, they said it would distort the impressionable minds of the young, if they believed that animals could talk to people.

A sad lot indeed!

Modern Technology

It's been nearly five decades since America had a man walking on the moon. Nevertheless they have still not learnt how to use a simple knife and fork, like the rest of the non-chopsticks nations. If you're going to blend in and look and act like an American, you are going to have to learn to chomp and smash all your food with a fork. Knives are only for cutting steak and placing back on to the table. This probably explains why the nation has become a burger munching society as hands only are required for this simple task.

Wildlife

A great variety of wildlife is found in the US. Second only to Africa for me. Well worth driving around Yellowstone National Park in Wyoming or Yosemite National Park in California, plus many more parks around the nation. America the beautiful, Yellowstone National Park. Just imagine less than two hundred years ago there were 60 million plus buffalo just waiting to get shot.

Jobs

There are plenty of resort type jobs available in seaside towns or gambling cities like Las Vegas, Reno, Lake Tahoe, Nevada or Atlantic City, New Jersey. It's very cheap to eat and live in gambling cities. Las Vegas is booming, lots of construction jobs. Remember it is mega, mega hot in the summer months as I found out when I worked in Reno. The neighbouring state of Arizona is also booming.

A Nice Little Earner – No Tax – No Social Security Card

While living in San Rafael I'd teamed up with my buddy American Pete. We were both working for a local construction company, labouring, doing the usual muscle building type work, i.e., pushing wheelbarrows uphill, digging ditches, mixing and shovelling concrete, unloading trucks, etc. You don't really want to do this type of work in the middle of a Californian summer. Anyway after work we all used to visit a nearby bar that used to have free bar snacks and half-price beer. A time to chill out in the air conditioning, play some pool, talk sport and work, the same scenario worldwide. After we'd downed a gallon or so of beer (very thirsty working in that dust and heat), the conversation had moved on to putting the world to right.

A woman in her early twenties came into the bar with a brief case, selling women's perfume and men's after shave, all neatly packed in little felt pouches. Well within half an hour she'd sold out and such was the demand she promised to return the following evening. Sure enough, the next night she returned to sell heaps more. After she'd finished her selling, Pete and I invited her over to our table for a beer. After a few more beers she was chatting away and being polite and friendly and she suggested that we could sell perfume and aftershave for the company she was working for, as they were always short of sellers. Myself and Pete looked at each other simultaneously and burst out laughing. She says, "No guys, seriously, both of you would make good salesmen," as she pointed out Pete was well spoken for an American and I had a strange accent. She carried on flattering us both by saying we were both good looking, fit and strong, and if we dressed up smart we would make plenty of sales, then she started to tell us about this other guy in the company who was inundated with female offers of dates. She then told us how much money she was making. While Pete and I were killing ourselves labouring for $60 per day, she told us that with her two visits to our bar she'd made over a hundred dollars. So we took her company card and said our temporary farewells and that we would see her soon, and she was off to deliver more orders that she'd taken during the day.

Well, when she went, we started going over everything she'd told us about how it all worked. Basically, one went around with a briefcase of bottles, selling them in shopping malls, office buildings, bars or parks where office workers had their lunch breaks. You sold them there and then, if you could, but if they didn't have the money you took a 25 per cent deposit and arranged to deliver later. For those that were uneasy about handing over a deposit, you gave them the company card and a receipt to reassure them. For every bottle sold, you made 25 per cent of the $20 price. Now we started thinking. Why don't we buy a perfume essence ourselves, take it to an industrial chemist, get them to mix it with medical alcohol to get the right mix, then buy the bottles and cork stoppers, order up labels and felt pouches, get ourselves syringes to fill the bottles, easy as cake, no office or industrial unit required.

So this is exactly what we did. We had two minor disagreements. Firstly I suggested that Pete carry on working and I'd set it all up and we split his wages as we were now partners, then he could quit work when it was all moving along. Pete's reply to this was, "Piss-off, you go to work and I'll set it up." So we came to a compromise – we both quit work. The second disagreement was, what do we call our perfume, it had to have a French name to have creditability.

Well our local pasta joint was called 'Guichards'. That will do, labels were made up, everything else was either picked up or delivered. One litre of perfume essence, when correctly mixed with the alcohol, became 66 bottles of 15 ml perfume, costing us about $1.50 per bottle. This was unreal, and after about two weeks we were making about $1000 per week each, after all expenses. Then we got five girls out selling on commission. This was going great. Heaps of dates as well. All good things come to an end. Two months later I broke my femur bone playing football.

After I came out of hospital I went back to Africa. I was longing for more African adventures. Pete carried on selling perfumes which paid his way through Berkeley University where he studied chemical engineering. I did do some perfume selling in South Africa, but Africa to me meant adventure, excitement, Wilbur Smith characters, not perfume selling.

On my travels I have come across perfume sellers in every western country. Remember no tax, no social security numbers required, just dress smart and have confidence in yourself. Also, many other similar types of jobs are available, from selling leather bags, reproduction paintings, all door to door. With little no social security documentation required.

Another good earner is selling ice-cream or popcorn from tricycles on piers, beaches, football and baseball games.

Agriculture

Every state has plenty of seasonal harvest work available. Most of this work is done by Mexicans or Chicanos (naturalized Hispanics). Black Americans do plenty of agricultural work in the southern states. A lot of these jobs pay cash in hand. When I worked in construction in Denver the construction was running ads through the newspapers for labourers. The ads were published every other week as the turnover of labourers was so high due to the fact that the job was an extremely hard one. After three days I got promoted to leading hand and got a dollar an hour increase in wages! Only in America man! All the foremen had to speak Spanish. I learnt quite a lot of Spanish on this job and this helped me out later on when I went to Mexico. I used my own social security number on that job.

Men Working With Women

When European companies send their employees over to the US to work, they often send their male employees on seminars first to initiate them in American office working protocol. This is due to the publicity that sexual harassment in the US work place has gotten.

Now some men in America are refusing to work alone with female employees. This is due to women jumping on the sexual harassment bandwagon. Things you can say in the office in the UK are definitely 'out' in America. Don't dare say, 'nice outfit you're wearing,' or 'you look good today.' or 'you smell nice.' Mind you they have a point, I mean you wouldn't say those things to a man, would you?

Another no-no is don't say to a woman, 'Have you got a rubber?' This will be taken as a sexual innuendo. Rubber means condom. A pencil mark remover is an eraser. Other words to bear in mind are: Fag in English is cigarette. American fag is homosexual. Faggot, is a meatball made from offal. Faggot is also a derogatory term for homosexual. Gay, meaning happy in English (the gay Caviller meant 'joyful' not homosexual). In the US you'll get the company sued and yourself fired, then future companies will look upon you as a risk, not worth hiring. Bear these things in mind so that you don't get yourself blacklisted by local companies.

Fishing Boats in Alaska

Huge amounts of money are to be made fishing for salmon. Forget it, nobody gets hired unless you are family of the trawler's owners or locals. How this story started about being able to get this kind of work I don't know. The only jobs going in the salmon industry are in the canning and packing plants and this in only in the summer time. It is still difficult to get taken on and the wages are not brilliant considering the cost of living in Alaska. If you are fortunate enough to get hired, the unloading and loading is done on piecework, so try and get in an all male loading gang, as very few females can pick up a salmon in each hand at the same time, whereas most men can. Therefore women slow you down, so less money is made.

If you're determined to go to Alaska to work, quite a few of the canning companies hire their labour from Fisherman's Wharf in Ballard an industrial suburb of Seattle and in Tacoma in Washington State. The main fishing centre in Alaska is in and around Dutch Harbour on Unalaska Island, there are flights, also some packing and canning plants on Kodiak Island, a good mate of mine Mario from the UK did a season in a canning plant on Kodiak, he's the chap who told me about not working with women in your crew as most of them cannot pick up a salmon in each hand at the same time. If you do get on a fishing trawler, highly unlikely unless you are a 'trawler man', you'll need a fishing licence first which covers you for insurance and costs about $200 per season. There is also seasons for other fish and crabs as well. You'll need two forms of US ID.

Labour ready: has heaps of offices in the US and Canada call toll free 1-800-555-1212.

As I've stated many times in this book already check the internet for latest up to date information and get the seasons right, no point turning up when the season is over.

Recommended reading is *The Students Guide to the Best Summer Jobs in Alaska* by John Groves, Mustang Publishing.

Natural Disasters

If you're in the right place at the right time, like when the Exxon Valdez went aground spilling millions of gallons of crude oil, there is a great chance of getting work as thousands of people in Alaska got hired to clean up Exxon's mess at $15 per hour. The clean up companies didn't bother with who was and who wasn't documented to work. The US gets more than its share of natural disasters ranging from hurricanes, tornadoes, torrential rain, fires, earthquakes, landslides, snowstorms and man-made disasters caused by riots, i.e., the LA riots, levies being breached in New Orleans.

Religion

Religion plays a massive role in the American way of life and government, more so in the Southern States. Nobody would ever get elected president if they admitted to being an atheist or if they were single. Atheists being on par with communists in the US. When senators are on the election campaign trail, they have to talk about God, at the same time as picking up babies for the cameras, (a cringe factor of 10 out of 10).

Written in the constitution, the other American bible, is the right to free worship. Although religion has been taken out of the state schools (something which should have been done in Northern Ireland a hundred years ago), it has not stopped the ever increasing fundamentalist religious advance. Every single religion on earth is present in America and they are all flourishing, with the exception of the ones who appoint themselves as 'the new Messiah' i.e., David Koresh and his band of religious followers who all perished in Waco, Texas at the hands of the FBI. A few years before they perished, another self-appointed Messiah called Jim Jones led his band of enlightened disciples down to the land of milk and honey, Guyana, South America, in 1979 where they all poisoned and shot one another. In all nine hundred of them died. This was the biggest mass suicide, murder ever, beating the previous record held by the Jews of Masada who killed them-selves rather than be taken prisoners by the Romans who were going to enslave them.

So if you are going to join a religious sect, make sure the leader has got most of his marbles intact. It's okay if he's just a space cadet. Make sure he's not the self-appointed new Messiah or you'll end up dead. Remember you're a long time dead and there ain't no heaven and Waco, Texas, is a long way from home as many British disciples found out.

In some states religion has tremendous clout (like Southern Ireland), they even make their own laws. A prime example being Utah, a Mormon state, where large families, and having lots of wives, is common practice. Alcohol is frowned upon and bible bashing is the order of the day.

The southern states and the wheat belt area of Kansas and Missouri in the mid-west are also much into bible bashing. California, which is well known for its offbeat life-styles, has all the obscure, little known Protestant offshoot sects.

This is all really very amazing as America is one of the most capitalist, greedy possession oriented countries I've been to and they all claim to be Christians, but if they were to read their New Testament, how would they explain their wealth to themselves. As Jesus said to a disciple, "If you want to be perfect go and sell all you have and give the money to the poor, and you will have riches in heaven." The disciple went away sad, because he was very rich. Jesus then said to his disciple, "I assure you it will be very hard for rich people to enter the Kingdom of Heaven. It is much harder for a rich person to enter the Kingdom of God than for a camel to go through the eye of a needle." (A narrow gate entrance into the walled old city of Jerusalem).

The bottom line is simply this: many people chase after material things which in the end don't really matter. What is important is the path you take in life. Jesus tells us that there are two paths in life. This all sounds like the teachings of Karl Marx to me. God forbid was Jesus a commie, or maybe Karl Marx was the born again Messiah. Both of them have had a profound influence on the human race. Also both of them were Jewish. Jesus founded Christianity which is thriving. Karl Marx's teachings were the foundation for communism, which is in decline, but Christianity has had its low points, especially when the Christians were being thrown to the lions in Roman times. Must have been great fun to watch at the time. Maybe communism will make a dramatic comeback after a low point. If the Messiah is born again as a reincarnation of Karl Marx, in America, they will probably fry him in the electric chair this time around for being a commie. All the catholic followers can then wear little electric chairs around their necks instead of crosses, and all the followers will have pictures of Jesus strapped to an electric chair in their bedrooms and living rooms.

Catholic Church

I have lived all over the world and every country that I've lived in has had its never ending scandals with the catholic priests molesting boys, and the church never throws them out, they just move them somewhere else to carry on with their paedophile activities. An organisation that attracts men who have to abstain from sex with women, is bound to always attract unbalanced undesirables. Apparently it hasn't always been vows of celibacy. It was a fourteenth century Pope who brought in the rules, obviously he didn't like women.

How can people go along with all this fear and damnation bullshit that they heap upon their followers, youngsters being brainwashed. Four of the biggest mass murdering war criminals in Europe last century have been Roman Catholics – Hitler, Mussolini, Franco and the Croatian Ustase leader, Ante Pavelic. The latter two dying of old age and all of them had the blessing of the Vatican and the Catholic Church.

The Croatian Ustasha slaughtered Serbs and Jews with such enthusiasm and gusto that their Gestapo masters left them to slaughter unsupervised and who were the first two countries to recognize Croatia as a state, who else but Austria and Germany. Now Croatia the darling of the west. What was the first thing they did? – Smash up all the monuments to the victims of Croatian genocide. No wonder Serbs felt let down, to say the least. Serbia was allied to us in two world wars.

A good buddy of mine from Africa, 'Mad' Sid, went and got himself killed fighting for a free Bosnia.

After the Second World War, the Vatican harboured and smuggled out countless thousands of war criminals all over the world, rather than have them face justice for their genocide crimes against humanity.

What Did The Catholic Church Have To Hide?

The Pope still refused to endorse birth control, when most of the catholic countries around the world are over-populated, hungry and living in miserable conditions, while the Vatican gets wealthier and wealthier.

As the Pope says, "It is better to produce more food," (by chopping down more rain forests).

I'd better not mention the Islamic faith or else I'll probably get a Salmon Rushdie type death sentence passed onto me by some raving Iranian Mullah.

A quote I heard recently: 'There's no fun in Islam' that just about sums it up about them.

Work and Visas

A social security card has a nine digit number. You can apply for one of these from the Social Security Department. You need a social security number to open a bank account, but the card you receive has 'Alien' stamped across it – 'not to work'?

If you build up American ID, starting with a driving licence, you can fill out the sections in the social security application form, so as to get a card without Alien stamped on it. Same goes for Australia. The Canadian one is tricky to get. In New Zealand, there is no problem getting a card, even with tourist stamped on your passport. Employers usually don't ask to see your card. They only want the number. You can use someone else's number or claim you're waiting for your card to arrive by post.

Unless your company transfers you to the US and arranges your visa, the only working visas available are through the BUNAC programme: British Universities North America Club, 16 Bowling Green Lane, London, EC1R OBD. Tel: 0171 2513472.

In Ireland for Irish citizens: USIT 19 Aston Quay, Dublin,

This is the I1, Q1 or H1B Visa, these are given out to students and voluntary workers.

For further in depth details contact the Visa branch of the US Embassy, 5 Upper Grosvenor Street, London, W1A 21B, or the Council on International Education Exchange, CIEE, 33 Seymour Place, London, W1 H 6AT. Tel: 0171 706 3008.

On the BUNAC scheme, they have programmes available like 'Work America Programme,' 4000 places are available on this course.

Summer Camps

The American Camping Association, 500 State Road, 67 North Martinsville, Indiana.

Summer Jobs USA published by Peterson's Guides, 202 Carnegie Centre, Princeton. N.J. 08543.

Camp America Department WW, 37A Queen's Gate, London, SW7 SHR. Tel: 0171 581 7373. Fax: 0171 5817377.

Camp Counsellors USA CCUSA, 154 Heath Road, Twickenham, TW1O GQX. Tel; 0181-332 2952. Fax: 0181-744 9252.

Childcare, Au Pair and Domestic Work. Au pair work is included on the Exchange Visitor Programmes with the J1 visa.

Au Pair Care Cultural Exchange, 101 Loma Road, Hove, Sussex, BN3 3EL. Tel: 01273 220261.

Au Pair, 74 Roupell Road, London, SE1 8SS. Tel: 0171 401 8004.

'Otesage', West Malvern Road, Malvern, Worcs, WR14 1DX. Tel: 01684 562577.

The American Institute for Foreign Study. AIFS, 37 Queen's Gate, London, SW7 5IR.

US Travel and Tourism Administration P0 Box 1EN, London, W1A IEN. Tel: 0171 495 4466, Fax: 0171 4954377

The Year Off Handbook Roger Jackson (mail order only) £9.95 Sabre Publishing Sabre House, 129 Mercers Rd, London, N19 4PY. This book is a bit old now but heaps of information in it that will still be current.

Another good book. How to Live and Work in America. From the how to series.

Born in the USA

Many women l have known over the years, when they reach the age of twenty-six to thirty-six decide it is time to have a baby. In many eases with or without a permanent partner. The stigma of being an unmarried mother has long passed in western nations. My own mother never got married until l was eight years old. In those days there was plenty of stigma and prejudice attached to being a single mother, not to mention wages were much lower for women doing the same jobs as men. So life was hard. Most people have great mothers, but mine was better than everybody's without a doubt.

The Fourteenth Amendment of the Constitution

States that a child born within the USA regardless of the citizenship or status of the parents, is automatically an American citizen no where else in the western world that I know of is this right granted.

Omnibus Budget Reconciliation Act of 1968

Was a provision that 'undocumented' illegal aliens must be given free emergency medical services, including maternity care, as part of the federal Medical program.

The mother then can use the baby to tap into a half dozen other welfare programs including low cost housing or rent paid in a private building with a rent voucher. You can then receive a WIC (Women, Infants, Children) Allowance.

At twenty-one years of age the now adult can sponsor in family members.

To pay for hospital treatment yourself without the state paying for you to have a baby is about $9,000-$15,000. (Obama care has properly altered this).

You may be thinking? What for? Why not have my baby at home.

Well in twenty year's time Europe might have no jobs, already Spain has over 25 per cent youth unemployment means in some areas will have 50 per cent unemployment, Italian and French youth unemployment is catching up on Spain.

The USA has always since the 40s had half the unemployment of the UK. This unselfish act of having your child in the US would give your child a tremendous opportunity and options in adulthood.

APPLICATION FOR US SOCIAL SECURITY CARD

SOCIAL SECURITY ADMINISTRATION

Application for a Social Security Card

Inside is the form you need to apply for a Social Security card. You can also use this form to replace a lost card or to change your name on your card. This service is free. But before you go on to the form, please read through the rest of this page. We want to cover some facts you should know before you apply.

IF YOU HAVE NEVER HAD A SOCIAL SECURITY NUMBER

If you were born in the US and have never had a Social Security number, you must complete this form and show us documents that show your age, citizenship, and who you are. Usually, all we need from you are:

Your birth certificate; AND some form of identity, such as a driver's license, school record, or medical record. See page 2 for more examples.

We prefer to see your birth certificate. However, we will accept a hospital record of your birth made before you were five years old, or a religious record of your age or birth made before you were three months old. **We must see original documents or certified copies. Uncertified photocopies are not acceptable.** You may apply at any age, but if you are eighteen or older when **you apply for your first Social Security card, you must apply in person. Please see the special requirements on page 4 if you were born outside the US, if you are not a US citizen or if you need a card for a child.**

IF YOU NEED TO REPLACE YOUR CARD

To replace your card, all we usually need is one type of identification and this completed form. See page 2 for examples of documents we will accept. If you were born outside the US, you must also submit proof of US citizenship or lawful alien status. Examples of the documents we will accept are on page 4. **Remember, we must see original documents or certified copies.**

IF YOU NEED TO CHANGE YOUR NAME ON YOUR CARD

If you already have a number, but need to change your name on our records, we need this completed form and a document that identifies you by both your old and new names. Examples include a marriage certificate, a divorce decree or a court order that changes your name. Or, we will accept two documents – one with your old name and one with your new name. See page 2 for examples of documents we will accept. If you were born outside the US, you must also show proof of US citizenship or lawful alien status. Examples of documents we will accept are on page 4.

HOW TO APPLY

First complete this form, using the instructions on page 2. Then take or mail it to the nearest Social Security office. Be sure to take or mail the originals or certified copies of your documents along with the form. We will return your documents right away.

IF YOU HAVE ANY QUESTIONS

If you have any questions about this form, or about the documents you need to show us, please contact any Social Security office. A telephone call will help you make sure you have everything you need to apply for your card.

Form SS-M9189) 6188 edition may be used until supply is exhausted.

APPLICATION FOR US SOCIAL SECURITY CARD

DOCUMENTS THAT SHOW YOUR IDENTITY HOW TO COMPLETE THE FORM

Here are some examples of identity documents that we will accept.

- US government or state employee ID card
- Driver's license

- Your passport

- School ID card, record, or report card

- Marriage or divorce record

- Health insurance card

- Clinic, doctor, or hospital records

- Military records

- Court order for name change

- Adoption records

- Church membership or confirmation record (if not used as evidence of age)

- Insurance policy

We will NOT accept a birth certificate or hospital record as proof of your identity. We will accept other documents if they have enough information to identify you. **Remember, we must see original documents or copies certified by the county clerk or other official who keeps the record.**

HOW TO COMPLETE THE FORM

Most questions on the form are self-explanatory. The questions that need explanation are discussed below. The numbers match the numbered questions on the form. **If you are completing this form for someone else, please answer the questions as they apply to that person**. Then, sign your own name in question 16.

1. Your card will show your full first, middle, and last names unless you show otherwise. If you have ever used another name, show it on the third line. You can show more than one name on this line. Do not show a nickname unless you have used it for work or business.

2. Show the address where you want your card mailed. If you do not usually get mail at this address, please show an 'in care of address', for example, c/o John Doe, 1 Elm Street, Any town, USA 00000.

3. If you check 'other' under Citizenship, please attach a statement that explains your situation and why you need a Social Security number.

5. You do not have to answer our question about race/ethnic background. We can issue you a Social Security card without this

information. However, this information is important. We use it to study and report on how Social Security programs affect different people in our nation. Of course, we use it only for statistical reports and do not reveal the identities of individuals.

13. If the date of birth you show in item 6 is different from the date of birth you used on an earlier application, show the date of birth you used on the earlier application on this line.

16. If you cannot sign your name, sign with an "X" mark and have two people sign beneath your mark as witnesses.

Form SS6 (9/89)
APPLICATION FOR US SOCIAL SECURITY CARD

SOCIAL SECURITY ADMINISTRATION
Application for a Social Security Card

Form Approved
OMB No. 0960-0066

1	NAME TO BE SHOWN ON CARD	First / Full Middle Name / Last
	FULL NAME AT BIRTH IF OTHER THAN ABOVE	First / Full Middle Name / Last
	OTHER NAMES USED	
2	Social Security number previously assigned to the person listed in item 1	___ - ___ - ___
3	PLACE OF BIRTH (Do Not Abbreviate)	City / State or Foreign Country / FCI (Office Use Only)
4	DATE OF BIRTH	MM/DD/YYYY
5	CITIZENSHIP (Check One)	☐ U.S. Citizen ☐ Legal Alien Allowed To Work ☐ Legal Alien Not Allowed To Work (See Instructions On Page 3) ☐ Other (See Instructions On Page 3)
6	ETHNICITY — Are You Hispanic or Latino? (Your Response is Voluntary)	☐ Yes ☐ No
7	RACE — Select One or More (Your Response is Voluntary)	☐ Native Hawaiian ☐ Alaska Native ☐ Asian ☐ American Indian ☐ Black/African American ☐ Other Pacific Islander ☐ White
8	SEX	☐ Male ☐ Female
9	A. PARENT/ MOTHER'S NAME AT HER BIRTH	First / Full Middle Name / Last
	B. PARENT/ MOTHER'S SOCIAL SECURITY NUMBER (See instructions for 9 B on Page 3)	___ - ___ - ___ ☐ Unknown
10	A. PARENT/ FATHER'S NAME	First / Full Middle Name / Last
	B. PARENT/ FATHER'S SOCIAL SECURITY NUMBER (See instructions for 10B on Page 3)	___ - ___ - ___ ☐ Unknown
11	Has the person listed in item 1 or anyone acting on his/her behalf ever filed for or received a Social Security number card before?	☐ Yes (If "yes" answer questions 12-13) ☐ No ☐ Don't Know (If "don't know," skip to question 14.)
12	Name shown on the most recent Social Security card issued for the person listed in item 1	First / Full Middle Name / Last
13	Enter any different date of birth if used on an earlier application for a card	MM/DD/YYYY
14	TODAY'S DATE	MM/DD/YYYY
15	DAYTIME PHONE NUMBER	Area Code / Number
16	MAILING ADDRESS (Do Not Abbreviate)	Street Address, Apt. No., PO Box, Rural Route No. / City / State/Foreign Country / ZIP Code
17	YOUR SIGNATURE — I declare under penalty of perjury that I have examined all the information on this form, and on any accompanying statements or forms, and it is true and correct to the best of my knowledge.	
18	YOUR RELATIONSHIP TO THE PERSON IN ITEM 1 IS:	☐ Self ☐ Natural Or Adoptive Parent ☐ Legal Guardian ☐ Other Specify

DO NOT WRITE BELOW THIS LINE (FOR SSA USE ONLY)

NPN			DOC	NTI	CAN		ITV
PBC	EVI	EVA	EVC	PRA	NWR	DNR	UNIT
EVIDENCE SUBMITTED					SIGNATURE AND TITLE OF EMPLOYEE(S) REVIEWING EVIDENCE AND/OR CONDUCTING INTERVIEW		
							DATE
				DCL			DATE

Form SS-5 (08-2011) ef (08-2011)   Destroy Prior Editions   Page 5

IF YOU ARE A UNITED STATES CITIZEN BORN OUTSIDE THE US.

If you are a United States citizen-who was born outside the US, we need to see your consular report of birth (FS240 or FS-545), if you have one. We also need to see one form of identification. See page 2 for examples of identity documents we will accept.

If you do not have your consular report of birth, we will need to see your foreign birth certificate and one of the following: a US Citizen ID card, US passport, Certificate of Citizenship, or a Certificate of Naturalization. Remember, you must show us the original documents.

IF YOU ARE NOT A US CITIZEN

If you are not a US citizen, you must show us your birth certificate or passport, and the documents given to you by the Immigration and Naturalization Service (INS). **We must see original documents, not photocopies.** Examples of INS documents are: your Alien Registration Receipt Card (Form I-151 or I-551) or Form L94. Because these documents should not be mailed, you should apply in person.

Even though you may not be authorized to work in this country, we can issue you a Social Security card if you are here legally and need it for some other reason. Your card will be marked to show that you cannot work, and if you do, we will notify INS.

IF YOU NEED A CARD FOR A CHILD OR SOMEONE ELSE

If you apply for a card for a child or someone else, you need to show us that person's original or certified birth certificate and one more document showing the person's identity. For example, for a child we will accept a doctor or hospital bill, a school record or any similar document that shows the child's identity. For an adult, see page 2 for examples of identity documents we will accept.

Also, if you sign the form, we need to see some kind of identification for you. Please see the list on page 2 for examples of documents we will accept. Be sure to answer the questions on the application form as they apply to the person needing the card.

THE PAPERWORK/PRIVACY ACT AND YOUR APPLICATION

The Social Security Act (sections Z) 5(c) and 702) allows us to collect the facts we ask for on this form. We use most of these facts to assign you a Social Security number or to issue you a card. You do not have to give us these facts, but without them we can not issue you a Social Security number or a card. Without a number, you could lose Social Security benefits in the future and you might not be able to get a job.

We give out the facts on this form without your consent only in certain situations that are explained in the Federal Register. For example, we must give out this information if Federal law requires us to, if your Congressman or Senator needs the information to answer questions you ask them or if the Justice Department needs it to investigate and prosecute violations of the Social Security Act.

We may also use the information you give us when we match records by computer. Matching programs compare our records with those of other Federal, State, or local government agencies. Many agencies may use matching programs to find or prove that a person qualifies for benefits paid by the Federal government. The law allows us to do this even if you do not agree to it. If you would like more facts about the Privacy Act, get in with any Social Security office.

We estimate that it will like you about 8 minutes to complete this form. This includes the time it will take to read the instructions, gather the necessary facts and fill out the form. If you have comments or suggestions on this estimate, write to the Social Security Administration ATTN:

Reports Clearance Officer, 1-A-21 Operations Bldg, Baltimore. MD 21235-0001. Send only comments relating to our estimate or other aspects of this form to the office listed above. All request for Social Security cards and other claims-related information should be sent to your local Social Security office, whose address is listed In your telephone directory under Social Security Administration the U.S. Government section of your of your telephone directory.   Form 85-6 (9/89)

CHAPTER 13
Mexico

As this book is not just about working around the world but also experiencing adventure, then those people who have earned their money working in the USA may be interested in heading south across the border into Mexico for some R&R (rest and relaxation).

Here follows some of my experiences in this wonderful country.

With winter rapidly approaching, I'm getting restless and longing for the warmth and sunshine.

The summer in Vancouver that year had been lousy, hardly any sun and heaps of torrential rain. The upside was that I'd made heaps of dough and I had a four-wheel-drive Land Cruiser paid for and I had friends to look after my surplus gear.

Well there's only one place to go and that's Mexico. I figure that three months in Mexico then back up to the US and Canada to catch the last of the skiing and then spring will be in sight.

Off I set, and instead of heading directly south, I head 400 miles east to a one man border post that borders the beautiful state of Idaho. No problem getting out of Canada. I fobbed the American immigration official off. I still had the edge in those days.

Down through the US through the famous Yellowstone National Park in Wyoming. The next destination I'm heading for is Denver. I had fond memories of my time in Denver a few years earlier. This time I'm not planning on teaming up with a woman, I'm meeting my buddy, 'Fruitcake' Giles.

Giles, I first met in Africa. He'd chucked in a promising career as a patent lawyer which required a degree in law and engineering. "Hey man, I ain't gonna shuffle papers all my life," that's what he told me when I first met him staring at the permanent daytime rainbow that is over Victoria Falls. It didn't take me long to figure out he was tripping on acid at the time, completely out of his head. A long and permanent friendship was developed on that day.

After picking Giles up, we're on our way. He's teaching me Spanish en route. We only have one near crash. The Land Cruiser was up on two wheels for a while anyway a miss is as good as a mile. I decided to take over the driving as I wasn't into his Evil Knievel stunts on two wheels and skidding all over the road, dodging in between semi-trailers who are blaring their hooters and shouting obscenities at us.

If any of you have seen the film *Young Guns*, it is about Billy the Kid and his gang of desperadoes. In the middle of the story there is a scene where the Indian in the gang finds and turns the boys onto the hallucinogenic cactus called Peyote. This cactus is extremely rare in the US today. It doesn't grow or reproduce very well, what ones were around, most of them got gobbled up by the hippies in the sixties and seventies. There is probably only one valley left in the whole world where this cactus grows and thrives. It is in Northern Mexico. The valley is kept secret and the plant is protected. The only exception made is for the Huichole Indians, who make a 700 kilometre round trip once a year to eat the cactus for one of their tribal rituals, where they fast for a few days then eat heaps of peyote so they can do their spiritual thing – talk to their ancestors and the likes.

There are probably no more than a dozen gringos who have been in to this valley in the twentieth century, and Giles is one of them. He's been to this valley half a dozen times over a ten year period. The ideal way in to this mountain desert valley would be by helicopter, followed by horse, or on foot, carrying plenty of water. It's at least forty miles from a tarred road. There is one perilous route in by four-wheel-drive and of course Giles knew the way, avoiding mounted rangers.

The peyote only grows at a certain altitude and because it only grows a few inches above the surface of the desert floor, they can't handle much snow or rain. Like most hallucinogenic plants, you eat it and because it's poisonous your body rejects the foreign substance, so you throw up. But as it's been in your body the chemicals enter your blood stream and bingo, you witness plants growing, sand moving and God talking, in the wind. After a few days of this, I'd had enough, but Giles hadn't, so he takes off the door panels from the jeep and stuffs them full with dried peyote for smoking later. We figured we'd have to leave before the rangers spotted us, so as to avoid paying them a backhander. The jeep wouldn't have out performed horses, so we were on our way. We reached the tar road, which is still a desert track with only about a dozen assorted vehicles per day passing along it, not what you would call a highway. We have decided to head south west so as to meet up with the Pacific Ocean and then hang out in some fishing villages to eat turtles and lobsters.

As you are driving throughout isolated Northern Mexico, every fifty miles or so one encounters enterprising Indian women usually in pairs, selling an array of desert goods. I used to wonder where they came from as there was usually no sign of habitation around. Some of them used to have horses hobbled nearby. Giles said that the ones without horses had lifts arranged, or walked out of the hills. Their goods varied from handmade clay bowls, woven blankets, chicken eggs, dried rattle snake and jack rabbit jerky and anything else they could get out of the desert.

A tough life indeed with no welfare payments like their cousins north of the border in US and Canada, although I can't blame them for getting drunk all the time and living off welfare as they had a great life not so many years ago. Galloping across the prairies hunting buffalo and stealing their enemies horses and women, until the white man put an end to it all and made life boring living on reservations.

Anyway, the first women we came across that day we stopped to see what they had for sale. Well, they had the usual chicken eggs, also they had half a dozen or so desert doves which I guess were for pets or for eating. To top it all they had a fledgling eagle. The size of a chicken, but it still had its juvenile feather down in places. I knew this bird was going to grow up to be a monster.

Giles was chatting away in Spanish to find out more about this bird. Apparently the Spanish name for the bird is a 'Royal King's Eagle', but it looked the same as a golden eagle to me. Giles decides he's having it.

I'm shaking my head saying, "Oh no man, how are we going to feed and train it?"

After a few minutes we are both seeing dollar signs. In the US it's illegal to own wild birds of prey, only birds bred in captivity are allowed to be owned. So there's a real shortage of tame eagles in America and they are fetching $10,000 plus. This Indian lady is wanting $20 for this tame fledgling. Opportunities don't come along like this every day, so a deal was struck. Before we departed with our new companion, I suggested to Giles we find out about the eagles eating habits from the Indian. The woman was so pleased with her sale she was more than willing to tell us how to look after the bird. In the next instant she reached over and grabbed one of the doves, that five minutes earlier had been sharing a perch with our eagle, and while she was talking she just ripped the head off the dove and offered the twitching carcass to the eagle, which immediately started devouring the offering from the inside out, through the neck cavity.

Giles, being a #fruitcake', just burst out laughing and said, "How are we going to catch doves every day man?" I was saying hang on a minute because if I was going to catch and kill birds then they were for me to eat, not song birds and the likes for that thing. Anyway, what the woman was explaining was that the eagle would eat any meat, lizards or snakes, as long as you opened it up and exposed the blood and innards to it.

I thought for a minute and said, "What about if we just bought it minced meat from the butchers," and she just looked at us in utter amazement as if to say, you're going to buy meat for the eagle. But she then told us that of course it would eat raw mince. The first of many problems solved. So we're off, the eagle perched on the top of the passenger seat back rest quite happy in its new environment. Little does this bird know it's going to migrate to America without a green card.

So there we are, driving along in 35°C to 40°C heat, the windows on the jeep unable to be opened because of the peyote in the door panelling which was jamming the windows shut. The eagle was getting hot also as it started to pant with its beak open. What a stench of rotting meat that was coming out of the bird's mouth – talk about 'eagle breath'. As with all birds when they eat, they just store it all in their gullet and let it be absorbed into the body, no problem if they are seed eaters, but with meat eaters, definitely enough stink to make one a vegetarian. This was unbelievable torture that we went through until we were able to get the windows open again.

We also found out that birds can't be 'house trained'. When the eagle wanted a poo it just lifted its tail feathers up and whoosh, splat, all over the back of the jeep or anywhere else it happened to be at the time. A few times I was on the verge of ringing its neck, but believe it or not I do like animals, especially ones that are dependent on you. They give you a sense of 'well-being' with their loyalty that they unquestionably give you, so we were both getting attached to this new companion of ours. Also it was going to make us a load of dough, so the first hurdle was to teach it to fly.

The first real flight was something I'll never forget. For a couple of weeks now, Giles had been running around with the bird on his arm and throwing it up into the air, whereupon the eagle would just flap its wings and land on the ground and then start walking around. By now the bird was fully feathered and we figured there was no reason why it shouldn't fly, but it wouldn't. Sometimes Giles would give it theory lessons on flying. He would talk to the bird in English and then in Spanish and then he would jump up and down flapping his arms up and down like we used to do at infant school playing 'spitfires'. To the sight of this I would be doubled up with laughter, it was painful to watch.

One evening we are sitting around our camp fire smoking peyote. Giles is very depressed. He's come to the conclusion that either the bird still only understands the Indian language, or it looks upon us as its parents and as we don't fly, it's not going to fly. I say no man, it was too young to remember Indian, also there's plenty of other birds flying around and it sees them all the time. Also you're putting too much emphasis on the bird thinking it's got the brain of a bird, because it is a bird. Maybe it just won't fly, like some dogs just don't bark. Hawkeye, (the bird's new name) must have heard all this, because the next day it flew, and what a flight it was.

Early in the morning, after coffee and Mexican refried beans which are brilliant, Giles decided to give our eagle another flying lesson before the weather got too hot. I guess it was exhausting running around and flapping one's arms in 30'C - 40'C.

So then ten minutes of theory of flight was explained to Hawkeye. Remember. Giles had a degree in engineering, so he used to go into real technical detail about slipstream and thermal air currents and putting flaps down for landing after your final approach was decided. Quite a feat in two languages. Hawkeye always used to perch attentively and turn its head to one side as if to take it all in. I'm on the floor again choking on the remains of the refried beans. If only I could have got all that on video I would have made a fortune. So off he starts running with Hawkeye on his arm. He throws his arm up and Hawkeye is airborne. He's flying like he owns the sky.

We are no longer in the desert now, we're just south of Puerto Vallarta, on the Pacific coast. We're at the location where the film *The Night of the Iguana* was filmed in the 1964, with a voluptuous Ava Gardner and a young Richard Burton.

So the vegetation has changed dramatically now we are in a subtropical region, with a rising forested hill around us. Hawkeye is flying higher and higher, around and around. Then he starts to fly out to sea. Giles is shouting, "Hawkeye come back, you're not a sea eagle, there's nowhere to land out there."

At that moment Hawkeye must have heard Giles, for he turned around and headed inland towards the forested hills behind us and into the forest he went, way out of sight. Giles is now frantic with despair. "Come on," he says, "let's go into the hills and look for him."

Somehow I managed to calm him down, which was a tremendous feat in itself. I explained that even if we see him, which I doubt, we'll never get him out of the trees. I suggested that we just put the meat out on the bonnet of the jeep at feeding time like usual, and hope he comes back. As I pointed out, he doesn't know how to look after himself as he is tame. To which Giles replied, "Yea, he's tame, that's why we have to go and look for him because he'll fly down to some peasant's back yard and they'll think he's after their chickens and kill him."

So I made a compromise, "You go up into the hills and look for him and I'll wait here just in case he comes back, because if he comes back and no-one is here, he'll be well and truly disorientated." Giles saw the logic of this and off he went.

A few hours later, at midday, Giles returns, almost suicidal with despair and no Hawkeye. I try and console him by saying that he still might come back at sunset when it's feeding time. As it's now midday and getting real hot, I go and lie on my air-bed in the shade. No sooner had I dosed off when Giles starts yelling, "Ralph look out!" I open my eyes and Hawkeye is coming in on final approach, straight towards me.

Of all the places Hawkeye could have landed, he'd decided to land on my air bed. Fortunately I rolled off at the last moment as two sets of eagle talons punctured the bed. Hawkeye was back and it wasn't even feeding time. We'd worked out our plan to get Hawkeye across the border. All we had to do was get the bird to associate food with the jeep, so meat was always placed on the jeep at feeding time. Giles knew a few really isolated crossings. So the plan was that I'd drive over first, being as the vehicle was registered in my name. I'd drive half a mile in away from the border post. Then Giles would release Hawkeye at feeding time; I'd have meat on the bonnet of the jeep; I'd blow into the whistle that we'd also taught him to recognise with feeding time. Being as Hawkeye was an eagle, and he had 'eagle eyesight', we later did a few dummy runs when the bird was flying. Well, he could spot the jeep from miles away. A really simple plan, then Giles would walk across the border and he would have no problem as he was an American. Selling was going to be the heartbreaking part but with the kind of dough we were looking at, it had to be done.

All over Mexico I found the Mexicans to be very friendly and helpful. When we used to go and drink in Canteenas in the isolated mountain regions, we always struck up conversations with the local vacairos (cowboys). Excellent quality drinks are available throughout Mexico, famous drinks come from here i.e., Tequila, Kaluha, Mescal and great beers, not Corona. The Mexicans thought that Britain was great as we had recently kicked the Argentinians out of the Falkland Isles, so we seldom bought drinks. Everyone in South and Central America dislikes the Argentinians, just like no-one in Europe likes the Germans. It's because the Argentinians look upon themselves as 'Europeans' and not mixed blood like the rest of South and Central America. Argentina looks upon herself as a nation with 'high culture', whatever that is.

The two English people that everyone knew at that time were, Bobby Charlton and Margaret Thatcher; Thatcher pronounced without the 'H'.

Pacific resorts are great places to meet rich American single women on holiday.

Maybe one day, in the next century, Mexico will regain its Northern States that the US took off them through its war of aggression in the 1830s. It won't be the Mexican army that retakes its land back, it will be the people crossing over on foot, back into California, Arizona, New Mexico and Texas.

Three months later, back in Canada after two months in Los Angeles working and then skiing, I get a phone call from Giles. He's suddenly remembered about the half pound of marijuana heads he'd hidden underneath the jeep battery, in a plastic bag, that fitted perfectly in the battery well, underneath the battery. What! I can't believe what he's saying. I'd crossed two International borders, risking a heavy fine, prison and vehicle confiscation. No wonder at the isolated border post that we'd crossed back into the US they'd put a dog in the jeep who went nuts, smelling the residue of the peyote and eagle shit and cases and cases of booze which we'd brought across. Me being in transit, en route to Canada I never had to pay duty.

Anyway I disposed of the grass appropriately. Good job I hadn't sold the jeep.

A Few Crucial Pointers

1. Never let Giles drive your vehicle.

2. Don't eat hallucinogenic plants. i.e., cactus and magic mushrooms – they are poisonous to your body. Don't do your head any good either. Same as LSD and ecstasy.

3. Don't carry illegal substances across borders, or at all.

4. Have a good four-wheel-drive vehicle doing a trip like ours.

5. Carry plenty of water in any desert region of the world.

6. Never let Giles start philosophizing to you about the teachings of Krishnamurti. He's read all his books and listened to all his tapes – really does one's head in!

Conclusion

A great trip was had with plenty of good times. A country I will definitely go back too. **Money was made**, without having to get up for work.

Jobs

The only jobs available that I heard of was teaching English in the cities or coastal resorts, as you're not going to make much money best to keep out of the heavily polluted cities. Living in Mexico City is the equivalent of smoking twenty-forty cigarettes per day.

Same story, all over teaching English if you're work through a school or college you're expected to be qualified, private lessons not so much of a problem.

Don't be tempted to smuggle dope as you can end up dead, and as I've stated before, one is a long time dead or if you're in a Mexican prison, you'll wish you were dead.

Note

If you have to choose between a Land Rover or a Toyota Land Cruiser for going off road, pick the Land Cruiser. They are far more robust and reliable. Your life could depend on it

The Lonely Planet covers Mexico.

Work Your Way around the World : by Susan Griffith. Has a Mexico chapter.

My get out clause – check out the internet.

CHAPTER 14
Women Travelling Alone

If you are going to travel through any of the third world or Islamic countries, you have to change your dress and western attitudes. It is no good getting on your high horse and preaching and ranting and raving about being pestered, abused, insulted and assaulted and then hopefully expecting western males to come to your rescue when you find yourself in an uncomfortable position.

In Britain the highest suicide rate amongst any one group of the population is Asian teenage girls. This is due to being brought up in a western society by parents who have their heads in their countries of origin, and who can't and won't come to terms with living in the decadent Western society with our freedoms and liberties and choices.

If you think life is hard and unfair – you're right. If you think you've got it tough, give a thought for the women of Saudi Arabia. They are totally oppressed by the male society, and are forbidden to go out alone. It is against the law for women to drive. They go their whole lives without meeting a male from outside their family. Their marriages are arranged, ideally to a cousin, and if they cannot sire male offspring, their husbands quite often take another wife or wives.

It is a sad sight to see veiled women in the burqa, totally engrossed in looking at glossy western woman's fashion magazines in book stores in the liberal Middle Eastern countries such a Bahrain, which I have witnessed whilst working in the Middle East after the Gulf War.

Here are a few excerpts I've copied from the *Rough Guide for Women Travellers*.

"All unmarried Moroccan men whom I spoke to about sex had their only experiences with prostitutes, apart from those who had been 'lucky' enough to meet tourists who would oblige them."

"No father would put his daughter at risk by letting her travel unless she was already worthless."

"Yemenis regard to modesty and chastity of their woman as paramount."

"White women, especially with fair hair, are the most hated, envied and desired of all. Any glance at the television screen makes it immediately obvious that white skin equals wealth and class in the Mexican popular imagination. Hence many Mexican men's desire to 'have' a white woman is matched by their secret (or sometimes not so secret) contempt. Mexican men can be both irritating and flattering. Men will ask outrageous questions about your sex life opening gambits like 'Tell me about free love in your country' are irritatingly common.

"In Morocco there are three kinds of women. I was often told 'Virgins, wives and whores'. It is as useful a proverb as any to keep in mind when you visit and start to understand the core of the country's culture – Islam and family." From the Rough Guide. For Muslim men there is no going out on the 'pull' on a Friday and Saturday night.

The Koran says that no man may touch the hand of a woman other than his mother or his wife. It is illegal to touch the hand of another woman, to see her face or even hear the sound of her voice. The Koran is clear. It says females are obliged to be covered, they must be kept at home and they must not work. That is their role. There can be no argument about this. The Koran also teaches that men and women should have equal opportunity – this has been bypassed by religious chauvinism. I myself have experienced great hospitality and generosity in the Muslim world, but it's all male orientated, you hardly ever see the women.

When I was in jail in Marrakesh, Morocco this chap I befriended told me about how he once had a girlfriend, and had sex with her and when her father found out he threw her out of the family home so she had to become a prostitute, and he was bragging about this to me.

In many Islamic countries you are not free to leave, as you have to obtain your husband's written approval. If you're not married then you have to have your father's permission or, the male head of the household.

Mandatory – in many Muslim countries the cloak, he-jab, burqa, tent-over-your head or whatever, it's called, inhibits vision and breathing. If you marry a Muslim, this can happen to you and it will be your own fault. Read *Not Without My Daughter* by Mahmoody & Hoffer before thinking of marrying a Muslim.

A sad sight in Bangkok to see the Arab women walking around under a tent, must be absolutely boiling underneath, meanwhile their men are walking around in tee-shirts and shorts. Talk about double standards.

An old Arab proverb, "A woman is for making babies, a boy is for pleasure."

Could all this be one of the reasons there is so much 'Rage' in the Muslim world, killing and slaughter, car bombs, suicide bombs shootings. It can't all be down to the West, Israel, George Bush and Tony Blair.

While I'm on the subject of Muslims, Syria has seldom been out of the news for the last few years. Yet when young British Muslims go and fight there, when they return they are charged, prosecuted, and in some cases jailed also lots of them are physically stopped from going. Yet how many British men and women went and fought in Spain on both sides in the 1930s? None of whom were charged or jailed, how many men went and fought in the Congo in the 60s? How many men went and fought in Angola in the 70s? How many men went to fight in Rhodesia in the 60s and 70s thousands of Brits went, myself included yet I was never charged, technically I committed treason as Rhodesia was a country then under British and world sanctions also many thousands of men went and fought for South Africa in the 60s, 70s and 80s. Also let's not forget about all the British Jewish men and women who go and do military service in Israel they never get charged. Maybe there's one law for them and one law for us!

On a lighter note

Heaven is an English policeman, a French cook, a German engineer, an Italian lover and everything organised by the Swiss. Hell is an English cook, a French engineer, a German policeman, a Swiss lover and everything organised by the Italians.

CHAPTER 15
Don't Upset the Powers That Be

Money will get you into any country and get you citizenship in any country. Usually, but not always so. The Al Fayhed brothers (who own Harrods in London, along with many other accumulated acquisitions through entrepreneurial business dealings) were originally from Egypt and have lived in the UK for more than forty years. Both of them have married British women and both of them have children born and bred in the UK. In 1995 they decided it was time they took out British citizenship as they have lived here so long and it was now their permanent home. Somewhere along the way to making their fortune they must have upset the almighty aristocracy, the powers that be, the true rulers of the land, because their application was denied and refused.

A few years earlier when Britain was struggling to put an Olympic team together, Zola Bud from South Africa was the new wonder woman of running. South Africa was then banned from fielding a team due to sporting sanctions that had been placed upon the country due to apartheid. What a golden opportunity for Britain! Here was a world great dying to run in the Olympics and even though she could hardly speak English, one of her grandparents had been British. That will do! Grab her before some other country does! Hey, presto – like magic, ten days later she is a British citizen with a brand new British passport. Zola has never lived in Britain except when she was running and now she lives at home in South Africa raising a family who are now also British citizens and are now entitled to live in Britain and so collect welfare benefits.

In 1999, the Portuguese colony of Macao was handed back to China. Portugal gave full Portuguese citizenship to the 100,000 plus Chinese citizens who were living in the colony. All of these then new Portuguese passport holders had automatically been given full right of abode in the UK, and access to the benefit system. This has come about by Portugal being one of the twenty eight EU members.

A Few Reasons to Hate Snakes

As a young lad growing up in a picture postcard village called Kemerton, which is five miles from beautiful Tewkesbury in Gloucestershire, every Springtime and early Summer, every weekend and school holidays were taken up by the pastime of 'birds nesting'. This hobby involved collecting an egg from each species of bird and then putting a tiny hole at each end and then blowing the egg yolk through the shell, (one of my Auntie's still has my collection to this day). Brilliant cliff and tree climbing skills were developed, which I'm sure in later life served me well for being a steel erector and other numerous types of jobs I've had which have involved climbing.

1. Being seven or eight years old, the water reeds, that I was walking through to try and get to a Moor hen's nest, were above my head. As I'm making my way to the water's edge, the ground is getting softer all the time. I took one more step and decided I had to start looking down at the ground so as not to sink in and get wet feet, or at worst get stuck in the mud. When I looked down, to my horror, there right in front of me stretched out with my foot only two inches maximum away from its tail, is an adder (European viper). If I'd trodden on that snake I probably would have been a child death, which happens periodically in Southern England. Luck was on my side, I made a hasty retreat, with my little heart pounding away.

2. Two years later, I'm in Hong Kong. I and my two buddies, Leslie and Denise, are in our den smoking a fag that one of us had acquired. As we were passing the cigarette around, a poisonous bamboo snake came slithering in through the entrance. It was probably more frightened than we were – we all made a rapid exit. We drew straws on who had to go back in and kill it with a stick, all macho stuff – guess who got the short straw!

3. Ten years later I'm in the rugged mountains of Morocco, fishing for trout. In an almost identical story to the first, I came inches away from treading on a North African viper. No heroics, just another quick exit.

4. Less than two years later I'm working in the cowsheds on a Kibbutz in Israel. We always had to look under the bottom row of stacked straw

bales as harmless big black mouse snakes used to look for mice and rats. On one of my days off, a Danish volunteer who was doing my job didn't look under the bottom row of bales and he was bitten by, not a harmless mouse snake, but a viper.

5. Four years later, I was working as a Cattle Ranch Manager in Rhodesia, now Zimbabwe. Every night l would go around checking that the windows and doors were locked. I would also place a gun, and whatever calibre ammunition it took, on a chair next to each window in case of a terrorist attack. When I went to the window that was in the verandah, as I reached out to release the brass locking latch to close it, I could see a movement around the catch. It's dark outside but fortunately it's a bright full moon. Instinctively I backed off and put the verandah light on. To my horror I see a poisonous African tiger snake wrapped around the latch. Without that full moon I would have been bitten. I killed that snake with a broom. I didn't get a wink of sleep that night, my heart was pounding like an African drum.

A few months later we put sunken logs in front of the windows. Supposedly to detonate rifle grenades, the downside though was the lack of light from the outside.

6. Six months later – same ranch. I had been drinking at the Lion and Elephant Hotel on the Bubye River, and when I came home I walked into the kitchen from the back yard. As I walked in half-pissed, there right in the middle of the floor was a fully erect cobra ready to strike. Unluckily for the cobra, I've got my seven shot shotgun in my hand. Bang! What a mess was made in the kitchen.

My South African boss had been bitten on the hand once by a black mamba and survived, and one of his brothers, while hunting in Botswana, (a classic quote I heard in Africa was 'White men go hunting, Black men go poaching') was bitten by a black mamba and he died.

I have heaps more snake stories, but I'd better stop now or else some snake lover will end up sending me a snake through the post. I also have plenty more stories about travelling. They will be in my next book.

Most of my days were spent dipping cattle. This is when farmers were most vulnerable for being ambushed. I would send two of my soldiers on patrol, when I was visiting the cattle dip. Usually they would find a shady tree and go to sleep. The other two, I would leave behind to guard the homestead.

Don't let snake stories put you off from travelling to exotic countries. Remember, most westerner's go their whole lives without seeing a snake in the wild. Probably half of all snake bites, maybe even more, occur because people antagonise the snake once they have seen it. Just leave it alone and walk away. Even looking at a snake from a safe distance can be dangerous. Cobra's spit venom and are deadly accurate up to fifteen feet or more, and if this venom hits your eyes, which they aim for, you'll have serious vision problems. Or if it hits an open cut or sore, venom can enter the blood stream. Black mambas are the fastest moving snakes, whenever I've seen one they move away like lightning. They can get disorientated and move at you and their venom is deadly toxic: if you get bitten it's usually curtains.

The World Health Organisation estimate 30-50,000 deaths per year from snake bites, worldwide. Much higher odds of getting shot in the USA on holiday.

BOY RECOVERING FROM SNAKE BITE

"A ten year-old boy who was bitten by a venomous adder in a park in Leicester is off the danger list at Leicester Royal Infirmary. While on a picnic with his mother, Samuel Kerr had tried to pick up the snake, which was basking in the sunshine." Leicester Mercury.

Leave snakes alone! Don't put hands in holes and wear boots or shoes in the bush.

The female mosquito kills way more people than all the other creatures on this earth put together. Over five thousand per day worldwide.

"Life must move forward, but it can only be understood backwards."

- Soren Kiekegaard

CHAPTER 16
Immigration and Over-Population

I have been at the receiving end of the Immigration's powers that be. It is not much fun when they alter your travelling plans, not to mention the money it costs you when you fall fowl of their wrath. I have heard horror stories. Even at the wealthy end of the travel market you can be inconvenienced, hassled and bullied. A friend of mine recently took a cruise ship holiday with his family out of Florida around the Caribbean Isles. Every stop was a pleasure and hassle free until they arrived at the American Virgin Isles. Everyone was searched and questioned when disembarking and same again when coming back aboard ship, only this time they were all kept standing around in the hot sun. You can imagine what the punters thought about this kind of treatment, especially when the kids started to play up and holler.

I have also entered the US through Florida. After taking one and a half hours to get to the front of the queue, this huge black immigration woman, who has probably only got the job through the affirmative action programme which was set up to advance women and minorities, (this law is way passed its 'sell by date' now and is not doing anybody any favours, it is just causing 'white male' resentment), takes one look at my port of entry card and says I've ticked one of the boxes incorrectly so go to the back of the queue and start again. I mean, how on earth can one be expected to have any respect for these power freaks. I learnt to fly in Florida once you can fly lots of opportunities to by pass customs and excise.

Taking the global picture into account I do see a need for strict immigration controls aimed at the third world to protect jobs and living standards in the West that we have worked hard to get and our forefathers fought for, not the western working traveller who is not duty bound to bring in all his/her extended family to the land of welfare, milk and honey, when they have made it. These controls should be enforced at the place of departure by the airlines. This would save a lot of heartache for the would be immigrant who gets turned away at his/her destination, not to mention the life savings needed in some cases to purchase the airline tickets in many cases. I cannot blame people for wanting to better themselves, to improve their lot, in some cases to get away from corrupt oppressive places.

This would only slow down the mass movement of the third world, as anyone who has been to Istanbul and witnessed the mass of people congregating from the Indian subcontinent, getting ready for their final leg of their journey into Europe. The same applies to Tijuana and Juarez in Mexico, where the Mexicans are getting ready for the dash across the Rio Grande River – hence the name 'wet back'.

Population

In the this century I see a major problem with the population explosion and everything that goes with it – global warming, de-forestation, polluted rivers and overused land. How will the planet cope when everyone in China and India owns a car and refrigerator? At the present time half of the world's population are either Chinese or people from the Indian subcontinent. China's population passed the 1 billion mark over twenty years ago and now at 1.4 billion, and this is with the one child per family law. When the communists finally relinquish power there will probably be a massive population explosion. Where will these people go? Already it is estimated that up to a third of the arable land is burnt out and overworked.

It is estimated that up to 100 million people within China are on the move looking for jobs in the cities from the land. They will migrate in every direction. Southern Siberia is already shown to be Chinese on the school geography text books. Siberia is relatively undefended and unpopulated.

Vladivostok in Siberia along with just about every other city in the world has a growing Chinese community. Tibet was gobbled by China in 1962, has lost most of its timber and now is rapidly losing its culture.

Every country in South East Asia has massive Chinese populations where they have little regard or respect for the wild animal populations of the world. The rarer the animal or reptile, the more it is in demand to be gobbled up for sexual aphrodisiac purposes. Any one who has seen the wildlife animal markets of Taipei, Bangkok and Manila will verify this, from drinking bile from the gall bladders of live imprisoned bears, to eating tiger's dicks and bones, rhino horns, rare bats, and carving up of elephant tusks and countless other rare exotic animals whose only purpose it seems is to be trapped, then tortured and then eaten by a Chinese man. When Viagra came along I thought this drug will save the rhino from extinction, guess what happened next, the crooks and gangsters started to mix crushed up Viagra with rhino horn, so this then proved without doubt that the rhino horn aphrodisiac really dose works, this in turn then creates more demand for the horn.

As the Chinese amass huge amounts of wealth through their running off the economies of SE Asia, the world's remaining wildlife will be under horrendous pressure in this century.

Joke: What has four legs that a Chinese person does not eat?
Answer: A table.

Nostradamus predicted a war to end all wars. A 'yellow race' would invade Europe and 'blood and corpses' would cover the land. The carnage would culminate in the year 1997 and seven months when from the sky will come the great king of terror. Predicted in the 1560. Could this be nuclear war? Hong Kong was handed back in the seventh month of 1997. (He got that one wrong.)

Indian Subcontinent

At least here wildlife is not under threat from being eaten, just from loss of habitat through over population and farming. India's population has now passed the 1.4 billion mark. Pakistan, Bangladesh and Sri Lanka add about another quarter of a billion people to the region.

I remember reading about a huge three metre cobra that came up from the sewers into the main business district of Calcutta. Cobras being the pet of the Hindu God, Shiva, are sacred, along with countless animals within mainly vegetarian India. The whole business district came to a standstill as people and traffic waited for the confused snake to find a suitable exit from its predicament. (Good job I wasn't there with my Rhodesian shotgun.)

In China there probably would have been a riot as everyone would have tried to devour the creature. I myself have a fear of poisonous snakes and shot plenty of them in Zimbabwe with my shotgun. Half a dozen or so of the ranch's calves died from snake bites in one year, about a dozen calves were taken by leopards.

India's population is set to double to two billion by 2033 rising at the present by 19 million a year. No wonder they want out and a better less crowded life in the West.

Indonesia

The fourth largest population of the world, was run by General Suharto and his family, who are now one of the wealthiest families in the world, and the Indonesian people are some of the poorest in the world. Australia has signed a defence 'non-aggression' pact with Indonesia. A worthless piece of paper. When the Indonesians have overpopulated their newly acquired territories that they took by force, Irian Jaya in 1964, East Timor in 1975, next will be Papua New Guinea and then their eyes will be on the sparsely populated Northern Territories and Queensland, Australia. Their northward expansion out of Borneo into Malaysia, Sarawak and Sabah was only halted by force by the British, New Zealanders, Australians and Gurkhas in the 1960s. How long would Queensland's Daintree Rain forest remain? It would be sold off to the Chinese or Japanese logging companies in no time at all and end up as hard wood concrete shuttering to be used once and then smashed up and burnt, like the rest of the tropical rain forests of South East Asia that the Japanese and Chinese have gobbled up like an out of control consuming monster.

The Japanese with a population of 120 million have less than 500 members of Greenpeace. They wouldn't stop forest destruction, any more than they can stop Japanese whaling and dolphin hunting (for scientific research).

Mass Migration: People on the Move

If, say, 3 million or so of India's 1.4 billion people were to have immigrated over a few years to, say, New Zealand, the effect on New Zealand's living standards and way of life would obviously be enormous, while the effect on India's low living standards would have been negligible.

An obvious example comes to mind – Fiji. Fiji was a democracy but the people voted along racial lines. The Indians had outbred the native Fijians, so they took over the country – not only the commerce and trade but the government as well. The native Fijians, who lacked the Indians entrepreneurial commercial skills, had traditionally joined the country's armed forces, so the only option open for them was to cancel the election and seize their country back of the immigrants from the barrel of a gun.

Vietnam's Boat People

Shortly after the communist victory and reunification of Vietnam a mass exodus of people started, as in all communist countries. People all over the world yearn to run their own lives, make their own decisions and go where they want and when they want within their own country. Communism must surely fail, just as apartheid in South Africa was doomed to failure. Systems of government without basic freedoms are bound to inevitable failure.

So, as the trickle of boats started to leave and the western democracies witnessed this tragic display of human bravery and endurance, they were queuing up to take these heroic people in. As soon as this became known back in Vietnam and Cambodia, the trickle rapidly became a flood of humanity, many of them were not persecuted at all back home many of them now were economic refugees jumping on the bandwagon to escape poverty. While this was happening, what were the prosperous countries in the region doing about this, with their incredible industrial growth rates, the dynamic economical miracles of this part of the world with tremendous resources of wealth. Japan – wealthy beyond imagination; South Korea and Taiwan – incredibly prosperous; Singapore – the Switzerland of South East Asia; what did they do? Nothing. How many people did they take? None. Thailand – what did they do? Thai pirates robbed, raped and murdered them in droves. Malaysia towed them back out to sea, the same with Indonesia – sent them on their way to Australia. The latter arrivals to Australia were processed in Port Headland, Western Australia, where they had to wait for three years before being admitted. This then became a benchmark, where new arrivals headed for. This has finally been stopped. What did the Middle Eastern Arab oil Gulf States do? Nothing. How many did they take with their phenomenal amounts of money? None. Hong Kong was also a destination as then it was British controlled, which meant fair play and civilised behaviour even though there was little or no room for them.

So where did they all go, as their Asian brethren had no time or place for them? They all went to the western world democracies – USA, Canada,

Australia, New Zealand and Europe. Britain took in 20,000 – as if we had plenty of jobs, houses and school places to go around.

When I was in Canada I tried to immigrate there. I had three companies prepared to sponsor me into the country. I fitted in like a hand in a glove. My application was turned down (my trade was not on the 'list'). In that one year Canada admitted 50,000 Vietnamese boat people. How do you think I feel? When you are in Canada today, all one reads about is the Vietnamese and Chinese Triad gang wars that are going on.

I've become very cynical, and I have reached the conclusion that the European races have incredible guilt complexes regarding other races from the third world, that they then play on to their advantage. With the western world's sperm count going down and down, we will probably become minorities within our own countries in the not so distant future.

League of Nations – Forerunner Of Today's United Nations

Shortly after World War II all the democratic nations of the world agreed to take in persecuted political asylum seekers from the tyrannical states that were around, and in a lot of cases are still around today. A very humanitarian gesture. Britain in the early 50s was accepting political asylum seekers who arrived on our shores, on average about 3000 per year. In many cases the asylum seekers had been tortured and were destitute. Now this has become a well organised criminal racket with up to 50,000 plus per year coming in, not to mention all the regular immigrants from extended families that come in every year.

Many of these people who come in and claim asylum have paid a lot of money to go on courses back in their countries of origin, just as I've paid to go to taxi cab training school in Sydney, flight training in Florida and welding school in Vancouver. Prime examples are Congo, Nigeria, Pakistan, Somalia, and Sri Lanka. They are taught what to say on arrival, how to claim benefits and housing, how to get one's case put back with the overstretched authorities dealing with them – basically how to get in and stay. The Chinese can always claim to be persecuted because they want more than one child, although most of them head for the USA. Cases of tankers running aground and illegals pouring over the sides to lose themselves within the nearest Chinatown have happened in the USA. All this going on is extremely unfair for the genuine political asylum seekers, who in some cases end up getting sent back to unspeakable atrocities.

Much of this lust for the West must be put down to the fact that nearly every village in the world now has a TV, DVD, or video run off generator electricity where they see the 'good' life to be had in the West which beckons them. Hollywood and Bollywood have a lot to answer for!

Sri Lanka

Over the last thirty years or so Sri Lanka has seldom been out of the news. Atrocities and civil war had been going on with no end in sight until the Tamil Tigers finally surrendered. The Tamils are not the original inhabitants of Sri Lanka (formerly known as Ceylon when it was peaceful under British rule). The Tamils are immigrants to the Island and were fighting a vicious civil war to get half of the Isle for their own state. Many thousands upon thousands of Tamils came to Britain claiming political asylum.

Ask yourself – Why do they want to settle in cold, damp, dark, overcrowded miserable Britain? When fifty miles away across the sea from Sri Lanka there is a state in India called Tamil Nadu which is half as large again as the whole Isle of Sri Lanka. Where the people are Tamils, where they speak Tamil, where they have the same religion – a tropical paradise with golden beaches with coconut palm trees stretching for 500 miles. This is where they originated from with no cultural barriers at all, with peace and no war, and political power. So why did they want to come to Britain?

Could it be, dare I say it, that we have a welfare state?

CV gets tourist barred from UK

When Mr Ben Coleman visited London he saw no double-decker buses and no Buckingham Palace. Instead, he spent five hours in a room at Heathrow Airport and was then deported on the next flight back to Australia. Mr Coleman, twenty-nine, had planned to backpack around Europe with his girlfriend and had sufficient money. Not checking his bank account, British officials thought his ten month return ticket was suspicious. Then they found a **resume** in his bag and concluded that he planned to work illegally in Britain. Mr Coleman, from Melbourne, had his resume with him because he had a job interview just before he left on March 22. He also needed written references if he were to get a temporary flat in London.

The Australian High Commission told him, he said, that Sundays were a bad day for immigration officials at Heathrow and if it had been any other day, he would have been let into the country. For Mr Coleman, it was a very expensive five hours in Britain. He wasted $2000 on his ticket and had to endure back-to-back international flights. The officials did give him the option of flying to the United States. Mr Coleman tried two airlines unsuccessfully but could not call any other US airline because he ran out of British currency, and officials would not give him change for the telephone. In the meantime, they had booked him a Qantas flight back to Australia. He called the Australian High Commission but it could do little for him.

Mrs Anna Bolger from Lonely Planet, publishers of travel guide books, said that the British Government had made its immigration regulations stricter in 1994, and was vigilantly enforcing them. "If you had a **resume** in your bag they would immediately be suspicious of you." Sydney Morning Herald. (So much for kith and kin.)

Remember – what I've said about carrying CVs or written job offers. Post them to poste restante or to a friend, or to follow on when you have an address. Carry no overalls, steel toe-capped boots or tools, unless you've a valid work visa. Watch out for incriminating evidence in your address book.

Remember – Immigration officials are heartless and ruthless with no compassion. They are out to get you. They have to make productivity quotas. They are the enemy. They are the same breed of monster all over the world. (A uniform and power).

Remember – you are a travelling tourist, you are not going to work, not even unpaid voluntary work.

I know, first hand, how Ben now feels – anger, frustration, disappointment and hatred. His plans are in ruins. He also now has a file with immigration on computer, like myself, in the USA. He, also like myself, had done nothing wrong. Don't let this happen to you! When it happened to me, I decided to write a book.

If any of you have hassles with these power freaks, write in and hopefully we can fight back with the pen. Someone once said that the pen is mightier than the sword.

"No beast is more savage than man when possessed with power answerable to his rage."

- Plutarch

My Story:

"Dear Sir or Madam,

As a regular tourist to your beautiful country, I would like to recount my recent experience with the US Immigration Service.

When I set off for a well-earned ten day skiing holiday to the USA, the last thing I expected was to be refused entry and sent back on the next plane! On 13 January 1994, having just completed an exhausting ten hour flight, I was subjected to a random spot check on arrival at Minneapolis airport, where I was cross-examined about my past by three armed immigration officers. When, in good faith, I told them about a minor previous conviction for possessing cannabis in 1973 (the same year that ex-President Clinton admitted smoking dope at Oxford University!) I was made to feel like a common criminal, photographed, finger printed and marched on to the next plane back to London.

My friends, who had not seen me for over a year, had driven for three hours to get to Denver airport to meet me, Denver was to be my next stop after Minneapolis.

What had I done that was so wrong? I was not a threat to anybody – I just wanted to see my friends again and have another skiing holiday, I would also have been spending several thousand dollars on goods and services whilst in the country.

To make matters worse I'd just returned from a two week skiing trip to Lake Tahoe, California,

I'd been back in London for five days putting my job on hold as I was having a 'down time'. This is what must have triggered alarm bells, they probably thought that I'd got myself a job lined up on the first trip and then gone back home to sort things out for a move back to take up employment, but this was not so I was living and working in London and into my skiing (for all you ski buffs Lake Taho is crap).

I wonder how many other people entering the USA have had a similar experience? Do such incidents make the Immigration Department proud? Do they use ceases like mine to help fill politically inspired quotas, so they can request extra taxpayers money to 'protect' Americans from people such as myself?

The hypocrisy of this is evident when two weeks after I was expelled, Jerry Adams, spokesman for the Provisional IRA, an organisation responsible for the murder of thousands of innocent people, was given a VIP welcome to the country. The 'special feeling' I once had for America is now dead. Yours sincerely, R Lloyd."

My letter was published by the New York Times in a weekend edition, May 94. They missed out the paragraph about President Bill and President Jerry.

On the plane back I was put in the smoking section, consequently picking up a throat infection that made me bedridden for a week. If ever I saw one of those immigration monsters drowning, I'd throw them a lead weight. All my life dealing with these people if only I'd kept my mouth shut, the one time I didn't, this is what happened. So be warned and be prepared.

Since this happened to me, I've been told that if ever they refuse you entry, stay put, you are within your rights to demand to see a state appointed lawyer.

Now though since the George Bush passed the Patriot Act you have zero rights, they could even send you to Guantanamo Bay detention centre and water board you to find out your intentions about America.

Canadian lawyers advise their clients who come to them concerned about what to put on

immigration forms for visiting the US, if they have a conviction for drug possession. The **advice** they give is admit to nothing put nothing down in writing because if you admit to anything they will not let you in and you will be blacklisted, so really it gives you no choice if you want to enter you lie if you tell the truth you don't get in, as simple as that.

Under the US justice system every conviction don't matter how minor stays with you forever until you're dead, hence the ever expanding growth rate of prisons. They are like a bull dog with a bone.

A different type of farm work

Five years later my buddy Big Belfast Bill the enforcer had moved into the indoor cannabis growing business in Vancouver, Canada, his first crop was so big that he needed a worker to help out for the harvesting, as his partner Finn who owned the barn was too busy with his daytime job to help out plus the fact that he was freaking out every time he came to the barn and saw just how huge the operation was. Being as the location was top secret, Bill needed someone who was hard working, reliable and trustworthy and an outsider, for security reasons, the call went out.

Being that I was available and I hadn't been back to Canada for a few years I was up for it, a working paid holiday not just cropping the plants but running repairs on the old barn had to be done to keep the rain out away for the electricity.

Vancouver now was known to many as 'Vancouverdam' after Amsterdam. Marijuana had become one of the top cash producing industries of British Columbia, Vancouver alone had over thirty 'grow shops' in the Yellow Pages. The Americans did not like this at all as most of the crop was going south of the boarder vie the courtesy of the Hells Angles who controlled the export market.

The only answer make it legal and then you get taxes and the criminals are taken out of the equation. Selling this idea to most politicians is like selling alcohol to the Saudi's. Finely the politicians of Colorado and Washington State have woken up and seen the light, about time to.

After the crop was picked, sorted, weighed and sold. I figured it was time to go and pay my buddy Pete a visit in Los Angeles. Now I needed a visa to enter the US, after that skiing fiasco five years earlier. To get this, one has to phone up for an appointment at their consulate in Vancouver no walking in off the street allowed. Phone calls were then charged at **$4 per minute** probably more now you are then put on hold for at least twenty minutes then you get to speak to someone.

When I had my interview I was told to go back to London to get a visa, what a load of nonsense anyway only one thing for it enter without a visa. Before I crossed over I checked out the crossing point, I'd been through this crossing many times before when I lived in Vancouver, we sometimes went to Mt Baker Washington for skiing if Mt Whistler was blanked by mist which happens a lot so Mt Baker was always our second choice.

The houses of the southern suburbs of Vancouver go right up to the border meeting the houses on the other side in Blaine Washington.

I parked my classic car a 1978 Oldsmobile Tornado that I'd bought, in a side street and walked across empty handed through the suburbs and went and had lunch in a local diner, after which I came back to Vancouver the way I'd come, (easy to cross like between two civilized European countries).

The next day myself and Bill drove down, I got out and walked across and Bill drove my car across as he's a Canadian he just sailed through, we meet up in the same restaurant that I'd been in the day before after lunch we said our goodbyes and he walked back also empty handed so not to look suspicious the way I'd gone the day before to pick up his car that was parked up.

Now I've heard that since 11 September 2001 they monitor the place like a hawk.

A week later I'm in LA having a beer and reminiscing about old times with Pete. Winter time and springtime in LA has a wonderful climate no wonder all the British actors, footballers and rock stars have mansions here. Two months later after commuting between Las Vegas and LA meeting up with Giles and other ex- travelling, working buddies, I'm living off my share of the farming enterprise so no need to work for a while yet. (Work the curse of the leisure class.) I get a phone call from London telling me that the tenants are moving out of my house, as I'd sacked the managing agent before I'd left, because he was hopeless. Nothing for it I'd have to go back to London to sort out new tenants. My house in London is my major asset so there's no way I'm losing it, repairs have to be done and mortgage payments have to be made. So with a sad heart I leave LA.

This had been my second stint in LA the first had been after the Mexican trip, I'd had quite a few women's address and phone numbers back then that I'd accumulated in the resort towns of Mazatian and Puerto Vallarta, I'd just had to say hello to them all on my way back to Canada.

Anyway I'm back on my way driving my wonderful car, it had power everything brilliant, even Jeremy Clarkson would have liked this car. I head over to Vegas for the last time, then head northwards on up through the Yellowstone National Park in Wyoming. Now the park in the summer time has traffic jams, unbelievable the wilderness with traffic bumper to bumper traffic.

Fifteen years earlier on my way to Mexico in my Toyota Land-Cruiser I'd driven through the park in October and I swear I was only vehicle in the park what a difference seasons can make. Although to me Jackson Hole the main town/resort of the area, I preferred the place on my first visit, then you had cowboy country music type bars with country and western singers who would play requests, you know the type of music I mean 'John Denver' *Take me home country road*, 'Gordon Lightfoot', 'Jimmy Buffet' and other great artists songs were sung. Anyway all those bars had all gone to be replaced by mega expensive restaurants catering for all the billionaire new inhabitants, the billionaires had now pushed out the millionaires. The town was still really nice to look at, but it didn't seem to have the atmosphere of before. Reminds me of a Joni Mitchell song, *We've found paradise so let's build an airport,* which has happened, one of the most spectacular places in the world surrounded by the Grand Teton mountain range, the Americans being so generous they have to share it with everybody. I wonder what Jim Bridger and the early mountain men would think if they could see the fruits of their exploring, they lived in a great time providing you could stay alive that is. I'd loved to have gone on the Lewis and Clark expedition of 1803, that was a real adventure.

A couple of days later I'm just out of the park heading towards Bozeman Montana as I go round a very sharp corner the fruit juice bottle that was on my passenger seat rolled off and fell onto the floor, as the bottle rolled I made a grab for it and missed, by doing this action I had a little swerve, nothing to write home about, just then a car overtakes me and the driver gives me a really strange look, oh well no big deal.

Twenty miles up the highway there's a cop waiting for me, he pulls me over the usual TV stuff, pulls you from behind stay in your car put your hands on the wheel. When he's ready he approaches me and says have you been drinking alcohol, the car that had over taken me just after the bend had reported me as a drunk driver, what a god dam jerk that guy must have been to do a thing like that to a fellow driver on a road with next to no traffic, if any of you are wondering I hadn't had a drink not alcohol only juice.

This cop tells me later he used to be an immigration officer and now he's a cop, one government department to another. As I've still got BC number plates on the car he wants to see all my documents passport, driving licence the works. At one time the cops wouldn't bother checking you out on your legal status but now all over the western world they checking people out, for their immigrant status once you've been pulled.

Well sods law this is all I need right now, I'm going to be in Canada in two days time. He quickly works out that I'm in the country illegally. I'm arrested I get ordered to put my stuff, two small bags in the boot of his car the remainder of my stuff is going to stay in the boot of my car, which he tells me will be picked up by a local towing company, leave the keys in the car, and a sticker is put on the car, to let other people know that this car is impounded not to be touched.

I'm handcuffed hands behind my back really uncomfortable, he's radioed ahead so I can be handed over to the immigration department about an hour later we rendezvous with two immigration guys. En route to a local lock up one of the guys tells me I was really unlucky to be picked by an ex-immigration guy as a regular cop would have just let me go as I hadn't done anything wrong (some consolation that was).

We make two stops en route for a break and refreshments the first place is a garage/store in the middle of nowhere, now I have a new set of cuffs on, not handcuffs but shackles they go around your ankles round your waist and around your wrists. These guys decided I wasn't a risk so they took off the shackles so I could go in with them for a drink, I wonder why I'd lost my appetite to eat. The next stop was an hour or so later, I needed a pee break, this place was a tourist rest centre with tables, chairs and barbecue pits with loads of families around so now I'm fully chained up again (just in case). So now I'm escorted through the multitude of bystanders who are grabbing their children to keep them out of harm's way, everyone is now looking at me because the two chaps are in suits and ties not uniforms and the car is unmarked everyone must have thought that I must have been a hardened, dangerous criminal and they must be FBI talk about embarrassing! The Yanks always have to go right over the top with everything.

We reached our destination, a small town in the middle of nowhere, they've decided to drop me off here as it's now night time, I guess it was getting too late to process me and they had homes to go to. This jail had only one cop officer and two cells with an interconnecting walkway between the cells, I was put in one cell and in the other were two Mexican cowboys not criminals just illegal workers, the cell doors were left open until night time, the walkway door leading to the cops office was kept locked.

Next morning the breakfast came I still couldn't eat anything so I gave my food to the one of the cowboys who spoke English. About mid-morning the younger of the two immigration guys came and picked me up in the same unmarked car, this time I was not shackled only handcuffed, hands behind back, much more uncomfortable than having hands cuffed in front.

We drive for about an hour to the town of Helena, here I'm put into a caged room inside the main office. Regular office work is going on, one of the office female workers came over and offered me coffee and magazines to read, also offered me the office standard food in America doughnuts. I took the coffee and, magazines but declined the doughnuts the cuffs had been taken off by now. Now they are doing a full check on me they phone my buddy Pete to let him know what's going on as I'm allowed to contact close friends and or relatives, as the immigration guys desk is right next to me, the other side of the bars, I could hear Pete pleading with them to let me go, to no avail. He then has a long conversation with the immigration department in Vancouver and also Sydney Australia, I reckon I'd made this guys week he must have thought he'd captured Carlos the Jackal or somebody of that stature.

The middle of the afternoon I'm taken into one of the senior guys office no handcuffs now, here they offer me a deal I guess they think I'm very vulnerable now to suggestions now after my ordeal. The deal is we take you to the airport and you pay for a flight to London, which would have involved a few connecting flights (not Vancouver because you're not Canadian) but you'll still be marked down as being deported, which means you can only apply for a visa if you want to come back after ten years, well I must admit I was tempted, or you go through the court system where you'll probably get deported anyway but you'll be able to leave under you own steam, meaning I'll be able to pick up my car and my things and drive back up to Vancouver, and I have a return ticket from Canada to London.

Anyway I chose the second option, I know my house is empty and I have to get back to sort it out, well I'll get Pete or Giles to phone the neighbours and tell them I'm temporarily unavailable and hopefully they'll keep an eye on the place, which the neighbours did for me.

So now I and the immigration guy set off once again, now he's getting comfortable around his captured desperado so leaves of the cuffs. Now we're heading for Butte Montana, the journey is going to take a couple of hours so we're chatting away, he's really surprised with my knowledge of the history of the Old West, as we're travelling along he's dropping hints about how him and his wife are due a holiday in a few months and as I'll be in

London by then, and as neither of them have been to Europe before London would be a great spring board for travelling around Europe especially if they had a place to stay. Well I'm almost speechless, I guess he'd been taking stock of the travelling he'd done in his life and then compared it with what he had found out about my travelling jaunts. Pete had filled him in on my humanitarian work I'd carried out in Africa!

This was an amazing turnaround the day before when I was handed over to this guy and his partner he gave me so much verbal abuse it was embarrassing. Anyway needless to say the offer wasn't forthcoming on my part, if he hadn't gave me the verbal abuse maybe as he would have been a challenge for me to try and teach him the errors of his ways.

The next holding cell I'm in there one night, this place only has one other prisoner, I meet him in the morning in the exercise yard we start playing one on one basket ball after which we start chatting, he's really despondent as he's just been sentenced and is waiting for a jail placement. I ask him what he's done and he tells me he had a marijuana grow operation and his cousin turned him in because he'd refused to pay him any more blackmail money which he'd been paying him.

He thought his cousin was bluffing being as he was family an all. Well he'd received a prison sentence of ten years with a $40,000 fine and his boat and truck to be confiscated, his lawyer did some plea bargaining and got the sentence reduced to five and five which is if you keep a clean record inside for five years they then give you five years parole, when you're released on parole you have to report in once a week and you're not allowed to go in a bar or leave the state. This is why the prisons are overcrowded and the percentage of Americans in prison is so high.

When he told me how big his operation was it was a quarter of the size that my mate Bill had.

I just didn't have the heart to tell him about what was going on up in British Columbia, in Vancouver people with grow operations who got busted were getting fines some confiscations of assists and confiscation of equipment plus your plants destroyed, very seldom jail time at least not for first offence. Even the electricity companies ran ads in the papers stating that they **do not** pass on electricity consumption details to any government departments, this was an attempt to stop people stealing electricity. My heart went out for this guy.

Later on an immigration bus arrived to pick me up, the shackles were back on now. Inside were my two Mexican companions and about a dozen other Mexicans. Over the remainder of the day we headed to Blackfoot in Idaho State picking up more unfortunate illegal Mexicans en route.

Blackfoot prison seemed like an open prison to me it was a mixed sex prison I didn't know there was such a thing but in the main recreation room men and women mixed, one of the women was assigned to wash and iron my clothes for me which I thought was most civilized. The major gripe I had was that when I was being processed I was put inside a single man type cage, not even enough room to swing a cat I was kept in here about two to three hours with nothing to read, most degrading.

Sleeping arrangements were we illegals had floor mattress inside the gymnasium there must have been about 80-100 of us by now. The next day we were all shackled and herded onto buses that then proceeded onto Boise the state capital, here we were driven right onto the city airport runway where we had to shuffle along onto a propeller type plane, as we were shuffling along this burly immigration guy tells me to get a move on and shuffle along like the rest of the unfortunates, where upon I lost my cool and told him in not so many choice words what he should do. He didn't like what I had to say fortunately for me nothing came of it. I was a bit put out to see that one of the unfortunates was a little old lady who must have been about seventy and could hardly walk.

Once on the plane still shackled we settled in for the flight all the seats had to remain upright there were twelve immigration guards all of them built like Arnold Schwarzenegger just like Con Air the prison escape film. What this is costing the American tax payer who knows?

The chap I'm sitting next to is twenty-four years old, we get talking and he tells me what's happening, we're going to El Paso Texas where we'll be sent over the border to Mexico. He tells me he and most of the offers will try and come straight back (a revolving door). As we get chatting I ask him, "How did you get into this mess and how long have you been here as you sound just like an American?" He tells me that he came here when he was four years old, I said, "What? Aren't you an American?"

He says, "I thought I was an American," it wasn't until he got into trouble with the law that he found out that he hadn't been naturalized so now he was being deported as an undesirable alien.

En route we're told we're making a stop in Denver Colorado where three of us will depart for processing again. I'm one of the three the other two are an Argentine and another South American.

From Denver airport we're picked up and taken to Wackenhut Corrections Immigration Processing Centre, Aurora about twenty miles from Denver, here I'm to be processed once again. After processing I'm put into one of the four dormitories each dormitory has between forty and sixty inmates one of the four dorms is for criminal illegals in each dorm there is a twenty-four hour full time warden and ceiling mounted surveillance cameras to keep an eye on everything, make sure no one dies either from fighting or suicide as this would not go down well with family and friends on the outside also makes bad press as there is a lot of controversy of the treatment of illegals in America, don't forget apart from the Native Indians every one is an immigrant some more recent than others.

In the dorm there is an open area with six tables and chairs at each end of the room there is a wall mounted television one for the Spanish speakers and one for the English speakers, the ten days I'm in here we never had more than about eight of us around the English table plus the warden would always sit with us being as they all had English as a first language daily newspapers and magazines in both languages were brought in.

Of all the English speakers none of them apart from me had English as their mother tongue, they were from all over a very diverse lot as far a field as the Philippines, Sri Lanka, China, and Ghana. The Ghanaian chap whose name was Okyia wasn't holding up very well mentally he'd been inside about three months he couldn't get anyone to post bail for him and his court hearing kept getting postponed as you cannot post your own bail I spent a lot of time with him over the next ten days, the reward I got for this was that one of the wardens told me since I'd been in there his mental state had defiantly improved. Okyia was a religious nut so I kept talking to him about Jesus and his trials and tribulations, I never told him that Jesus was a man only as there is no such thing as god. Okyia had fallen for the immigration ruse of, they phone you up, they have your details they then convince you to come into one of their offices so they can upgrade your status with a green card as your doing such valuable work etc. Okyia was a mental health nurse and they were in short supply being as he was a mental health nurse (quite ironic) this is why he didn't want any medication from the prison pharmacy.

This method of entrapment saves them time and money I've heard of this ruse being used in Australia as well, so if any of you get the phone call it's time to change your job, phone number and address until they move on to a new victim, they are not going to spend heaps of time and money on you unless you've gone down the criminal pathway.

Okyia had been advised by his lawyer that was provide by his hospital that he worked for to try and claim political asylum, but he would not go down that route being as the President of Ghana at that time was Flight Lieutenant Gerry Rawlings, who he greatly admired for getting Ghana out of a terrible mess caused by African corruption that is everywhere on the sub continent, I've witnessed it myself.

Now the chap from Sri Lanka, he was trying to claim political asylum, he was making out that he'd was a persecuted Tamil, I guess he was hoping to fool the authorities as I knew straight away that he was a Sinhaless no way was he a Tamil as the Tamils are almost black and he was fair like the Sinhaless are. Everything about him was a story, he was still in there when I left, maybe he succeeded in getting to stay.

If one wanted to you could work in the kitchen and get paid a $1 per day, I opted to read and watch TV, everyday six people in the dorm on a rooter system were designated to be on cleaning up the room, tables, toilets and showers detail.

When it came to my turn I refused to be on a work detail where upon I was taken to the main office to explain myself, looking back I guess I was having a rebellious tantrum. (They are probably laughing to this day still every time they have a beer together.) I stated that I was a political prisoner so I did not have to work as only common criminals had to work. I thought what are they going to do, throw me in jail! I was already in jail. To my surprise the officer just said all right then and left it at that.

Being as I'd had my great victory the next day I made one of the work detail guys stand down and I went back into the work roster. I did not want to be seen by the other guys as a shirker, as I was accepted by them all because I was the Gringo who played football with them in the exercise yard.

Each day we'd have an hour's exercise each dorm would rotate with one another you never knew what time the exercise hour would come around as it was changed every day I guess to stop planned escapes. In the exercise yard there was basketball, weights and football or you could do nothing or you could go to the prison library.

Okyia would stay in the dorm and kneel next to his bed and read his bible 'in peace'.

On my third day in there I got him out and got him to play basket ball, I reckon this is what helped turn his mental state around. The football was great, myself and Hocho, who was my new found Mexican friend who spoke great English, would be on opposite sides both being a bit older than the rest of the guys we naturally became the 'midfield generals'. The day I left I was in the middle of a football game when they came for me to be released, I asked if I could finish the game first, Americans being sticklers for the rules said no.

Hocho also had a hard luck story. He'd been in the US just under nine years when he was caught. When he came to the US with his wife they worked three jobs each to enable them to buy a house. He'd just missed the seven year rule, which was if you kept yourself clean of any misdemeanour's and paid your taxes for seven years with proof you could get a green card he had just missed it by three months because it was raised to nine years and three months before the nine years was up he got turned in. His wife and kids had already moved back down to Mexico, he was going to met them in Cancun a resort town in the Yucation peninsular, where he was from and there he was going to open up a restaurant with proceeds from his Denver house sale at least his kids were now American, being as they were born there.

About on the fifth or sixth day the exercise time came round really early about 9.a.m, being as I hadn't had a shower or shave yet, as there were only about six mirrors and showers in the place so you had to take turns for use of the mirrors. First thing in the morning you were given a disposable razor to be handed back after use. I thought, no bother I'll just put the razor in my locker trunk that was placed under my bed to be retrieved and used it after the exercise hour has finished. On the way out everyone is dropping their razors in the razor collection bucket, I thought nothing of it. Where upon when we returned to the dorm the place had been turned upside down by the wardens, everyone thought that they were just having a 'shake' down.

Of course when I looked for my razor it had been found and was gone I'm thinking, 'Oh bloody hell what bull shit is going to happen to me now.' Anyway nothing! Nothing said and nothing happened, I mean they know it was me who had kept the missing razor as it was under my designated bed.

Anyway near the end of my stay at the expense of the hard working never complaining put upon American taxpayer, I'm having an evening conversation with one of the wardens, we've got to know each other quite well by now as we've had many interesting conversations over the last week or so, which I did with all of them, they were in a different 'mould' to your average cop or immigration guy.

He says to me, "You seem like a really interesting level headed guy to me."

To which I reply, "Thanks."

Then he says, "I shouldn't really tell you this but you've been on suicide watch ever since you've been in here."

I says, "What!" And laughed.

Of course now it's all starting to fall in place. Nothing was said when I refused to be on the work detail and nothing was said after the razor blade escapade, they (someone) thinks I'm unhinged. I then start to question the chap on how did this decision come about that I was to be placed on suicide watch.

Apparently when I was being processed once again, this time by the detention centre nurse who was giving me a medical questionnaire. This they do to see what, and if you need any drugs i.e. for gout, high blood pressure, diabetics etc. We're chatting away, which is nice as I haven't spoken to a female since I was processed in that office in Helena. She tells me she's been to England quite a few times as her husband is English, well this is all good natured and she seems to be very amicable with a sense of humour, well one the last questions was have you ever had any suicidal tendencies, which I replied, no not until I got in here, British sense of humour! She must have been covering herself by ticking the 'yes' box.

In the dorm we had a phone box for use with prison phone cards which we had to buy with our own money, on Fridays the phones were switched off due to that was the day that inmates were shipped out to by aeroplane to El Paso and they did not want last minute hurdles with lawyers and such phoning up disrupting the process when I told my lawyer about this she was very interested as they were probably breaking some human rights of sorts.

I'd sorted myself out with a local lawyer Lichter Korkin and Associates, they took a retainer of $1,200 off my credit card then they organized my bail which was set at $2,000, set very low as I was considered a low flight risk. As I said earlier you cannot put up your own money so four of my friends on the outside guaranteed bail for me Giles, Pete, Lane and Bill $500 each.

When I'm in the governor's office for my final processing after saying my goodbyes, I comment to the governor what dose OTM stand for at the top of one of the blackboard columns that has every ones name on written in chalk he tells me it stands for Other Than Mexican, at the time I thought it quite funny.

Finally after ten days I was out with a court date set for six weeks time.

Giles in the meantime had arranged for me to stay with his friend Bob and his wife Jane and two teenage boys Bobby and John plus Biff the dog. I knew Bob from when I'd been working in Denver a few years earlier he'd been a bit of a wild character then to say the least, so I figured we'll get on just fine which we did and I'll be ever grateful for the generous hospitality they all showed me in the coming weeks. I'm now outside the building sitting on the grass waiting for Bob to arrive. I'm glad to be out even if I did have to cut my last football game short. Bob picks me up and I start telling about what's been happening, then he tells me one of his recent escapades.

Bob's Story – briefly

Bob seeing me waiting sitting on the grass he tells me what happened to him a couple of years earlier, he'd just completed a thirty day prison sentence for drunk driving, no accident involved just, failing a breathalyser test. He's waiting outside the prison for his wife Jane to pick him up, sitting on the grass enjoying his freedom in the sunshine. He's been there about ten minutes when outcome the cop prison guards who have now strapped on their guns, as when they are on the inside they do not carry them in case an inmate gets hold of one. Bob is rearrested and charged with loitering with intent. They pointed out that there are signs clearly stating no loitering, Bob hadn't seen these signs as they are all positioned at the edge of the grass embankment facing out onto the road. To no avail Bob is rearrested, when he goes to court after having to pay more lawyer's fees, he's then hit with a heavy fine and more hours added to his already community service order, his lawyer with a bit of plea bargaining got the fine reduced a bit and the hours on his community service order was reduced a bit also. Needless to say Bob doesn't have much time for the overzealous, overbearing rule of law, some people would say a police state.

After a few days of recuperating from my ordeal, Bob drops me off at the down town bus station so as I can go up to Montana to retrieve my dearly beloved car. When I get to the car pound, the car is there undamaged and the proprietor's bill was only about $170. I'm sure if this had been a car pound in 'rip off' Britain the bill would have been astronomical.

I check inside the glove compartment and the book that I slipped in there as I was being arrested was still there, inside I had slipped my California driving licence and my social security card, the arresting officer had flicked the pages of the book while searching me and my belongings but I had jammed the cards against the spine of the book he missed them as they did not fall out. As I'd been driving a Canadian registered car I'd given him my British Columbian driving licence. All North American licences weather the US or Canada are only valid for five years. I've picked up driving licences from loads of countries on my travels. Then to top it all off the car started first time, brilliant I'm now back on the road in the summer time in the beautiful state of Montana.

I spend about a week in Montana staying in hostels and backpacker guest houses, courtesy of *Jim's Backpacker's Bible* by Jim Cordova this is the second plug I've given this book, well worth buying can save you heaps of money on accommodation bills.

Everyone who goes to Montana must check out the Little Bighorn Battlefield, Custer's last stand, I won't go into the history of the battle as everyone has seen a Hollywood film about this, there has been over hundred films made about this battle, Errol Flynn was there so was Dustin Hoffman and my personal hero Sir Harry Flashman he was there and he got away the lone survivor!

An Englishman at that.

Once back in Denver I went out to Aurora, the detention centre, to give some magazines and my phone card that still had credit on it to Okyia, (they said that the phone cards worked on the outside but they didn't) but he had finally been shipped out to where I don't know as they wouldn't tell me, my other good friend Ocho had been shipped out before I left. I passed on the magazines and phone card to a woman that was in the reception waiting to see her loved one.

A few days later I then drive down to see Giles who's now living in El Paso Texas. After a week with Giles it's time to set off back to Denver for my court hearing. Thirty miles in from El Pasco on all roads leading out of the city away from the border of Mexico there are immigration check points, they don't stop you on the way in but on the way out they do, me having BC plates was an open invitation to be pulled and processed once again, I'm now starting to feel like a piece of processed meat, these people are unreal —talk about the land of the free.

Anyway the court day, my hearing to be deported has finally arrived, the lawyer has assured me that I'll shortly be on my way, I'm taking no chances I tell Bob he can have my car if worst comes to worst and I'm locked up.

My turn comes I'm in front of the judge my lawyer (solicitor) she's next to me. The judge has his head lowered as he's reading my case I can see him slowly shaking his head from side to side and raising his eye brow's, as if to say under his breath what the hell have these immigration idiots done now.

When he's finished reading he says to me what have I got to say for myself. I say your honour I was on my way back to London where I have to get back to urgently via Vancouver as I have the second half of a return air ticket from there, I was almost at the border when I got stopped, the Canadians will let me in as they are part of the British Commonwealth and I don't need a visa to get into Canada also I have sufficient funds to look after myself.

He seemed pleased with what I had to say, he then says to me, "I'll give you three months to leave the country," now I have a visa, a three month one at that. Now why couldn't they have given me a visa in the first place?

That night I take Bob and the family out for a meal and a celebration drink, next day we say our goodbyes and I'm on my way again, I head up north again through the Yellowstone park again.

As I said earlier in the book I feel guilty if I don't pick up hitch-hikers, so I picked a few up en route. One dude who I picked up on the north side of the park was going all the way to Alaska to get there for the autumn fish canning season, he had been doing this for a number of years hitching between Wyoming to Alaska, doing such varied jobs as a cowboy, oilfield worker, building labourer, to fisherman.

As he wanted to come all the way to Vancouver with me as he offered to share driving and petrol (gas) money which suited me down to the ground. We stayed at hostels from Jim's guide book on route. When we entered Idaho he asked if we could make a slight detour to go and visit some friends of his, to which I replied sure thing. Well after driving down a dirt road for a few miles we come to the headquarters of an Idaho white supremacist Militia group signs were up all over the place saying 'WHITES ONLY' just like the old South Africa, once inside the reception area he introduces me to some of the people that he knew. There were posters up all over the place with things like, Jewry Communism=Enslavement, Vigilantes of Christendom, God's call to Race, and many other books and posters were all over the place. He tells them about my recent persecution by the totalitarian establishment, so I'm well received and they offer their condolences on my recent misfortune.

The conversation revolves around how we all have to be armed and prepared for when the Jewish, communist government tries to enslave us all by using the unwitting blacks to do their dirty work for them. I replied that I was ready as I've been reading Flashman and Wilbur Smith all my life and I'd been armed up to the teeth when I lived in Rhodesia so I knew all about weapons. They give me some posters and pamphlets for me to read on our journey.

After a couple of hours it's time to hit the road as we've got to get to the next overnight stay. This chap I'm travelling with was very interesting with his view of the world, quite a bit different from mine though. It transpired that he was a big shot in one of the Alaska Militias, he did seem somewhat unhinged to me, but this is travelling, one meets all sorts of characters on the road, much different from your average Joe Blow down the pub talking football (soccer to any Americans reading this).

Two days time we cross over with no hassles whatsoever through an isolated border post, back to civilized Canada, finely away from all the America bureaucratic nonsense. After two miles driving I go round a sharp bend in a heavily forested river valley, when I almost run into the largest flock of wild turkeys I've ever seen in my life, I had a flash back then to the huge guinea fowl flocks I'd witnessed in Africa.

We part in Vancouver, I wish him well on his next leg of his long journey. Now it's time to catch up with Bill, Les, Viking Eric and a few other friends over a few beers. When I'm back at Bill's place where I'm staying he tells me he's got another crop ready for harvesting can I help him out as the last crop worked out so well. This was great news as I needed to replenish my funds by now, London could wait another week or so. I also needed to sell my car which was going to break my heart, this had been the best car I'd ever had. When I eventually sold it I sold it for the same price that I'd paid for it and I'd put 15,000 miles on the clock.

Back in London after sorting through a mountain of mail I find a letter from my Solicitors that I'd used in Denver inside was a rebate cheque for $240. Who said all Lawyers are crooks? Lichter Korkin and Associates are definitely not.

What do I think of America after all that had happened to me? Well I love the place and the people except of course the over the top, overzealous cops and immigration officials. Who won't let go like a bull dog with a bone.

CHAPTER 17
Having Made the Decision to Work Abroad

Many of you will be apprehensive about going too far from home. Your sights will focus on Europe as the logical place to start your working travels from. It is easy to get to, plus we've all got right of abode and work in all the twenty-eight EU countries, plus reciprocal health agreements with each State within the EU.

I myself, started my working travels in Jersey, one of the Channel Isles, after I'd spent a few years working around England with Irish navvy gangs. Later on I picked grapes in France, and later on again I worked in Denmark at a horse riding school and as a kitchen porter in Copenhagen. In those days there were plenty of jobs to be had. It wasn't that I was scared to go further afield, it was simply down to funds, or should I say lack of funds, that kept me close to the UK.

With my experience of working and travelling overseas, I have found that it is far easier to make out in Australia and New Zealand, than it is in Europe; they even drive on the same side of the road as the UK.

USA and Canada, Except Quebec, Are Easier Than Europe

Basically they are all mainstream, English-speaking, Protestant nations that are easy to blend into without much difficulty. Here are a few paragraphs I've copied from Time Magazine, by their European correspondent, Jay Branegan, **I copied** this article way back in 22.2.96. Not much has changed since then, it could easily be now. After reading this chapter, you won't want to stay in Europe. With hindsight we should have stayed out of the EU and kept with our 'Kith and Kin' relationship with our dominion commonwealth. They fought and died for us in numerous wars and we thanked them by saying goodbye, we have now got new friends to trade with, big, big mistake.

We practically had right of **abode** in Canada, Australia and New Zealand and now we would have been even closer to the US, through our ties with Canada.

"Europe's teeming unemployed, of more than 20 million. Restructured – the new euphemism for cutting costs by shedding jobs. I guess my position was just too expensive. I worked for thirty years. Maybe that was enough. Despite all the rhetoric, by governments," says Peter Coldrick of the European Trade Union Confederation, "reducing unemployment is no longer the top priority."

"In 1993 the European Commission in Brussels tumbled out a 'jobs and competitiveness' programme that held out the promise of 15 million new jobs by the year 2000. Yet after two years of solid growth, the commission announced this month that December unemployment had jumped back to 10.9%, the same figure as a year earlier."

"As the century slogs to a close, the plight of Europe's jobless seems as hopeless as ever." French economist, Alain Grielen, foresees, "the creation of a two-speed society: on one side those who work, on the other those who don't, which could lead to destructive social convulsions. Future societies will have to get used to this, rather than chasing an unattainable level of employment for all."

"Nowhere, it seems, are governments able to muster the political courage or popular support to dispense the harsh medicine that Europe's crisis requires. Europe's chronic inability to create jobs are many and complex. Central to the problem are heavy taxes, high minimum and average wages along with other employment costs, feather bedding labour laws, lavish welfare benefits and a blanket of regulations that smother new businesses and entrepreneurship. For Europe to start generating jobs, it will have to scale down, if not dismantle, the rococo welfare edifice constructed over the past fifty years."

"America, facing the same pressures as Europe, has a low minimum wage that has not kept up with inflation; weak unions; great freedom to hire, fire and set pay levels; low taxes; a thriving entrepreneurial culture, and a booming high-tech sector. This has lead to a stinkingly different outcome: the 5.8 per cent jobless rate, half the size of Europe's.

"America and its workers pay a price: no job security; wage inequality; a drop in real wages for the bottom rung workers and stagnant pay for most of the rest; and a growing cadre of the 'working poor' people with full time jobs who are still stuck in poverty.

"The Clinton administration claims that since January 1993, America has created 8 million jobs while the fifteen EU members have added only 296,000. Why? Because of high minimum wages that price workers out of jobs, and high non-wage costs, Europe's employers are reluctant to expand their payrolls even in good times. Better to pay existing workers overtime for longer hours, than take on new workers.

"An expensive plan to help the long-term unemployed through subsidies and tax breaks, has purportedly led to the hiring of 152,000 people, but with an unforeseen side effect: in favouring older, long-term jobless, employers are shunning younger job applicants who are equally plagued

by high unemployment rates."

"No job programme can work in any European country, without robust economic growth. Alliance for jobs. We agree there has to be a radical change, but we don't want an American-style free-for-all that destroys the social safety net." says David O'Sullivan, a top aide to Padraig Flynn, the European Commissioner for Employment.

There Is A Third Way

Efforts to clear these obstacles show some success. In Britain, where the jobless rate is 8 per cent and still falling, some 500,000 small businesses were created last year. But for every step forward, there seem to be two steps backward. The down-town business district of Brussels last year enacted a wrong-headed $34 annual tax on every business/computer screen on the theory that computers 'kill jobs'.

In Berlin, Norbert Bauer, forty-one, has no incentive to expand his small cash-register business because taxes and other costs would take 70 cents from every dollar of extra profit. "On Sundays the politicians preach about improving conditions for small businesses, then on Monday they vote to raise taxes."

Labour Costs: Europe's manufacturing wages are often far higher than competitors in Japan and the US, while high minimum wages ($8 an hour in

France for instance) prevent the creation of millions of additional low level service jobs in the hotel, retail, recreation, health care and personal service industries. Generous employee benefits (mandated by union contracts), payroll taxes and other non-wage costs add further to the burden and are disproportionately high for low-paid jobs. German firms, as a result, invested roughly $29 billion abroad last year, five times the private capital outlaid within their own country.

Welfare Benefits: For many people safety nets have undeniably become hammocks. "We can create low-level jobs, like street sweeping, but the French won't accept them. They can get by without working on the basic welfare payment," says Jean-Marie Chevaliar, an Economist Professor at the University of Paris. Chancellor Kohl last month complained that, "About a third of those on welfare rejected jobs offered to them," and noted that construction sites around Germany are filled with foreign workers while Germans sit idle.

In Ireland, a married couple with two children can get from unemployed assistance $214 a week – it is significantly higher than the average after tax wage of $167. In Italy, Marina Salaman, President of a textile factory in Treviso, says, "A lot of times I hold off hiring, because once you've hired someone, it's very hard to get rid of them." And that, say experts, is an all too common problem in many European countries, along with limits on part-time work and temporary contracts. Such measures keep people out of jobs in the name of protecting those already employed, and should be eased to encourage more hiring.

Europe's labour unions regard efforts to reduce employee protection as a virtual declaration of war on the worker and a sure way to lower living standards for all. "Saying a low-paid job is better than no job is like saying it's better to be alive than dead."

Labour's economists argue that evidence on the benefits of lower minimum wages is weak and that without job security both employee and employer lose the incentive to invest in upgrading skills. Charles Bean of the London School of Economics concedes, "We really don't know enough about the causes of Europe's high unemployment to know exactly how to cure it."

Britain, which had no minimum wage and under Margaret Thatcher adopted the toughest labour stance in Europe – crushing the Unions and deregulating markets – is the best test case. Richard Jackman of the London School of Economics, estimates that the dramatic changes have helped lower the unemployment rate two to three percentage points. He argues that the drop would have been more impressive if it weren't for the poor education system. There's little prospect, however, of a Thatcherite revolution on the Continent. "Any political party that tried would run into a cultural wall. They'd be kicked out in one day." Written by Jay Barnegan.

Conclusion. After reading all that, who really wants to go and work in Europe. Not only will you find high unemployment, unless you speak the language of the country you are in you'll be down a rung on the employment ladder, below the locals, but above the wave of immigrant workers from the old Eastern Block and North African countries who have flooded into Western Europe. Fortunately a lot of them don't speak English, but plenty of them speak German, and French which is a popular working language in Europe today. Also many of the migrants from countries like Poland are prepared to work mega hard doing anything for just to have a piece of the good life in the West.

Driving a car around Europe, one needs to own a gold mine just to pay for the diabolical price of petrol, and motorway tolls. In France it's about £6.50 per gallon and most of that is tax. In the USA that would buy four or five gallons. You'd also get five or six gallons of LPG gas in Australia for that.

To stop in a restaurant for a meal or a night in a cheap hotel, add twenty percent for VAT on top of the bill. Outrageous! Why is everything so expensive in Europe; to pay for everything that's mentioned in the last chapter. Not to mention the billions that go to support the EU Agricultural Policy, so we can have mountains of surplus foods, lakes of wine and olive oil that is so expensive no-one can afford to buy any of it, so we have to give it all away in Foreign Aid.

Who benefits besides the Mafia and other terrorist organisations like the IRA doing scams and the rich land owners who now get paid over £90 per acre not to grow anything. Not bad if you're landed gentry and you own 10,000 acres – that's nearly a million pounds a year for doing sweet FA on top of all your other wealth. So, who pays for all this? Have a guess!

Let's help the Third World. They need to trade not aid. Let's buy their agricultural produce at the real world market value i.e., beef from Botswana, Argentina, Namibia or Brazil is also much tastier as the animals are grass feed on the open range and safer – no mad cow disease from their beef. Then sell them finished goods instead of subsidizing our EU farmers, some to the tune of £5 million per year.

Japan does the same. They pay their farmers to grow rice, then ban imports of rice so the people have to then pay ten times the 'world price'.

In the USA, the maximum a farmer can receive in government subsidies is about $60,000 per year. Ever wonder why the food is so cheap in the USA? But US farm subsidies have destroyed many emerging third world country's agricultural, development – for further in-depth facts check out; Agricultural subsidy – Wikipedia the free encyclopaedia.

I remember reading about the Marquis of Bath, one of the wealthiest landowners in Britain. He is the owner of the world famous Longleat Estate and his personal fortune is said to be worth over £150 million. I wonder how he's going to make out in the new classless society. As if titles are going to disappear and the estates of the landowners are going to be split up amongst all the offspring, instead of the eldest 'male' heir taking all – title, mansion and land.

A classic example was Diana Windsor, formerly Spencer, who was having to get by on royal handouts, whilst her younger brother inherited over a £100 million plus the Spencer Earldom. No justice. No wonder she had an eating disorder before her terrible tragic death, if ever there was an add for wearing seat belts this terrible car crash was it, four people in the car and the only survivor was wearing a seat belt. Another travesty of justice, her ex-husband Charlie is going to inherit a Kingdom and his youngest brother Edward has to go out and work. Unreal man, no justice at all.

The Marquis of Bath was said to be a real 'rebel' in the seventies. He went and lived in a cave up the Amazon River somewhere. Big deal, anyone can do that when you're sitting on a fortune. I would have admired him if he'd given his money away first and then went up the Amazon doing jobs to pay his way, like the rest of us would have to do. I wonder if his cave had room service included, or did he take his own servant?

This ain't a worker travelling, this is having a holiday. One of the above ought to try and live on an inner city council estate for a while, where, if you're rich enough to own a broken down car, you have to take the tax disc out of the windscreen every night.

Hereditary Peerage

This ancient law is not only sexist but unjust. The powers that be, the ruling, titled, land owning class, with their inbred 'blue blood' lines, will close ranks when needed to preserve this medieval privilege.

The previous Lord Moynihan, absconded from Britain after living a life of deceit and fraud, only to surface in the Philippines where upon he led a life of drug dealing, combined with running massage parlours, pimping for prostitution and any other racket he could get into. During this period of his life he married a number of Filipino women who bore him male heirs who, under our own laws, one of them is entitled to the Moynihan Peerage. Well, talk about shock waves through the aristocracy establishment. No way were they going to have a Eurasian sitting in the House of Lords. Good God man, it's unthinkable, a sacrilege, not to mention his mother's dubious background.

To reverse this desperate situation Colin Moynihan, his half-brother, a former Tory minister, saved the Establishment. A pretender for the title. Just like when they brought in William of Orange another pretender.

The closing of ranks was last witnessed when Lord Lucan bolted after killing one of his employees.

With this Peerage bullshit, the late Tony Benn must have had field day in the House of Commons as he had relinquished his hereditary tile.

Do It, Stop Talking, Just Go

When you are getting ready to go, quite a few people will try and talk you out of going. People do this for differing reasons. Quite often the people who are doing this are concerned for your welfare i.e., close family. They are frightened of you leaving the nest and you making your own way,

without their guidance and knowledge. Today we still want the security of the 'tribe' so leaving can be a difficult decision to make.

Other people will try and put you off because deep down they are jealous of you being able to do something they are unable or unwilling to do –I've heard it all.

A classic is, "Work hard and save when you're young and then you can travel and enjoy yourself when you're older." Bullshit! Have you never heard about old people trying to find the 'fountain of eternal youth!'

Always remember – nobody lives forever! And you're a long time dead.

Ask yourself, do I want to reach forty-five-fifty years of age and only be able to write my life story on a postage stamp? Well, do you?

It is one of the great myths perpetuated in our society, that working long, hard hours will make you wealthy. Working long, hard hours for someone else can leave you very disillusioned when you end up poor. I am amazed at the number of people who throw themselves into, or even devote their whole working lives to, someone else's cause.

As I stated in the beginning of this book lots of jobs have disappeared, mainly down to technology, but other ways of working and making money have emerged, and best of all these new ways of making money give you a limited amount of freedom away from the daily grind of 'commuting'. There are thousands of people making a good living from eBay, Craigs List,

Amazon and many other internet sites. All of this can be done from a £300 laptop computer.

I myself dabble on the US stock market, best not to use the UK market if you want to play the market, as you then have to have a UK broker, who charges outrageous buying and selling rates plus an annual subscription fee, we did not get the title of 'rip of Britain' for nothing. It starts with the government ripping us off, in return we feel as if we have to rip off the government, and this starts a cycle of everyone ripping one another off. Sad but true.

It's a bit of hassle to open an American account but well worth it as all the best internet financial sites are for US market. There are loads of brokerage houses, most of them will let you have a one month dummy $50,000 account trial run on their trading platforms, you only need $2500 to open an account with most brokers. If you do decide to get involved with trading stocks keep well away from penny shares off the OTC market known as the over the counter market the 'pink sheets', these are volatile, manipulated and hyped only whiz kid Timothy Sykes the penny stock share guru makes any money on this market, because he is able to sell the shares 'short' using an offshore brokerage house in the Bahamas as most brokerage houses do not allow you to trade penny shares and just about next to none of them allow you to sell 'short'. Hence I've lost dough on penny shares check out the site PUMPs&dumpS. Also keep well away from the Forex (foreign exchange) market the only people who make money on this market are the brokers and multi millionaires.

If you want to check stock trading out, check out Barchart.com, Marketwatch.com, Yahoo!Finance, Google Finance and watch YouTube Basics of Trading Video Course from Informed Trades.com also MarketToolBox.com with a twice weekly webinar featuring Doug Newberry, Jeffrey Brewer and Bill Mickinly.

After trading, vehicles, weapons, wildlife, black market currency, gold Kruger Rand coins, fake tradesman certificates, counterfeit goods, cigarettes, rolling tobacco, booze and drugs, I figured I'd check out the stock market, less bloody risk involved (some people say more crooks).

I myself have two brokerage accounts one is with Tradeking.com they charge $5 to buy and $5 to sell, a very good trading platform but my other account is with Just2Trade.com and they charge $2.50 buy and $2.50 sell. Not such a good platform but they have a very good free live streaming chart which I use all the time. If you decide to go down the stock trading route and play 'safe' by buying high paying dividend stocks, just remember that as a non American citizen you have to pay 30 per cent tax on earned dividends regardless if the stock price goes up or down.

So if you go down the dividend route use an offshore broker such as SureTrade.com based in the Bahamas, offshore brokerages are also based in Cyprus and the Isle of Man.

To be British

Must like bacon sandwiches, roast beef, fish and chips, no vegetarians and drink beer, lots of.

Sport must like football, rugby is for big guys who can't play football, cricket a good game for football players when it's too hot to play football, polo for the landed gentry, boxing not a sport.

The four best British footballers in recent years George Best, Laurie Cunningham, Paul Gascoigne and Ryan Giggs. If you don't agree with all of the above statement you can't be British.

My Hero's

Robin Hood, Major Richard Sharp, General Sir Harry Flashman, Captain Horatio Hornblower, Sir Francis Drake, Captain Blackadder, Lord Horatio Nelson, Sir Winston Churchill, King Richard the Lion-heart and King Harold.

BRITISH NATIONAL INSURANCE CARD

Application for a National Insurance Number Card

We will be able to deal with your application more quickly if you complete all relevant boxes in full using CAPITAL LETTERS.

1 Surname

2 Other names

3 If you are male put 'M' in the box, if female put 'F'

4 Your date of birth

5 If you have had a different surname, please say what it was

6 Your National Insurance number, if you know it

7 Your address - please write each normal line of address on a different line. Leave a space between each word and write only one letter in each box.

In case we have any enquiries please give your daytime telephone number.

8 Please sign here _____ Date _____

Form CF88

IRISH APPLICATION CARD

WORK PERMIT APPLICATIONS IMPORTANT NOTICE

An employer making an application for permission to employ an alien should read carefully the

"Conditions for issue" on the application form. The following points should be noted

1. A work permit is issued only on condition that the Minister for Enterprise and Employment is satisfied that all reasonable steps have been taken to recruit a suitably qualified national of the European Economic Union or a national of any other country covered by the European Economic Area (EEA) Agreement for the job.

2. With effect from 1 January 1994, work permits are not required for national of Austria, Finland, Iceland) Norway and Sweden as a result of the entry into force of the European Economic Area (EEA) Agreement.

3. Completed application form must be accompanied by two recently taken passport sized

photographs of the person whose employment is to be authorised and documentary evidence of the employers efforts to recruit someone of EU or EEA nationality.

4. (i) Where a person the subject of a work permit application is married to an EU or EEA national,

(a) the birth certificate or copy of passport or certificate of naturalisation and

(b) the marriage certificate of the subject's spouse must be furnished.

(ii) Where the subject of a work permit application is a dependant child or child under 21 of an EU or EEA national. the application must be accompanied by: (at the birth certificate of the dependant child or child under 21 which states the full name of the parent who is an EU or EEA national and (b) documentary proof that the parent is an EU or EEA national such as a birth certificate, a copy of passport or certificate of naturalisation. If any of the original documents are not in English a translation of the original must be supplied and certified as such, by a reputable authority.

(iii) Where the subject of a work permit application has an Irish born child, who is dependent on the applicant the birth certificate of the child should be furnished.

The work permit fee is normally waived for such applications which are generally granted.

5. Once an applicant has been lodged, the procedure may take some weeks to complete.

Representative bodies, profession associations and immigration authorities must be advised that the application is being considered and must be allowed time to prepare and lodge objections.

6. **It is not possible to deal with personal callers in respect of any application on hand**. Should an employer wish to give additional details in support of the application, they should be sent in writing to the Work Permits Section, Room 105, Davitt House, Adelaide Road, Dublin 2.

7. To help defray administrative costs, a fee is charged for each permit issued but this fee may be waived in some cases. Details of the amount due will be sent to the employer when the permit has been approved.

8. The period of validity of a permit will normally commence on the date of commencement of employment and will in any case not exceed one calendar year. In some cases it may be possible to grant an extension to a permit but application for an extension must be made in good time, as the same procedure will be followed as with a new permit.

IRISH APPLICATION CARD

PLEASE ENCLOSE TWO RECENT PASSPORT SIZE PHOTOGRAPHS OF THE PROPOSED EMPLOYEE.

DEPARTMENT OF ENTERPRISE & EMPLOYMENT

APPLICATION FOR A WORK PERMIT TO EMPLOY A Non-EEA national

(The EEA comprises the European Union together with Iceland and Norway).

Section A: Particulars of Employer

Employer's Name ___

Registered name of employer's business ___

Address___

Nature of employer's business ___ Tel. No

Number of EEA_ nationals employed___

Number of non-EEA nationals employed ___

Section B: Particulars of proposed employee

Surname___ Male/Female

Other Name (s) (as on passport) ___

Present Address ___

Date of Birth__ Place of Birth __ Nationality___

Passport Number ___ Date and place of issue of passport ___

Martial Status ___ Nationality of spouse ___

(If Married to an EEA national, please furnish birth certificate of spouse and marriage or certificate; or certified copies thereof)

Has he/she any \Irish born dependants __ Was he/she previously employed in the State Name of previous employer ___

Section C: Title of the post on offer

Title of post on offer

Proposed period of employment: from ___ to ___

(please specify exact dates)

Department of Enterprise and Employment, Davitt House, Adelaide Road, Dublin

An Roinn Fiontar agus Foslaiochta, Teach Davitt, Bothar, Adelaide, Baile Atha Cliath

Tel: (0I) 661 4444 Ext.   Fax: (01) 676 9047   Telex 93435

IRISH APPLICATION CARD

Section D: Details of the post on offer

Main functions of the job _____

Salary or wages offered £ _____ per _____ Other Benefits (car, etc.)

Number or hours of work ___ Number of days per week

Reasons for employing a non-EEA national :

Special qualifications for the job :

Section E: Efforts to recruit an EEA worker

(This section dose not have to be completed if the application is being made to employ a non-EEA national)

Detail any efforts made to recruit an EEA national for the position, including full details of advertisements placed

(Documentary evidence should be attached)

Detail any plans to train an EAA national for the position in the future.

Which unions represented in firm cater for the grade or category of worker to which this vacancy refers.

Have these trade union been consulted re this application and if so, with what result

CONDITION FOR ISSUE OF A WORK PERMIT

(A) Issue of a work permit in respect of a named non-EEA national does not in itself authorise such a person or reside within the state. Admission to the State and authorised duration of stay is subject to the control of the Immigration Authorities. All-non-EEA nationals must be registered with the Aliens Registration Office.

(B) Application for J work permit, including a renewal, should be made six weeks before the non-EEA national is required to take up employment or a current permit expires.

(C) Work permits are issued for a maximum period of one year.

(D) A fee, as determined by um Minister |for Enterprise and Employment is payable by the employer, in respect of each work permit granted.

DECLARATION

I hereby solemnly declare the particulars given in this application are true, to the best of my knowledge and belief and I apply to the Minister for Enterprise and Employment a work permit as required under the provisions of the Aliens Act, 1935, the Aliens Order, 1946, and 1975 and the European Communities (Aliens)Regulations,1977 in accordance with the conditions referred to in this form.

Name of Employer ____ (BLOCK LETTERS)

Signature ___ Date _____

(In the case of an incorporated company this form must be signed by a director or the other responsible person whose position must be stated.)

Undercover Cops

If you're going to do anything that's not quite 'Kosher' (best to stick to the straight and narrow). Just bear in mind that the 'old bill' come in all shapes, sizes and colours, female as well, and in most countries they are armed and in some countries they are prepared to use their guns, clubs or tasers on you.

Here are two of my many experiences with cops, one recent one not so recent.

One night while riding the tube back to my house in west London after a night out in a restaurant. I'm seated wearing my 'whistle & flute' reading a magazine. Across and down from me there's this drunk in his mid-twenties yelling and shouting abusive language at everyone. The usual dribble that alcoholics spout off. So of course everyone that's sitting in his vicinity, vacate their seats and move further up the carriage.

He didn't bother me, I didn't feel threatened by his obscenities, even though some of them were directed at me. I don't rise to a drunkard's bait I just ignored him and carried on reading. For a brief moment he stopped performing at the same time as the train stopped at a station. Where upon a middle aged woman boarded the carriage and sat down near to him, she being unaware of the performance that had been going on before her arrival.

Now the guy has a new victim to abuse, he dutifully started the next act. The lady wasn't having any of his abuse so she started to tell him what she thought of him, I'm thinking, 'Oh no why couldn't you have just moved away like everyone else had done.'

He's now getting really aggressive towards her, I'm thinking, 'If he hits her I'm going to give him a mighty big 'slapping' and then I might end up ruffling up my new suite.' I now start looking around to see if there's anybody else who is likely to put an end to his antics.

Of course everyone else is looking away or pretending nothing is happening, the only other person who is half taking any notice of what's happening is a Rasterfairan with a 'walkman' on his head over his tea cosy hat. He's wearing torn jeans, a scruffy bomber jacket and dirty trainers. 'Not much chance of him intervening then,' I thought, even though he had now put the walkman in his pocket. Just then the drunk dutifully started to assault the woman. Well before I even had time to blink, the Rasta had the drunk, face down on the floor, arms behind his back handcuffed and a radio out asking for assistance with an arrest at the next station. Well, the odds I thought of him being a copper, would have been a million to one.

Story number two

A few years earlier, I was living in Hillbrow, Johannesburg South Africa. – Today an extremely dangerous place to be especially at night.

One Friday night after a night out a few of us decide to go back to one of the couples' place, for a night-cap and a smoke. After a few more hours of abuse to my body, l decided enough is enough, it's time to go home and crash out. As I only lived a short distance away, I'd decided against crashing out on the floor, or the couch, l was starting to get soft. I closed the front door to the block of flats and proceeded to make my way to the road, through the gardens.

All of a sudden, out of the bushes three black guys jumped on me so fast all at once, giving me no time at all to react. Within seconds I'm face down on the ground, with one guy's boot on my neck, another is on the back of my legs and the other one is handcuffing my hands behind my back. (I would have needed the strength Arnold Schwarzenegger to have got them off.)

Just then out of the corner of my eye l see a car pull up and a white man who is driving shouts out in Afrikaans, "Let him go he's not the one we want he didn't bother to get out of the car to apologise or anything silly like that."

One of the black guys then says to me as he's taking the cuffs off, "Sorry boss you'd better go now."

Well, before they could change their minds I'd done hundred yard dash faster than Usain Bolt.

Moral of the stories never underestimate plain clothes (old Bill).

All of my dealings with police I have found them to be much more reasonable than dealing with immigration officials. Also remember, in many third world countries if you tangle with the authorities you could end up face down in a river as crocodile meat.

A few addresses I've come up with before I come to the end of this book.

VSO – Voluntary Service Overseas: 317 Putney Bridge Rd, SW15 2PN: Teachers, mechanics, midwives, builders, business advisers and journalists.

British Red Cross Society: 9 Grosvenor Crescent, SW1X 7E1

Medical register, nursing administration, engineering and agricultural specialists to serve in disaster areas. Three to six months.

EU Vacancies – The Overseas Placing Unit c/o Rockingham House, 113 West St.

Sheffield S14 ER Phone: 01 14 2596051

The Weak Link in the EU – For South Africans

If you're from, say South Africa of European descent or of mixed race, and you've decided to migrate due to the lack of opportunities available to you due to the newly enforced affirmative action where you are racially discriminated against when applying for a job, and want to escape the ever increasing escalating, never ending violence that is now all too prevalent, but you don't have a grandparent from Europe, so you can't claim another nationality (all your ancestors arrived, too far back). Don't despair just yet!

Hungary is the weakest link in the EU followed closely by Romania and Bulgaria. Hungary is issuing well over a hundred thousand new passports per year to people with, very tenuous ancestry links. In theory and I'm sure in practice, it shouldn't be that difficult to get a Hungarian passport. Legally one can change your name by deed poll in any country, if you were to check out the most common Hungarian names through Google and look for names the equivalent of John Smith, James Brown, Peter Black etc. or Koos de la Rey, Jan Smuts, Chistiaan de Wet, Louis Botha or Van de Mare. Change your name get all the relevant ID in your new name learn a few phrases of Hungarian, then you make up a story, like your granddad escaped from the Soviet invasion in 1956 when the tanks came rolling in to crush our new found independence, he then made his way to South Africa, I'm sure some did as a quarter of a million people fled in a period of a few months. You were never taught Hungarian as your mother was Afrikaans or English. You then go to Hungry for a few months **learn** to become Hungarian then apply for a passport. Once you have a passport you can live and work freely in all twenty-eight EU countries.

Another way if you're a young fit bloke is to join the French Foreign Legion. The minimum sign on period is five years, and after you've completed your service they give you French citizenship, the British army does not do this. Remember if you join an army you have to be prepared to get shot at and you must be prepared to shoot back.

As of July 2014 the cheapest and one of the easiest ways to get an EU passport is to invest in Malta it costs 1.5 million Euros that's about 22 million Rand also you must have one year's residency. Cyprus offers a similar deal with 2 million Euros invested, all the legal infrastructure in both counties is based on the British system, English is spoken in both countries.

Know before you go

> For up-to-date travel advice and tips, check the Foreign and Commonwealth Office (FCO) website at www.fco.gov.uk/travel or call 0845 850 2829.

> Get a good guidebook and find out about your destination. Make sure you know about local laws and customs and follow them on arrival.

> Tell family and friends where you are going and leave them your contact details. Leave copies of your passport, insurance policy (including a 24-hour emergency number), ticket details, and your itinerary and/or store online using a secure data storage site.

> Register with the FCO's LOCATE service via the FCO website. Entering details of your trip as well as emergency friend and family contact details will help the FCO to find you in the event of a crisis and inform next of kin of your whereabouts.

Insurance

Get adequate and comprehensive travel insurance and check that it covers all the activities you plan to undertake. Be sure your policy provides for:

- an air ambulance, in case you need to be flown home
- all medical bills (which can be expensive)

- any pre-existing medical conditions

- any potentially hazardous sports activities

- bringing the body home, in the event of a death

- bringing your family home, in the event of your illness or injury

- replacing and/or bringing your car home. Plan to stay healthy

- Check what vaccinations you need with your GP as soon as possible before you travel.

- Check to see if you need extra health precautions for the country you are visiting (e.g. malaria zones).

- Check if your medication is legal in the country you are visiting. Pack it in your hand luggage.

- If you are taking prescribed medication, take a copy of the prescription with you, and find out if you will need to take a doctor's letter with you.

- If you're travelling within the European Economic (EEA), get an EHlC www.dh.gov.uk/travellers, ring 0845 606 2030 or go to the Post Office. But remember you still need travel insurance.

Passports and Visas Before you go...

- If you want to travel overseas, including journeys through the Channel Tunnel, you will need a passport.

- Check that your passport is still valid for a minimum of six months at return date, that it is in good condition and make a note of its number, date and place of issue.

- Make a photocopy of the last page and leave it with family/friends.

- Write the full details of your next of kin in your passport

- Check if you will need a visa — travel agents can advise.

- Children under 16 (including babies) not already included on a valid passport, need their own individual passports. Children already included on their parents passports can continue to travel on these until they reach 16, or until the passport on which they are included on expires. When travelling to the USA, children must hold a passport of their own.

- Take another means of identification (preferably with a photograph).

When you are there...

- Keep your passport in the hotel safe and carry a photocopy with you.

Drugs

- Avoid any involvement with drugs – the penalties are severe and could include the death sentence.

- Don't carry parcels or luggage through customs for other people.

- Don't cross land borders with people you don't know, i.e. hitch-hikers.

Money Before you go...

- Make sure you have enough to cover emergencies.

- Find out if traveller's cheques are appropriate for your destination and keep a separate record of their numbers.

- Find out how your traveller's cheques and credit cards can be replaced if lost.

- Check the expiry dates on your credit or debit card(s) and make a separate note of their numbers.

When you are there

- Carry only as much money as you need for the day leave the rest in a hotel safe.

- If you have to carry a lot of money, ask your partner or a friend to carry some of it for you.

- Use a money belt or secure inside pocket.

- Don't carry all your cards with you – leave at least one in the hotel safe.

- If your money, passport or anything else is stolen abroad, report it at once to the local police and obtain a statement about the loss as you will need one to claim against your insurance. You will need to take steps to cancel any cards or travellers cheques, so take relevant phone numbers.

Consular assistance

British Consular Officers are ready to help you help yourself. Make a note of the telephone number of the nearest British Consulate. You can find this out from the FCO website (below) as well as hotels, tour operators and police. Working hours vary: it is better to telephone first. Most British Consulates operate an answer hone service outside office hours, giving working hours and an emergency number for other times. For more detail on what support you can receive, consult www.fco.gov.uk/travel.

Safety

As you would be in the UK, be alert and observant, and report any unattended items of suspicious activity by individuals to the local police or appropriate authorities.

Under Twenty-six Only

For an annual payment of just £10 those lucky enough in be under twenty-six years of age can get substantial discounts on flights worldwide and on Eurostar journeys, 10 per cent off travel gear from YHA Adventure Shops, savings of up £5 on Rough Guides, cheaper international phone and voice-mail facilities, as well as reductions on some accommodation, museums and galleries across Europe For more information contact Under 26(0171-823 5363).

Gap Year Contacts

Gap year advice (www.gapadvice.org) 01494 673448

Foreign Office Travel Advice Unit (www.fco.gov.uk) 0845 8502829

Gapyear.com (wwwgapyear.com)

Year Out Group (www.yearoutgroup.org) 01380 816696

Project Trust (www.projecttrust.org.uk) O20-7796 1170

Community Service Volunteers (www.csv.org.uk) 0800 374991

Year in Industry (www.yini.org.uk) 02380 597061

Raleigh International (www.raleigh.org.uk) 0207371 8585

i-to-i (www.i-to-i.com) 0800 0111156

Gap Sports Abroad (www.gapsportsabroad.co.uk) 0870 837979

GAP Activity Projects (www.gap.org.uk) 01184959 4914

Students Partnership Worldwide (www.spw.org) 020 7222 0138

lnterVol (www.lntervol.org.uk) 0845 6014008

Trekforce Expeditions (www.trekforce.org.uk) 01444 474123

Gapwork (www.gapwork.com) 0113-266 0880

TImebank (www.timebank.org.uk) 0845 4561668

Volunteering England (www.volunteering.org.uk) 0845 3056979

Safety Tips for Young Travellers

- Be aware of people acting suspiciously

- Obtain comprehensive travel insurance

- Do not flaunt (relative) wealth

- Read up on local laws and customs

- Check what inoculations and healthcare you need

- Drugs: be aware of the consequences

- Keep your drink with you at all times. Drugs are sometimes used in rape and once added to a drink they cannot normally be detected

- Make comes of tickets, Passport, insurance policy, itinerary and contacts, and leave one set at home

- Take sufficient money. British consular staff can't send you home if you run out

- Consider taking a roam-enabled mobile phone with you and use e-mail to keep in touch with home

- Check cars for explosive devices

- Find out about local scams used on tourists

- Never carry packages through Customs for others

- Stay at locally owned accommodation and try to eat in locally owned restaurant

- Respect local dress codes; think about what you wear

- Always pick up the Hotel or Guest House, wallet size card or leaflet or pamphlet.

Printed in Poland
by Amazon Fulfillment
Poland Sp. z o.o., Wrocław